WAR SINCE 1945

CONTEMPORARY WORLDS explores the present and recent past. Books in the series take a distinctive theme, geo-political entity or cultural group and explore their developments over a period ranging usually over the last fifty years. The impact of current events and developments are accounted for by rapid but clear interpretation in order to unveil the cultural, political, religious and technological forces that are reshaping today's worlds.

SERIES EDITOR
Jeremy Black

In the same series

Sky Wars: A History of Military Aerospace Power
David Gates

Britain since the Seventies
Jeremy Black

WAR SINCE 1945

JEREMY BLACK

REAKTION BOOKS

For Mark Jackson

Published by Reaktion Books Ltd
79 Farringdon Road
London EC1M 3JU, UK

www.reaktionbooks.co.uk

First published 2004, reprinted 2005

Printed and bound in Great Britain
by Biddles Ltd, King's Lynn.

British Library Cataloguing in Publication Data
Black, Jeremy
    War since 1945. – (Contemporary worlds)
    1. Military art and science – History – 20th century
    2. Military art and science – Developing countries – History
    – 20th century
    I. Title
    355'.02'09045

ISBN 1 86189 216 0

Contents

Preface

This book seeks to provide a short and accessible introduction to war since 1945. Much coverage of modern warfare is taken to mean discussion of the period beginning with the outbreak of the French Revolutionary War in 1792, with an emphasis, for the twentieth century, on World Wars I and II, and a postscript on the Cold War; the great ideological and 'super-power' stand off between capitalism and Communism, and their leaders, the USA and the Soviet Union, that lasted from the close of World War II until the Soviet collapse in the early 1990s. The focus for other conflicts discussed is on those involving Western powers, especially the USA and particularly the Vietnam War, and the organizing principle is often that of the triumphs and travails of Western weaponry and methods, an approach that links the Vietnam War to the two wars with Iraq in 1991 and 2003. As the new century advances, however, it becomes increasingly difficult to determine how best to present the second half of the twentieth century. For a long time, this period was understood in terms of the Cold War, and it was possible to see the 1990s in terms of the winding down, or consequences, of that war. Now, however, it appears less convincing to analyse the second half of the century in these terms and more necessary instead to search for new approaches and concepts; this book is a contribution to that process. The Cold War thesis subordinated events throughout the world, especially in the developing world, to the confrontation to an inappropriate degree, obscuring other trends. The emphasis in this book will be on the variety of post-1945 conflicts and the diversity of goals and methods. In addition, there will be an effort to show how war has played a major role in the history of the period; this is true both of conflict itself, particularly in South-West, South and South-East Asia, and in Africa, and of preparations for warfare. The coverage will be thematic, although these themes will be chronologically delimited.

Jeffrey Clarke made extremely helpful comments on an earlier draft and kindly provided journals and other material not readily obtainable in the UK. Stan Carpenter and Bill Gibson also offered useful comments. Discussions with other scholars while thinking about and writing this book have also been of value. In the period of writing, I benefited from invitations to speak at Assumption College, Boston University and Clark University, the University of Massachusetts at Boston, Roger Williams University, the Worcester Polytechnic Institute and Radley College, and to the Foreign Policy Research Institute and the New York Military Affairs Symposium. It is a great pleasure to dedicate this book to a good friend and much valued colleague.

Chapter 1

Introduction

The First and Second World Wars still dominate popular interest in war, and establish the parameters within which the Western public thinks about it. This was also very much the case after 1945, when, to many, it seemed obvious that future wars would follow the model of World War II. This conclusion was not restricted to the public. In the aftermath of the war, the campaigns were carefully scrutinized by military commentators seeking indications about how best to wage war in what appeared to be the imminent conflict between the Soviet Union and the group of non-Communist powers that allied in 1949 in the North Atlantic Treaty Organization (NATO). Atomic weaponry had appeared to suggest that there had been a paradigm shift in military capability and war-making, with aircraft able to drop those bombs as the war-winning tools. However, after 1949, when the Soviet Union unexpectedly exploded a nuclear bomb, the threat of nuclear devastation led to revived interest in conventional operations; although, at the same time, the prospect of nuclear devastation was employed as a deterrent with the American doctrine of 'massive retaliation'.

Concerned about conventional operations, the Americans took a close interest in the experience the Germans had acquired in fighting the Soviet Union. In the late 1940s they used German veterans to acquire information about the Soviet navy,[1] and in the 1950s they persuaded Luftwaffe commanders to write a series of reports. In addition, Franz Halder, head of the German army's General Staff in

1938–42, was employed by the American army's Historical Division for fourteen years, and indeed received the American Civilian Service Award in 1961. In their plans for conflict in Europe, both Soviet and, later, NATO forces came to focus on manoeuvre warfare, and there was great interest on both sides in the successful Soviet campaigns of 1943–5 against Germany, especially the concept of 'deep operations'. Similarly, the impact of the German and American submarine campaigns in World War II encouraged NATO to devote much attention to anti-submarine capability in the North Atlantic. Soviet willingness to sustain the losses seen in World War II made the Soviet Union subsequently appear to be such a threat to the West.

The legacy of the war also included among the victors a sense of righteous struggle, an affirmed nationalism, and a pride in military achievement. Politicians from the war years continued to be influential, the Americans electing General Eisenhower as President in 1952 and 1956, and the French turning to General de Gaulle. Conscription continued, or was revived for the Cold War, providing a collective experience of manhood. By 1958, 70 per cent of eligible young American males had served in the military, either as draftees or as draft-induced volunteers. The attitudes reflected and developed in this experience helped underpin willingness to serve in the Korean War and, at least initially, the Vietnam War.

The applicability, however, of the military lessons of World War II was lessened not only by the spread of atomic capability and the availability of improved weaponry, but also by the fact that most of the wars in the period of the Cold War were very different in type to World War II. The closest in operational terms were the wars between states where armour and airpower could be used by both sides, particularly the Arab–Israeli wars (indeed, Basil Liddell Hart saw Israeli operations as another instance of *Blitzkrieg*) and also the India–Pakistan war of 1965.

The most 'typical' wars, however, were those that involved at least an element of insurrection. This was true of the conflicts of decolonization, such as the British in Malaya, Kenya, Cyprus and Aden, and the French in Vietnam and Algeria, in which political will and the battle to win or intimidate 'hearts and minds' were as important as conventional military operations. This was also true of the American engagement in Vietnam, a conflict that very much indicated the limited value of doctrine and strategy derived from both World War II and Cold War confrontation with the Soviet Union. Instead, the need to rethink military practice (and history) in order to give due attention to the range of challenges that might have to be confronted by major powers was made readily apparent.

Even so, all too many commentators continued to place their trust in the paradigm power and conflict approach to war, with the related assumption that a particular operational method and/or type of military technology would lead to increased capability and success. This book focuses instead on the variety of war, not the paradigm. As such, it contests the dominant meta-narrative of war, which is one securely located within the Western intellectual tradition. The stress in this meta-narrative is on the material culture of war, and the explanatory approach focuses on the capabilities of particular weapons and weapons systems, and a belief that progress stemmed from their improvement. This is an approach that extends across time; thus, for example, with the Iron Age replacing the Bronze Age, the emphasis is on how the superior cutting power of iron and the relative ease of making iron weapons led to a change in civilizations.

Improved technology, not least in the shape of mechanization, plays a major role in the dominant modern concept of war, as the capability of weaponry takes precedence over the purpose of conflict. In spatial terms, this relates to the collapsing of distance, strategically, operationally and tactically. The entire world is literally under the scrutiny of surveillance satellites. Missiles and planes benefiting from mid-air refuelling can deliver warheads continents away, and units can be rapidly transported to and around the battlefield. Once there, they can use real-time information to increase their effectiveness. Space no longer appears an encumbrance, let alone a friction.

This technologically driven approach to war, however, has serious flaws. In particular, it pays insufficient attention to the diversity of military force structures, methods, goals and cultures that exist and have existed. The conventional Western approach is an idealistic one that assumes a clear paradigm of excellence, as well as an obvious means by which capability is to be ranked: in terms of the quality and quantity of resources applied in accordance with an effective doctrine and organization. In short, the world is seen as an isotropic surface: the space employed is one that is unvarying, and, from that perspective also, space has ceased to exist as an issue. This has been a particular problem with airpower theory, much of which has found it difficult to relate to low-intensity conflict, and to devise an appropriate doctrine.[2] Specific issues also arise from aspects of air capability. For example, the ability to transport units rapidly to the area of conflict and to 'insert' them into battle means that troops who are not always ready for the particular nature of the sphere of operations are exposed too swiftly, a problem that faced American forces in the Vietnam War.

In practice, across the world, there is a variety in military structures, methods, organizations, goals and cultures that raises serious questions about the conventional understanding of war. The method of approaching this issue, and the order in which aspects of it are considered, pose problems, as there is a danger that Western analytical concepts will prevail in a misleading fashion when discussing the remainder of the world. At the same time, it is necessary to give due weight to the variety of the 'non-West' or 'Rest'. For example, to suggest that the Western military approach places particular weight on battle, while the non-West does not, may well be valid in terms of the guerrilla and irregular campaigns of the 1950s, '60s and '70s, especially in the wars of decolonization, but is less valid as a general conclusion. Nevertheless, such a contrast, between battle and non-battle as goals, does capture the important role of anti-tactics and anti-strategy in warfare; for instead of imagining that two sides in conflict approximate to the same methods, it is more pertinent to note the degree to which the advantages of one power are countered not by emulation (so that the key spatial model is diffusion), but by the choice of weaponry, tactics, operational methods, strategy and doctrine that nullify, or seek to nullify, the affects of these advantages; in short a model that sees contrasts, and, thus, boundaries.

To focus on battle for a moment, there is another problem stemming from the assumption that the 'face of battle', the essentials of war, are in some fashion timeless, as they involve men being willing to undergo the trial of combat. In practice, the understanding of loss and suffering, at both the level of ordinary soldiers and that of societies as a whole, is far more culturally conditioned than any emphasis on the sameness of battle might suggest, while the experience of the harshness of war is in part affected by the nature of the society in question. The supply of toilet paper (and much else more serious) was an issue for the British forces sent to the Persian Gulf in 2003; for some other armies, such a shortage would not have led to public complaints. To put it bluntly, the willingness of societies to suffer losses varies, and this helps to determine both military success and differences in combat across the world in any one period. Cultural factors can also be seen in organizational issues such as discipline. This includes forces that are encouraged by alliance partnership toward inter-operability. Thus, the punishment for being a sentry asleep on duty is far harsher in the Turkish army than in its American counterpart; although both are NATO members.

Contrasts are readily observable in both chronological and geographical cultural parameters. To contrast the willingness of the Western powers to suffer heavy losses in the World Wars, especially World War I, with their reluctance to do so subsequently, and also the different attitudes towards casualties held by the Americans and the North Vietnamese in the Vietnam War, is to be aware of a situation that has a wider resonance. It is far from clear that variations and changes in these 'cultural' factors, and related norms, should play a smaller role in the history of war than weaponry. Linked to this is morale, the single most important factor in war, while, as a related point, success in war, seen as an attempt to impose will, involves more than victory in battle.

It is unclear how far the Western will to win remains able to cope with the uncertainty and losses of war. At a time when as far as aggregate demographic and economic consequences are concerned, high casualty levels can be readily survived, Western sensitivity to casualties has become stronger over recent decades, producing powerful operational constraints. This sensitivity has grown at the same time as the threat of civilian casualties in the West has dwindled. Some commentators blame this on politicians, the media and public opinion, implying that the military is largely free of that sensitivity, although operational and tactical practice suggests otherwise; and an awareness of the conditional nature of military service in volunteer forces is clearly important. Sensitivities about casualties extend to a reluctance either to inflict heavy casualties on opponents, or to cause civilian losses, and both affect planning. Thus, the sinking of the Argentine warship the *General Belgrano* during the Falklands conflict in 1982 was used to criticize the Thatcher government even though the ship was a threat to the British naval task force. Similarly, concern was expressed about the killing of retreating Iraqi forces in 1991. Concern about civilian losses greatly affected targeting for the air offensives on Serbia in 1999 and Iraq in 2003, and also produced a political reason to accompany the military desirability of 'smart' bombs.

Organizational issues – how troops are managed on the battlefield, the nature of force structures, and the structuring of societies for conflict – also vary greatly between countries. Instead of assuming that these issues are driven by weaponry, specifically how best to use weapons, and possibly also to move and supply them, it is necessary to appreciate the autonomous character of organizational factors and their close linkage with social patterns and developments. Thus, militaries that are the product of ethnically divided societies (such as Nigeria) frequently display attitudes and practices in their recruitment patterns and command structures that are different to those that lack such divisions. Linking back to earlier paragraphs, there are also cultural differences between conscript and volunteer militaries, not least in their degrees of willingness to engage in combat, although it is important to locate this issue in particular contexts as there is no invariable linkage between recruitment systems and zeal for conflict. A parallel case can be made with the causes of war, which can also be seen as an independent variable and one that does not conform to a chronology determined by technological developments.

Looked at differently, military forces are organizations with objectives, and in assessing their capability and effectiveness it is necessary to consider how these objectives have varied and changed, and how far such variations and changes created pressures for adaptation. This adaptation can be seen both in terms of changes in organizational character, and with regard to the responsiveness to opportunities, for example those offered by advances in military (and related) technologies. In short, a demand-led account that focuses on the 'tasking' of the military has to be set alongside the more familiar supply-side assessment that presents improvements in weaponry or increases in numbers without adequately considering the wider context. 'Tasking' is certainly very important for force structures. Both the setting of goals and the definition of optimal force structures owe much to government policies. As a result, military history is an aspect of the total history of the period.

That, of course, begs the question of how best to describe the latter. Whereas nationalism, democracy and industrialization had been major themes in the Western world in the nineteenth century, in the twentieth they were important across the world. So also, especially in the West, was individualism, with its stresses on personal rights and consumerism; moral socialism, with its emphasis on the role of the state in ethical conduct; and the technological revolution of applied science. The most potent of these developments for conflict in the period after 1945 was not applied science but rather the nationalism that helped undermine empires.

Chapter 2

Aftermath Conflicts

The end of World War II in 1945 was followed by peace in some areas, especially the occupied Axis states; but elsewhere saw the continuation or fresh outbreak of warfare. This reflected the degree to which World War II was an umbrella conflict that encompassed many struggles, some of which had preceded the war and continued after it. Furthermore, the end of the war itself left issues that were clarified by the use of force. More generally, the militarized character of the late 1940s and early 1950s in part reflected the difficulty of moving to a peacetime situation. This was particularly apparent in the occupied Axis territories, as in place of peace treaties and rapid disengagement, there was an attempt to organize large-scale reconstructions of civil society that ultimately rested on military strength. Thus, in Eastern Europe, North Korea, Sakhalin and the Kuriles, Communism and state ownership were enforced in the shadow of Soviet military power, while in what became West Germany there was a process of disarmament and de-Nazification. In Japan, where the occupation lasted until 1952, the process was anchored by socio-political changes, including land reform, although in both Germany and Japan wartime industrial companies continued intact into the post-war period. The numbers of troops involved in support of these occupations were considerable, and represented important military commitments that affected the ability to demobilize. Furthermore, the troops used for these occupation duties were available for force projection, so that when the Korean War broke out in 1950,

American and Australian units in Japan were available for reinforcing South Korea.

The most dramatic aftermath conflicts occurred in East and South-East Asia, the largest being that in China, where civil conflict had followed the fall of the monarchy in 1911. In a complex process, the Nationalists (Kuomintang) under Jiang Jieshi (Chiang Kai-shek) emerged as the dominant force in the 1920s, defeating the warlords who controlled much of the country. The small, urban-based Chinese Communist Party was largely destroyed in the 1927 Harvest Moon Uprising, after which control was increasingly taken by agrarian reformers under Mao Zedong, who pressed for a rural revolution. Despite a series of offensives, the Nationalists were unable to destroy the Communists in the 1930s, and their position was increasingly challenged by Japanese aggression, with full-scale war breaking out in 1937. Once Japan over-ran China's coasts and valleys, destroying the Nationalists' urban power bases, capturing Shanghai and Nanjing in 1937 and Canton in 1938, the Communists were able to make a greater impact in rural areas, where the Nationalists had little interest or control. In opposi-tion to the Nationalists, Mao had developed a three-stage revolutionary war model, and during World War II was able to use a combination of clandestine political and social organization (Stage 1) and guerrilla warfare (Stage 2) in order to advance the Communist position, but was unable to move successfully into the conventional realm (Stage 3) until after the Japanese withdrawal.[1] The Nationalist government was gravely weakened by the long war with Japan, being particularly hard hit by Japanese advances in 1944 and 1945, and despite American support was defeated anew after World War II by the Soviet-backed Communists. This defeat would have been less likely were it not for the war: prior to the Japanese attack on China, the Chinese Com-munists had been in a vulnerable position in their conflict with the Nationalists, but, following that attack, the Communists benefited from having become, during the 1930s and early 1940s, the dominant anti-Japanese force in northern China. Nevertheless, they were still weaker than the Nationalists at the close of World War II.

The Chinese Civil War was the largest in terms of number of combatants and area fought over since World War II, and it proves an instructive counterpoint to the latter, indicating the difficulty of drawing clear lessons from the conflicts of the 1940s; although it ought to be stressed that there has been far less scholarship on the Chinese Civil War, and much of the work published on it has reflected ideological bias. In China, technology and the quantity of *matériel* did not triumph, as the Communists were inferior in weaponry and, in particular, lacked air and sea power. However, their strategic conceptions, operational planning and execution, army morale and political leadership proved superior, and they were able to make the transition from guerrilla warfare to large-scale conventional operations; from denying their opponents' control over territory to seizing and securing it. The Nationalist cause was weakened by poor leadership, inept strategy, and, as the war went badly, poor morale, while corruption and inflation affected civilian support. Indeed, the *China White Paper* published by the US State Department in 1950 blamed the Nationalists' failure on their own incompetence and corruption. Nevertheless, the classic treatment of the war as a Communist victory of 'hearts and minds', that indicated the superior virtues of Communism over the Nationalists, as well as the strength of the People's Liberation Army and its brave peasant fighters,[2] has been qualified by a greater emphasis on the quality of decision-making during the civil war and on the importance of what actually happened in the fighting.[3]

Until 1948 the Nationalists largely held their own. When the American use of atomic bombs led to Japan's sudden surrender in August 1945, the Communists liberated much of the north of China from Japanese forces, capturing large quantities of weaponry. Negotiations with the Nationalists actively sponsored by the USA, which sought a unity government for China, broke down as the Communists were determined to retain control of the north; and the ceasefire agreement that was negotiated did not apply in Manchuria where the Japanese forces had been defeated in a Soviet invasion in August 1945. In 1946 Nationalist troops transported north by the

American navy occupied the major cities in Manchuria, China's industrial heartland, but most of the rest of the region was held by the Communists. The following year 'a hybrid operational doctrine in which both guerrilla and mobile warfare were employed'[4] enabled the Communists to sway the struggle in Manchuria, increasingly isolating Nationalist garrisons, although further south the Nationalists overran the Communist-dominated province of Shensi, capturing Yenan in March. Despite pressure in the USA to intervene on the Nationalist side, particularly from the Republican opposition, which raised the charge of weakness toward Communism, the Truman administration decided not to do so, and took a lesser role than in the Greek Civil War, although that conflict was more containable and more propitious for Western intervention.

In 1948, as the Communists increasingly switched to conventional, but mobile, operations, the Nationalist forces in Manchuria were isolated and then destroyed, and the Communists regained Shensi and conquered much of China north of the Yellow River, although, in the valley of the Yellow River, Kaifeng was recaptured after it fell to the Communists in June 1948. Communist victory in Manchuria led to a crucial shift in advantage, and was followed by the rapid collapse of the Nationalists the following year. The Communists made major gains of matériel in Manchuria, and it also served as a base for raising supplies for operations elsewhere.[5]

After overrunning Manchuria, the Communists focused on the large Nationalist concentration in the Suchow–Kaifeng region. In the Huai Hai campaign, beginning on 6 November 1948, each side committed about 600,000 men. The Nationalists suffered from poor generalship, including inadequate coordination of units and poor use of air support, and were also hit by defections, an important factor in many civil wars. Much of the Nationalist force was encircled thanks to effective Communist envelopment methods, and in December and January 1948–9, it collapsed due to defections and combat losses.

Jiang Jieshi, the Nationalist leader, resigned as President on 21 January 1949, and the Communists captured Beijing the following day. They responded to the new President's offer of negotiation by demanding unconditional surrender, and the war continued. The Communist victories that winter had opened the way to advances further south, not least by enabling them to build up resources. The Communists crossed the Yangzi river on 20 April 1949, and the rapid overrunning of much of southern China over the following six months testified not only to the potential speed of operations but also to the impact of success in winning over support. Nanjing fell on 22 April, and Shanghai on 27 May, and the Communists pressed on rapidly to overrun the other major centres. Jiang Jieshi took refuge on the island of Formosa (Taiwan), which was all he retained control over. It was protected by the limited aerial and naval capability of the Communists and, eventually, by American naval power, but, until he intervened in Korea in 1950, Mao Zedong prepared for an invasion of Formosa, creating an air force to that end.[6] Jiang, in turn, used Formosa and other offshore islands he still controlled as a base for raids on the mainland. Meanwhile, in the spring of 1950, the island of Hainan and, in 1950–51, Tibet were conquered by the Communists, the capital of Tibet, Lhasa, being occupied on 7 October 1950. The new strategic order in Asia was underlined in January 1950 when China and the Soviet Union signed a mutual security agreement.

A separate set of conflicts arose from the reimposition of colonial control after the defeat of Japan in World War II. The Dutch proved unable to sustain their attempt to regain control of the East Indies, while the French also faced a growing insurrection in Indo-China. There, Ho Chi Minh, the Communist head of the Viet Minh, exploited the vacuum of power left by the Japanese surrender, and seized power across Vietnam in August 1945, proclaiming national independence and the foundation of the Democratic Republic of Vietnam on 2 September 1945. The French, however, refused to accept the loss of colonial control, and on 22 September 1945 French troops landed in Saigon. The following month saw both guerrilla operations against the French in the south and negotiations; after the latter failed, large-scale conflict broke out in December 1946. The Viet Minh was unsuccessful in conventional conflict and resorted to guerrilla operations, with the French gaining control of the major centres.[7]

In Europe, there had already been fighting in Greece before the death of Hitler: German evacuation in 1944 led to an accentuation of conflict between left- and right-wing guerrilla groups, and then, in order to thwart a left-wing takeover, to military intervention by the British on behalf of the right. Having arrived in October, the British were fighting the Communist National Popular Liberation Army (ELAS) on behalf of the returned exile administration two months later. A fragile armistice was negotiated in February 1945.

Attempts to reach a compromise failed, however, leading to a second stage of the war in 1946–9, which was to be exacerbated by the developing Cold War. The Communists' inability to achieve their goals by political means led them to turn to a guerrilla insurrection, and in this they were backed by the newly established neighbouring Communist administrations of Bulgaria, Yugoslavia and Albania. In response, the Greek army became more effective as a consequence of its abandonment, in 1948, of a policy of static defence, and its adoption of an offensive policy with a systematic clearance of guerrilla forces out of particular areas. The Greek army was also helped by the extent to which the population supported the administration, and by the Communists' adoption of more conventional methods of fighting – a political decision, taken in 1947, and resting on the belief that by establishing a Communist administration in parts of northern Greece near the Communist states, it would be possible to secure Soviet aid to counteract that from the USA. However, it proved impossible to recruit the manpower anticipated, the Soviets did not provide the heavy weaponry that was sought, and the Communists' reliance on position warfare led to their defeat: they were driven back to their strongholds in western Macedonia and finally defeated there.

Foreign intervention had been important, particularly the provision of US military and economic aid (but not troops) to the government under the so-called Truman Doctrine proclaimed in March 1947, when President Truman announced that the USA would oppose totalitarianism. The following year, General James van Fleet was selected by Truman to train and revive the Greek army. The eventual cutting of aid to the Communists, especially after the Tito–Stalin breach of 1948 brought the first major division between Communist states, was also significant, for, by supporting Stalin, the Greek Communists wrecked their relations with Yugoslavia.[8] The Communist defeat in Greece in 1949 was not to be followed by Western 'roll-back' of Communism further north in the Balkans, despite efforts to support the overthrow of the Hoxha regime in Albania, but it did ensure that the Communist presence in the Mediterranean and near the Middle East was weaker than it would otherwise have been. This was seen as a crucial success for containment, and was to be anchored when Greece joined NATO in 1952.

Elsewhere in Eastern Europe force played a major role in the wholesale expulsion of millions of people from their homes, especially Germans, particularly from Bohemia in the modern Czech Republic, but also Poles, Ukrainians and others; and in the imposition of Communist control. The role of Soviet forces in driving the Germans out of most of the region in 1944–5 was crucial, and helped to undermine non-Communist political movements then and subsequently. After the war Soviet forces remained in place, for example in Poland where they helped the Communists. There and elsewhere, some of the non-Communist resistance was arrested, and show trials were used to wreck the leadership and disrupt the organization of non-Communist political movements. Although a degree of political pluralism was initially accepted, the Soviet Union in 1947–8 pressed for Communist control in Eastern Europe. Force and intimidation were widely used; in Poland ensuring that in the general election of 1947, the Communists won a majority and then went on to incorporate or disband independent organizations. In Romania, King Michael was forced to abdicate after the palace in Bucharest was surrounded, at the close of 1947, by troops of the Romanian division raised in the Soviet Union. A coup brought the Communists to power in Czechoslovakia in 1948, and the Skoda works there was to provide much of the Communist world's export arms, including large quantities of small arms to Castro in 1960. In Yugoslavia, where the Communist guerrilla movement under Tito had eventually played the leading role in the resistance, the Axis defeat was followed by the large-scale slaughter of its supporters, especially of

Croat quislings, contributing to a spiral of hatred that was to revive in the 1990s.

The movement of peoples, as they were expelled from their homes after the war, in some cases involved military units. This was true of Poland where the army was employed to move Ukrainians forcibly from south-east Poland to Ukraine. The Ukrainians resisted, and the Ukrainian Partisan Army attacked Polish villagers. In 1946, the Polish army was used to remove the 200,000 Ukrainians still in Poland and to relocate them to lands acquired from Germany and cleared of Germans.

Anti-Communist guerrillas in Albania, the Baltic republics (the Forest Brethren), Bulgaria, Poland, Romania, Ukraine and Yugoslavia, some of which were based on resistance opposition to the Axis, were all suppressed. Despite efforts by the USA and Britain, particularly in Albania, Poland, Romania and Ukraine, the guerrillas received little effective support from the West,[9] although Western efforts contributed to Soviet paranoia, encouraging Stalin toward a more aggressive posture, not least with his approval for the invasion of South Korea in 1950. This was an important aspect of the way in which Western covert action played a role akin to its Soviet counterpart in exacerbating insecurity and sustaining hostility.[10] Some of the conflicts in Eastern Europe involved substantial forces and heavy casualties, although many are obscure; this is true, for example, of Soviet campaigns in the Baltic republics and Ukraine in the late 1940s. It has been suggested that the Soviets lost 20,000 men in suppressing opposition in Lithuania alone, and such figures are a reminder of the importance of non-conventional warfare in the late 1940s and early 1950s. This was also seen in the Korean conflict, which had a strong guerrilla war aspect at first with left-wing uprisings against the government in South Korea.

Other instances of failed insurrections included post-war attempts to challenge the Franco regime in Spain and a rising, in 1947, against Jiang Jieshi by native Taiwanese.[11] The Spanish insurrection, which was at its height in 1944–8, with up to 10,000 guerrillas in action, was the last stage of the Spanish Civil War (1936–9), which had left General Franco in power as a right-wing dictator. The insurrection officially ended, according to the government, in 1951, although it continued at a low level thereafter. In addition to Republican soldiers hidden in the mountains, the government faced guerrillas operating on the French border in the Pyrenees, and they became active after the German occupation of France ended in 1944. The government won in part by a ruthless policy of hunting down the rebels, supported by very punitive action against any sign of local support. It also benefited from divisions within the opposition between Communists and anarchists; from popular exhaustion with conflict after the travails of the Civil War; from its use of food rationing in order to influence popular support; from the strength of Francoist support in some areas close to the Pyrenees, especially Navarre; and from the extent to which the French government, initially sympathetic to the insurrection (when it was a post-war coalition containing Communists and Socialists), became more hostile to it from the end of 1946. Because the reliability of the conscripts in the Spanish army was doubted, Franco's government used the Civil Guard, which developed appropriate tactics, doctrine and brutal forcefulness.[12]

THE KOREAN WAR

These conflicts were overshadowed by the most important 'aftermath war' involving a Western power, that in Korea in 1950–53. The Communists had won in the Chinese Civil War, but the Americans were determined that they should not be allowed further gains in East Asia. At the close of World War II, in a partition of Korea, a hitherto united territory that had been part of the Japanese Empire, northern Korea had been occupied by Soviet forces and southern Korea by the Americans. In the context of the difficulties posed by Korean political divisions, and growing American–Soviet distrust, both of which sapped attempts to create a united Korea, they each in 1948 established authoritarian regimes: under Syngman Rhee in South Korea and Kim Il-sung in North Korea. There was no historical foundation for this division, each regime had supporters across Korea, and both wished to govern the entire peninsula. The regime in North Korea, whose military buildup was helped by the Soviet Union, was convinced that its counterpart in the South was weak and could be overthrown, and was likely to be denied American support. The South Korean army, indeed, lacked military experience and adequate equipment, while the Korean Military Assistance Group provided by the USA was only 500 strong.

The bitter rivalry between the two states, as each sought to destabilize the other – which, from 1948, included guerrilla operations in South Korea supported by the Communist North – led to full-scale conflict on 25 June 1950, when the North launched a surprise invasion of South Korea. They attacked with about 135,000 troops, using T34 tanks and Yak aeroplanes provided by the Soviets that gave them an advantage over their lightly armed opponents. The South Koreans were pushed back, but enough units fought sufficiently well in their delaying actions during their retreat south to give time for the arrival of American troops. American forces were in combat in Korea from 30 June.

The North Korean invasion led to intervention by an American-led United Nations coalition, which was determined to maintain policies of collective security and containment, and was concerned that a successful invasion of South Korea would be followed by Communist pressure elsewhere, possibly on Berlin or on Taiwan. The leading UN contingent was American, and the second largest was British. Among the large number of international participants, the Turks were prominent. The Americans also provided most of the air and naval power, as well as the commander, General Douglas MacArthur, their Far East Commander in Chief. The UN forces benefited from the backing of a stable South Korean civilian government and from a unified command: MacArthur's control over all military forces, including the South Korean army, provided a coherence that was to be lacking in Vietnam. American capability was enhanced by the presence of their occupation forces in Japan, and by the logistical infrastructure and support services provided by Japanese facilities and resources.

Nevertheless, although the Americans were better able than they would have been in the 1930s to fight in Korea owing to their major role in World War II, since 1945, thanks to post-war demobilization as the 'peace dividend' was taken, there had been a dramatic decline of available manpower and *matériel*. The number of amphibious ships had fallen from 610 in 1945 to 81 in 1950, there was a grave shortage of artillery units, and in 1949 the US army contained only one armoured division. Compared to 1945, fighting effectiveness had also declined, as was shown by the experience of some American units in the first year of the Korean War. Many of the National Guard units sent were inadequately trained and equipped.

After almost being driven into the sea at the end of the peninsula in the first North Korean onslaught, the Americans, who held the Pusan perimeter there against attack, managed to rescue the situation by Operation Chromite. This was a daring and unrehearsed landing on the Korean west coast at Inchon on 15 September 1950 that applied American force at a decisive point. Carried out far behind the front, about 83,000 troops were successfully landed, and they pressed on to capture nearby Seoul, wrecking the coherence of North Korean forces and their supply system, which had been put under great strain by the advance towards Pusan; as well as achieving a major psychological victory. The capture of Seoul enabled the American forces in the Pusan area in the south who, once reinforced, had convincingly held the perimeter, to drive the North Koreans back into their own half of the peninsula and north toward the Chinese frontier, advancing across a broad front against only limited resistance. On 7 October 1950, American forces crossed the 38th parallel.

However, the advance was affected by serious logistical problems that owed much to a lack of adequate harbours, but even more to the poor nature of ground routes, especially in the mountainous interior. In addition, MacArthur's insistence on a landing on the east coast at Wonsan robbed the American Eighth Army's advance on Pyongyang of logistical support, was delayed anyway until 25 October by the extensive mining of the harbour, and, as had been predicted by American staff officers, was rendered superfluous because Korean troops advancing up the east coast had already seized the town on 11 October. Thus, much as Chromite had been a success, the double envelopment failed to achieve its goals, not least of cutting off large numbers of North Koreans.

The American advance was not welcome to the Chinese, who suddenly intervened in October 1950, exploiting American over-confidence. Mao Zedong felt that UN support for Korean unification threatened China and might lead to a Nationalist *revanche*, and was also keen to present China as a major force, and to punish the USA for supporting the Chinese Nationalists; while Stalin, the dictator of the Communist Soviet Union, to whom Mao appealed for help, wanted to see China committed against the USA. This was the price for meeting Chinese requirements for assistance with military modernization.

No such intervention had been anticipated by MacArthur, who had believed that by maintaining the pace of the offensive and advancing to the Korean-Chinese frontier at the Yalu River he would end the war. In this, he had been authorized by the Joint Chiefs of Staff, and there was encouragement from CIA reports that direct intervention by China and the Soviet Union was unlikely. Despite a Chinese warning, via the Indian envoy in Beijing, of action if the UN forces advanced in North Korea, it was believed that the Communist leadership was intent on strengthening its position within China and that China lacked the resources for foreign intervention.

MacArthur ignored the more cautious approach taken by Truman and his Secretary of State, Dean Acheson. Concerned about the Chinese response, Truman instructed MacArthur to use only South Korean forces close to the Chinese border, but MacArthur was insistent that American troops be employed. MacArthur told Truman that it was too late in the year for the Chinese to act in strength, and, after they initially intervened from 18 October in fairly small numbers, he ignored evidence of Chinese troops in Korea. The operational success MacArthur had shown in the Inchon operation was not matched by adequate strategic assessment. Although his hubris was partly respons-ible, there were also weaknesses in American command and control reflecting the improvised way in which the conflict was being fought. In addition, the belief that airpower could isolate the battlefield led to misplaced confidence. From July 1950 the Chinese appear to have begun preparing for intervention, and certainly built up large forces near the border. Success in the Chinese Civil War had encouraged Mao Zedong to believe that technological advantages, especially in airpower, could be countered; not least by determination, but, as with the Japanese in World War II, American resilience, resources and fighting quality were underestimated in this, the sole war between any of the world's leading military powers since 1945.

Attacking in force from 20 November, against the over-extended and, because of an advance on different axes, poorly coordinated coalition forces, the Chinese drove them out of North Korea in late 1950, capturing Seoul in January 1951. The Chinese, nominally Chinese People's Volunteers, not regulars, proved better able to take advantage of the terrain, and outmanoeuvred the coalition forces, who were more closely tied to their road links. The fighting quality and heroism of some retreating units limited the scale of the defeat, but nevertheless, it was a serious one. Thanks to control of the sea, however, it was possible to evacuate some units that had been cut off by the Communist advance, especially the US 1st Marine Division from Hungnam, thus limiting the losses.

The naval dimension was an important element in the conflict, and the Americans were able to deploy and apply a formidable amount of naval strength. The firepower of naval ordnance from Task Force 95 and from the carrier aircraft of Task Force 77 was of operational and tactical value, not least for ground support,[13] while naval control permitted resupply from Japan. Concerned to limit the war, the Soviet Union did not attack the American naval supply routes, not that they would have been able to do so successfully, and the small North Korean and Chinese navies were in no position to do so: in the Chinese Civil War, the Nationalists, not the Communists, had controlled Chinese naval power. Equally, there was no American or United Nations blockade of China, and the Chinese forces deployed in coastal regions that appeared threatened with an American invasion, for example near Tianjin, were not tested in battle.

MacArthur had requested an expansion of the war to include a blockade of China, as well as permission to pursue opposing aircraft into Manchuria and to attack their bases, to bomb bridges along the Yalu River, and to employ Nationalist Chinese troops against the Chinese coast (as a second front) or in Korea. These proposals were rejected by the Joint Chiefs of Staff as likely to lead to an escalation of the war, with the possibility of direct Soviet entry. This was seen as a threat to Western Europe, which was regarded as particularly vulnerable. Had the Soviets attacked in the west, there would, indeed, have been no reinforcements to spare for Korea.[14] American restraint therefore helped ensure that the conflict did not become World War III, or a nuclear war, and the war served as an important introduction for American politicians to the complexities of limited warfare. In turn, Stalin did not wish to take the risk of formal Soviet entry into the war.

The Americans encountered resistance in the air space over North Korea. The Chinese, who had only created an air force in November 1949, and whose Soviet-trained pilots lacked adequate experience, and were equipped with out-of-date Soviet planes, were supported by the advanced MiG-15 fighters of the Manchurian-based Soviet 'Group 64', and the war saw the first dogfights between jet aircraft, with MiG-15s flown by Soviet pilots fighting American F-86 Sabres. The rotation system employed greatly undermined the Soviet pilots' continuity of experience, and thus their effectiveness. The Americans inflicted far heavier casualties and were able to dominate the skies, with serious consequences for respective ground support, although the absence of adequate command integration limited the American exploitation of this advantage. The Soviet refusal to heed Chinese pressure for Soviet air support of Chinese ground forces was a major advantage for the Americans, as well as helping limit the war.[15]

During the war, the Chinese made a full transition to a conventional army, with tanks, heavy artillery and aircraft, continuing the process started during the Chinese Civil War. The UN forces, however, were now a more formidable opponent than when the war started. The Chinese were fought to a standstill in mid-February and in late May 1951, as UN supply lines shortened, and as Chinese human-wave frontal attacks fell victim to American firepower, particularly in the 'Wŏnju Shoot' on 14 February. Even the Chinese Fifth Offensive, that on 22–30 April 1951, pushed the UN forces back toward Seoul, suffered very heavy casualties. Heavy Chinese and North Korean losses of men (about 160,000 casualties in April and May 1951) and equipment, including the surrender of large numbers of soldiers, plus the arrival of American reinforcements, led the Chinese commander, P'eng The-huai, to abandon the attack in late May. The Chinese advance had also greatly increased the logistical burden of supporting China's large commitment of troops.

Thereafter, the war became far more static, with the front pushed back by a UN offensive between 20 May and 24 June to near the 38th Parallel. The attritional conflict that MacArthur had sought to avoid by Operation Chromite now prevailed, and he himself had been relieved in March 1951 for insubordination. Truman's patience with MacArthur was exhausted, and he was also under pressure from his allies concerning the General's views.

The advantage given to the defence by Korea's mountainous terrain was accentuated by the politics of the conflict. Operational intensity and casualties both fell, and lengthy negotiations became more important, with offensives tied to their course. As trench replaced manoeuvre warfare, the role of artillery became more important, while, as the defences on both sides became stronger, the tendency for a more fixed front line was accentuated. With the Americans seeking an exit strategy from the war in the shape of the territorial *status quo* and a ceasefire, there was no attempt to move forward from stalemate.

Nevertheless, there were still costly clashes. For example, in August–September 1951, American and South Korean forces captured the Bloody Ridge group of hills in order to prevent its use as an observation base for artillery fire. In September and October they pressed on, with French support, to take Heartbreak Ridge to the north, in a series of assaults that recalled the methods of World War I trench warfare: UN forces suffered 60,000 casualties between July and November 1951; their opponents about 234,000. This was the last major UN offensive of the war, and after October 1951 the front line changed little. Casualty rates were too high to justify the continuation of the UN advance. In the summer of 1953 the Chinese mounted a series of attacks in order to win advantage in the closing stages of the war. The Chinese made territorial gains, but only at the cost of very heavy casualties.

More positively, containment – both by UN forces of the Communists, and of the nature of the war – prevented the risk of escalation. It was still difficult, however, to end the conflict – the goal of Dwight Eisenhower, who was elected US President in late 1952 – as

Mao Zedong, convinced that his opponents lacked the necessary willpower to persist, felt it appropriate to fight on. However, he was weakened by a shift of Soviet policy after Stalin died in March 1953, a shift accentuated by anti-government riots in East Germany and Poland, and by the serious strain that the war was placing on the Chinese military. The eventual armistice, signed on 27 July 1953, left a military demarcation line along the 38th Parallel with an unfortified demilitarized zone two kilometres deep on either side.[16]

The United States Air Force (USAF) claimed that its conventional bombing caused much damage in North Korea, and helped lead America's opponents to accept the armistice. Heavy damage was certainly inflicted, for example, in 1952, to hydro-electric generating capacity with the attack on the Suiho dam complex; although it is not clear that the bombing campaign was as effective as was to be claimed, and it certainly did not break the stalemate of the last two years of the war. Looking ahead to the Vietnam War, the bombing in the Korean War was also more limited than it had been in World War II. Aside from the decision not to use atomic bombs, USAF suggestions, in 1950, to firebomb the major industrial cities in North Korea were not initially implemented. Once the Chinese had entered the war, major incendiary attacks were launched on North Korea, but there was no hot pursuit of Communist aircraft into China.[17] The USAF also devoted considerable effort to attacking North Korean supply lines, particularly rail links, but it failed to inflict the anticipated logistical damage, not least because of the extent of opposition, and due to repairs and to the night movement of supplies, again anticipating the situation during the Vietnam War.

By the time the Korean War ended in 1953, with over three million dead (of whom 33,741 were classified as American battle deaths, with 2,827 non-battle deaths), the pattern of the Communist–Western confrontation known as the Cold War was set. The majority of casualties were Korean, and for Korea the war was very far from limited: the South Korean military alone lost 415,000, and the war closed with the partition of the peninsula between two states well entrenched and with their mutual hostility unlanced. Indeed, the conflict had seen many of the symptoms of civil war, not least with the harsh treatment of opponents by advancing forces, both North and South Korean.

The war ceased with an armistice agreement, not a peace treaty, and tensions, exacerbated by the war, remained high in Korea. Although Chinese forces were withdrawn from North Korea, a process completed in 1958, the USA still retains a strong military presence in South Korea in order to deter North Korea from invading.

Outside Korea, there was a process of radicalization that further helped entrench ideological and political differences. Thus, Mao Zedong used conflict with the USA in order to consolidate the position of the Communist Party within China, and to push through land seizures, killing large numbers in the process. Furthermore, the war led to a process of militarization and a major increase in military expenditure, especially in the West. For example, in the USA, it rose, as a percentage of total government expenditure, from 30.4 per cent in 1950 to 65.7 in 1954, and a military–industrial complex came to play a greater role in the US economy and governmental structure.[18] Unlike after World War II, the USA did not disarm. Conscription was revived, and the size of the armed forces greatly expanded, with the army being increased to 3.5 million men. The Americans also put pressure on their allies to build up their military. Indeed, the Korean War helped ensure that NATO was transformed into an effective alliance.

In the Soviet Union, militarization was already well established, thanks to World War II, but the late 1940s saw a Sovietization of the militaries of Eastern Europe. This involved those which had fought alongside Germany in World War II before changing sides: Romania and Bulgaria; Hungary, whose forces had largely disintegrated under Soviet attack in 1944; as well as Poland and Czechoslovakia, where the military was based on units that had fought the Germans with Soviet support. The Soviets disbanded the non-Communist Polish Home Army. Soviet officers were appointed to the East European forces: Marshal Konstantin Rokossovsky, a Pole by birth, having been Commander of the Second Byelorussian Front and then, in 1945–9, commander of Soviet occupation forces, became deputy chairman of the Polish Council of Ministers and, later, Polish Minister of Defence.

The Korean War also greatly increased American sensitivity to developments and threats in East Asia, leading to an extension of the containment policy towards the Communist powers, the maintenance of American army, navy and air-power in Japan (where bases were preserved after the occupation was ended), and a growing commitment to the Nationalist Chinese in Taiwan, a marked shift from the position prior to the war when Truman had considered accepting a Communist invasion of the island. The outbreak of the war, and China's subsequent intervention, instead led to a marked increase in aid to the Nationalists and, in June 1950, to the move of the American Seventh Fleet into the Taiwan Strait. The American military presence in the region was fostered precisely because it could serve a variety of purposes, countering North Korea, China and the Soviet Union, but also providing an important element in relations with Japan.

More generally, a sense that the situation might slip out of control through a 'domino effect', as the fall of one country to Communism led to that of others, encouraged the US government to take a greater interest in the course and consequences of the Western retreat from empire, especially in Indo-China where the French were under great pressure. Also, in 1953, a CIA-instigated coup led to the overthrow of the Iranian nationalist leader Mohammed Mossadegh. Nationalist movements throughout the 'Third World' were to be viewed increasingly by Americans through the perspective of their struggle with Communism. The *realpolitik* of intra-state relations was perceived in ideological terms by both the USA and its Communist opponents, helping to ensure that tensions remained high, and encouraging the development of covert operations.

Yet, the Korean War was more than a bridge between World War II and the Cold War. It also links some of the other topics in this book, in being, in part, a war between non-Western powers, in this case North and South Korea; and, as Allan Millett has pointed out, the conflict requires rethinking 'as a war of postcolonial succession, a People's War of revolutionary national liberation, and a war of regional and global great power intervention'.[19] Such a rethinking is more generally required, not only for individual wars, but also in order to discuss conceptually how best to align and assess these varied categories. As they serve as a reminder of the range of causes and interests to be seen in particular conflicts, so they draw attention to the variety of taskings that affected forces, and thus the difficulty of judging success.

Chapter 3

Wars of Decolonization

The most important shift in global power after World War II was the fall of the Western empires; with the exception of that of the USA which still remains in its Pacific territories, with Hawaii, as a state, part of the metropolitan USA. This was a shift that involved a large amount of conflict, although much decolonization was accomplished without warfare. Decolonization, however, fuelled the Cold War, providing it with a series of battlefields and areas for competition, and provided the context, and often cause, for struggles within newly independent states.

Initially, there were major attempts to reintroduce Western imperial control in colonies where it had been disrupted during World War II. This was peaceful in some territories, such as the British colonies of Hong Kong, Malaya and Singapore, but led to conflict in the Dutch East Indies, French Indo-China, and the French colonies of Madagascar and Syria. Syria had been granted independence by the French in 1944, but Anglo-French occupation continued, leading to fighting, which began in 1945 and escalated with the French shelling Damascus. French and British troops were finally withdrawn in April 1946. The following year, there was an anti-French rising in Madagascar, but this was firmly repressed, as the Sétif rebellion in Algeria had been in 1945.

The Dutch were less successful in the Dutch East Indies (now Indonesia). Returning after the end of the war, they were unable to suppress the resistance of nationalists, who had been encouraged during the Japanese occupation and who had declared independence in 1945. Nor did the Dutch prove able to cope with the political challenge of nationalism. In November 1946, they negotiated the Linggajati agreement, recognizing the legitimacy of the nationalist government on Java and Sumatra, and undertaking to cooperate in the creation of a democratic federation; but the Dutch commitment to the agreement was limited and, when it lapsed in June 1947, following divisions within the nationalist movement, the Dutch made a major attempt to secure their position.

Thanks to a large-scale deployment of troops – about 150,000 men – and the support of local allies, especially on the outer islands where there was hostility to the predominantly Java-based nationalists, the Dutch, in two 'police actions' – one in late 1947 and a second in December 1948 – did limit the extent of the nationalists' control on Java and Sumatra, and by the end of 1948 the Dutch were in a strong position. However, a combination of American anti-colonial pressure, post-World War II weakness, guerrilla warfare and nationalist determination forced the Netherlands to accept an armistice on 1 August 1949, and Indonesian independence on 2 November 1949. The Indonesians then moved into Dutch Borneo, the Celebes, the Moluccas, the Lesser Sunda Islands and West Timor;[1] although western New Guinea (still then held by the Dutch) and East Timor (still then held by Portugal) did not follow until later. The Americans were willing to press the Dutch to withdraw, a very different position to that adopted towards the French in Indo-China, because their opponents were viewed as nationalists ready to stand up against Communists.

The British were also involved in a process of imperial withdrawal in the late 1940s. The most important departure was from British India. There, World War II had helped undermine British rule, and post-war volatility made it impossible to provide a level of stability sufficient to serve as the basis for a restoration of the processes of accommodation that ensured widespread consent. The rise of the Congress Party had challenged the British position; not least by reducing the effectiveness, morale and business interests of the government. In addition, the increased sectarianism of Indian politics, with the rise of the Muslim League and its distrust of Congress, made imperial crisis-management, let alone control, impossible. The British hope for a quasi-federation of Muslim and Hindu India fell victim to their inability to reach compromises, leading to a reluctant agreement to partition. The British decision to withdraw in August 1947 was marked by large-scale violence, which was inter-communal, rather than directed at the British. India was divided between the new states of India and Pakistan. The following year Burma (now Myanmar) and Ceylon (now Sri Lanka), also achieved independence.

Inter-communal violence, in this case Arabs versus Jews, was also central in Palestine. There, the British mandate was abandoned in 1948, with the government keen to get an embarrassing problem off its hands. It had found it impossible to maintain order, and had also faced major difficulties at sea, trying to prevent illegal immigration by Holocaust survivors.[2]

THE MALAYAN EMERGENCY

Elsewhere, however, the British made a major attempt to maintain their imperial position. The surrender of Japan was followed by the reimposition of control in occupied areas, including Malaya, Singapore and Hong Kong, and, from 1948, a serious effort was made to resist a Communist insurrection in the economically crucial colony of Malaya. In what was termed the Malayan Emergency, the British initially failed to devise an effective strategy, but this changed with the development of successful, and intertwined, military and political plans. 'Hearts and minds' policies restricted the appeal of the Malayan Communist Party, which was largely based in the minority Chinese population, although these policies also relied on the ability to coerce. Local economic growth, which benefited greatly from the Korean War, also helped. British effectiveness owed much to the use of helicopters and transport aircraft; to improvements in their intelligence system; and to the use of counter-insurgency forces skilled in jungle craft and understanding of the local situation. Rather than requiring protection, a problem with force-deployment in many counter-insurgency struggles, such forces could take the war to the guerrillas. This was complemented by steps to control the population that included the careful supervision of food supplies and the resettlement of much of the rural population, a crucial move. British assistance to the Greek army in the Greek civil war had played a role in the evolution of British experience with counter-insurgency operations.

Partly due to Malaya's geographical isolation, and certainly to the absence of a neighbouring Communist state, the Communists lacked adequate Chinese or Soviet support; they also failed to create a parallel system of government, while the British did not allow the Emergency to deter them from their political course: moves towards self-government (1955) and independence (1957), which the British saw as the best way to defeat the Communists. On the local level, there was a parallel move toward normality, with pacified areas benefiting from an easing of the emergency regulations.

Having largely beaten the insurgents by 1954, the British maintained the pressure over the following years, in particular by the effective use of the now well-developed intelligence apparatus, further weakening the Communists, and were rewarded with mass surrenders in December 1957.[3] In the 1960s, British success in Malaya was to be contrasted with American failure in Vietnam. The contrast frequently focused on greater British commitment to, and skill in, 'hearts and minds' policies, and on the deficiencies of the American stress on fire-power.[4] While this was correct, the situation facing the Americans in Vietnam, in terms both of the political situation there and of the international context, was more difficult.

FRANCE IN INDO-CHINA

France was less successful in Indo-China in 1946–54; in part because, unlike the British in Malaya, the French faced an opponent that, after the Communists won the Chinese Civil War in 1949, had a safe neighbouring base. Important differences of interest affected the degree of support that was provided, but Chinese assistance during 1950 helped ensure that the Communist and nationalist Viet Minh pushed the French back from their border posts in the Le Hong Phong II offensive in late 1950. The French reliance on the road system to link their positions led to a vulnerability that the Americans later were better able to avoid thanks to their vastly greater air transport capability. The French also lacked any recent experience in sustained, large-scale counter-insurgency operations. However, the Viet Minh were defeated when they switched to mass attacks on French *hérissons*, fortified hedgehog positions, in the open areas of the Red River delta in North Vietnam in 1951 and 1952, for example at Vinh Yen and Mao Khé, and in the Day River campaign. In these campaigns the French benefited from a vigorous command and from the ability to employ their conventional forces and airpower, which used napalm among other weapons.

Nevertheless, the Viet Minh were helped by the extent to which, in contrast to the British in Malaya, French forces were spread out over a large area of operations. The French also faced more numerous opposition and enjoyed less domestic support, which affected their capacity to use existing local administrative systems to win support. The French strategy of creating a puppet independent state under Bao Dai, the former emperor, which led, in December 1950, to the Convention of Saigon, did not win much popular support. In 1952, the vigorous command of Lattre de Tassigny, commander from December 1950 until late 1951, was replaced by the less adroit generalship of General Salan. The cumbersome advances he ordered were vulnerable to Viet Minh attacks on their lines of communication.

From 1952, the Viet Minh, who were receiving more Chinese help than hitherto, were increasingly successful in taking over the north-west of Vietnam, threatening both Laos (part of Indo-China) and the French-allied tribes on the Laos–Vietnam border. This area produced opium, and its profits were a valuable support to the French, not least by financing local allies. The opium crop was captured by the Viet Minh in 1952, but recaptured by the French the following year; hitting Viet Minh finances and affecting their operations. In 1954, the Viet Minh succeeded in defeating the French in position warfare at Dien Bien Phu, a forward base about 200 miles by air from Hanoi near the border with Laos. This position had been developed from November 1953 by French parachutists, in Operation Castor, in order to protect native allies and the opium crop, threaten an invasion route into northern

Laos, and lure the Viet Minh into a major battle which it was hoped would enable the French to negotiate from a position of strength.

The French parachutists who arrived on 20 November 1953 rapidly overcame the small garrison at the airstrip in Dien Bien Phu, and, by March 1954, the French had a force of close to 11,000 men in the valley, dug in in a series of strongpoints. General Henri Navarre, the French commander in Indo-China, had assumed that, if the Viet Minh attacked, they would only choose to use one division, but, in the event, Vo Nguyen Giap, the Viet Minh commander, deployed four. During the battle, the French were to add another 4,000 men to the garrison, but Giap was able to commit even more reinforcements.

Viet Minh attacks began on 13 March 1954, and were helped by the French failure to occupy the high ground from which their bunkers could be bombarded; by the folly of the French assumption that their artillery could overcome Viet Minh guns; and by the weakness of French airpower. The Viet Minh had American 105mm cannon, captured by the Chinese Communists in the Chinese Civil War, and also Chinese anti-aircraft weapons and Soviet Katyusha rockets. During the siege, the Viet Minh fired 350,000 shells. Artillery bombardment of the airstrip prevented the French from landing planes after 27 March, and, instead, they were dependent on reinforcements dropped by parachute. The outgunned and poorly chosen French strongpoints were successively stormed, although, thanks to their mass infantry attacks, the Viet Minh suffered far more casualties in combat. The cost of these human-wave attacks led Giap to shift to the use of advancing trench positions. The last assault was launched on 6 May. By then the net had been drawn so tight that air-supply drops were able to bring only scant relief to the garrison; indeed most fell into Viet Minh hands. The remains of the isolated French force finally surrendered on 7 May, their bases overrun. A total of 6,500 troops were captured.[5]

The poorly led French had finally proved unable to defeat their opponents in either guerrilla or conventional warfare. The French army had shown an ability to learn during the war, and had developed counter-insurgency tactics, but it could not respond adequately to the Viet Minh's dynamic synergy of guerrilla and conventional warfare, a synergy that reflected their organizational and doctrinal flexibility, and their successful logistics. After Chinese participation in the Korean War in November 1950 led to greater American concern about Communist expansionism and Chinese policy in East Asia, the Americans, who had begun to supply assistance in May 1950, provided massive quantities of military equipment to the French. In 1952, the USA pressed France not to make peace with the Viet Minh, and by 1954 was paying over three-quarters of French costs in the conflict, but this could not sway the outcome. American policy was both an aspect of the new strategy of containment, and an effort to support France that owed much to concern about the implications of developments in Indo-China for the defence of Western Europe. In this way NATO and Indo-China were linked.

After Dien Bien Phu, the French, who suffered from growing domestic criticism of the war, abandoned Indo-China; although fighting continued into the summer and the French were still in control of the centres of population. However, France's will had been broken by defeat and the US was unwilling to help with a wide-ranging military intervention. Instead, under a new government led by Pierre Mendès-France, a critic of the war, 1954 saw a ceasefire and the Geneva Conference which led to a provisional military demarcation line in Vietnam along the seventeenth parallel, with the hope of reunification once elections had been held, and the guarantee of the independence of Cambodia and Laos. This was not to be a lasting settlement: neither North Vietnam nor the government of South Vietnam were happy to accept partition, but it was a solution that enabled the French to leave.

FRANCE IN ALGERIA

The French were also unsuccessful in Algeria, despite committing considerable resources to its retention. French forces in Algeria rose from about 65,000 in late 1954 to 390,000 in 1956, after first reservists and then conscripts were sent. The dispatch of both these groups was unpopular in France, and greatly increased opposition to the conflict there. In order to concentrate on Algeria, which had been declared an integral part of France (and thus not a colony) in 1848, the French granted independence to its protectorate of Tunisia in 1956, even though nationalist guerrilla activity there, since 1952, had had only limited impact in the towns. The French protectorate in Morocco, where guerrilla activity had become widespread in 1955, also ended in 1956. Algeria was different. It was dominated by a settler population (*colons*) of over a million, and the eight and a half million native Moslems had no real power and suffered discrimination. Attempts to improve their position, for example the Loi-Cadre of 1947, were limited and not pressed home. An insurrection by the Front de Libération Nationale (FLN) began in October 1954, much encouraged by French failure in Vietnam, but at first it was restricted to small-scale terror operations. This destabilized the French relationship with the indigenous Moslems: thousands of loyalists were killed by the terrorists, while the French army found it difficult to identify their opponents and alienated Moslems by ruthless search and destroy operations. Relations between *colons* and Moslems also deteriorated.

In 1955, the scale of FLN operations increased and the war intensified, with massacres, reprisals and a commitment by the French to a more rigorous approach, which led to more effective French tactics: static garrisons were complemented by pursuit groups, often moved by helicopter. These helicopter assault forces were stepped up in 1959, in large part in response to the introduction of significant numbers of large helicopters: Boeing Vertol H-21 helicopters, called *bananes*, which could fly entire units as well as light artillery. Eventually, the French deployed 175 helicopters, as well as 940 aircraft. The designation of large free-fire zones, cleared by forced resettlement, in which aircraft could bomb and strafe freely, increased the effectiveness of the aircraft. Unlike later insurgent forces under air attack, the FLN lacked anti-aircraft missiles, while the terrain was far more exposed than the forested lands of Indo-China. The indiscriminate character of the French use of strafing and bombing was, however, all too characteristic of a failure to distinguish foes from the bulk of the population.

Air reconnaissance and attack and helicopter-borne units took part in a series of sweeps in north Algeria in 1959, killing large numbers of insurgents, while *harkis* – locally raised auxiliaries – served to consolidate control in swept areas. These sweeps gravely damaged the FLN within Algeria, although other FLN units remained outside, attacking French positions from the Tunisian frontier, across the Morice Line which the French had built.

In some respects, the Algerian War prefigured that of the Americans in Vietnam, although the French were more determined than the Americans were to be and, by now, also had more experience of counter-insurgency warfare. Learning from their experience in Indo-China, the French had developed a 'theory of parallel hierarchies' which they applied to Algeria, putting significant resources into intelligence and civilian organizational efforts. The FLN was badly damaged in 1959, just as the Viet Cong was to be in 1968, but the continued existence of both, and their intractability, made the military option appear a dead-end and, in each case, created pressure for a political solution. In France, the pressures of the war helped to bring down the Fourth Republic in 1958 and helped to set General de Gaulle, who had formed a government in 1958 and become President at the close of the year, against the *colons* and much of the military leadership in Algeria, who were opposed to negotiations with the FLN. In January 1960, the *colons* tried to seize power in Algiers, but were faced down by de Gaulle, who wished to retain control of Algeria (as well as influence over Morocco and Tunisia), but was more concerned about France's other political and strategic interests and, in the last resort, was willing to abandon Algeria.

The granting of independence to most of France's other territories in Africa in 1960 made her position in Algeria appear anachronistic, and the French faced serious financial problems and mounting international pressure to negotiate. In particular, the FLN sought to accentuate US concerns about French policy, in order to prevent the French from using the issue of the Cold War to win valuable international support. Convinced that France would fail and worried that backing France would alienate Arab opinion,[6] the Americans were indeed increasingly unwilling to support the French. In early 1961 de Gaulle ordered a truce, and in April the Generals' Putsch, an attempt by some of the army who were angry with negotiations with the FLN to seize power in Algeria, was unsuccessful. The Organization Armée Secrète (OAS), an illegal terrorist movement that wanted to keep

Algeria French, then began a terror campaign against both Gaullists and Moslems. The resulting three-way struggle between the government, the OAS and the FLN led to extensive slaughter in 1962 as independence neared. The eventual agreement with the FLN provided for security for the *colons*, but most fled to France, as did the *harkis*.

A summary of this conflict illustrates the general difficulty of mounting effective counter-insurgency operations. Tough anti-insurrectionary measures, including widespread torture, which was seen as a justified response to FLN atrocities, gave the French control of Algiers in 1957. However, although undefeated in battle and making effective use of helicopter-borne units, the French were unable to end guerrilla action in what was a very costly struggle. And French moves were often counter-productive in winning the loyalty of the bulk of the population. There were also operational problems: aside from the difficulty of operating active counter-insurgency policies, there was also a need to tie up large numbers of troops in protecting settlers and in trying to close the frontiers to the movement of guerrilla reinforcements, so that much of the army was not used for offensive purposes.[7]

Although it is easy to see the failure of the French as a failure of European imperialism, the Egyptians militarily were to be even less successful in Yemen in 1962–7 (see pp. 120–22), while Algeria returned to civil conflict in 1992 as the FLN state proved unable to meet expectations, was perceived as corrupt and Westernized, and proved unwilling to respond to the popular will. The fundamentalist terrorists of the FIS (the Islamic Salvation Front) destabilized the state by widespread acts of brutal terror, and, in response, the government adopted the earlier techniques of the French, including helicopter-borne pursuit groups, large-scale sweep and search operations, and the use of terror as a reprisal; all, to the present day, with only partial success.

BRITAIN AND DECOLONIZATION

The intractable nature of this conflict, which is still continuing and has led to major casualties, especially civilians slaughtered by the FIS and, allegedly, by the government, suggests that it is misleading to see

Western military and political structures and methods as necessarily at fault in the failures of counter-insurgency operations in the 1950s and '60s, a point that was also to be borne out by Vietnamese problems in Cambodia. It is also appropriate to note Western successes, such as the Malayan Emergency and the British suppression of the Mau-Mau uprising in Kenya in 1952–6. In the latter the British benefited from a wide-ranging social reform policy, including land reform, in which the government distanced itself from the white colonists and sought to win 'hearts and minds'. The move from the initial defensive stage, in which the British suffered from not learning the lessons of Malaya, to a recapture of the initiative, in which these lessons were applied, was crucial. This move entailed the development of a system of command and control encompassing army, police and administration, and the introduction of appropriate tactics. In 1954, in Operation Anvil, the British isolated and combed the capital, Nairobi, a move that denied the Mau Mau urban support. The successful use of loyal Africans, including former insurgents, was also important, as were (until 1955) larger-scale sweep operations and, later, air-supported forest patrols. From 1955, success led to the withdrawal of British troops, and this was accelerated after the capture of Dedan Kimathi, the leading Mau Mau commander, in October 1956. The following month, the police took over responsibility for operations.[8]

The British also sought to resolve their problems in the Middle East with the use of force. In 1951 a dispute with the nationalist government in Iran over its nationalization of British oil interests led to Plan Y, the plan for a military intervention by the seizure of Abadan, the centre of the oil industry. It was not, however, pursued, in large part because in the absence of the Indian Army, which had been a vital prop to British power during the colonial period, it no longer seemed militarily viable. This was a major contrast to 1941 when the availability of the Indian Army had helped in the occupation of Iraq.

In 1956 a more assertive stance was taken towards Egypt, in what was seen as a more threatening situation. Britain and France attacked Egypt in an intervention publicly justified as a way of safeguarding the Suez Canal, which had been nationalized that July by the aggressive Egyptian leader, Gamal Abdel Nasser, and that now appeared threatened by a successful Israeli attack on Egypt (see p. 125) with which Britain and France had secretly colluded. Nasser's Arab nationalism was seen as a threat to Britain's Arab allies and to the French position in Algeria, and the British Prime Minister, Anthony Eden, saw Nasser as another Fascist dictator. References to the manner in which the 1930s had shown the dangers of appeasement were a good example of the perils of using inappropriate historical parallels, but decision-makers felt that it was important to stop a dictator in his tracks.

Although poorly planned and badly affected by shortages of equipment, both reflections of the limited amphibious capability of British forces,[9] the invasion saw a major display of military power, with a large force sent to the eastern Mediterranean and the extensive use of warships and air attack, including helicopter-borne troops and parachutists. Much of the Egyptian air force was destroyed as a result of air attacks on its bases. Nevertheless, the invasion was rapidly abandoned, in large part because of US opposition, although the Soviet threat to fire missiles against Anglo-French forces also helped raise tension. Concerned about the impact of the invasion on attitudes in the Third World, the Americans, who were ambivalent about many aspects of British policy, refused to extend any credits to support sterling, blocked British access to the International Monetary Fund until she withdrew her troops from Suez, and refused to provide oil to compensate for interrupted supplies from the Middle East. US opposition was crucial in weakening British resolve and led to a humiliating withdrawal,[10] although, had the British and French persisted, it is unclear how readily they could have translated battlefield success into an acceptable outcome, a point that was to be recalled before the attack on Iraq in 2003. In 1958, both the USA (in Lebanon) and Britain (in Jordan) were to deploy forces in the region as Syria's espousal of left-wing Arab nationalism threatened friendly regimes, but these commitments were easy to contain as they were in support of friendly governments.

The Suez crisis revealed the limitations of British strength, encouraging a new attitude towards empire in Britain, which led to rapid decolonization, especially in Africa, but also in the West Indies and Malaysia. Decolonization was also hastened by a strong upsurge in colonial nationalist movements. The combination of nationalism and the extensive mobilization of people and resources that had character-ized industrializing nations in the nineteenth century in part spread to the non-European world and helped to undermine the logic and practice of colonial control. The 'right to rule' colonial peoples could not be sustained in the political climate of the later twentieth century. There were examples of successful military counter-insurgency, but the political contest was lost as imperialism came to seem ideologically and politically bankrupt, and this factor was to be more important in the collapse of Western control over most of the world than changes in military capability. In the British empire, nationalist movements caused problems, particularly in West Africa, which policy-makers did not know how to confront, as they sought to rest imperial rule on consent, not force. It also proved difficult to control events in Cyprus during the Greek Cypriot insurgency of 1954–9, although regaining the military initiative in 1956, again by applying the Malayan lessons, helped contain the crisis, while the use of sympathetic Cypriots was also important.[11]

Decolonization proceeded on the simple assumption that Britain would withdraw from those areas that it could no longer control, or, equally importantly, from those areas where the cost of maintaining a presence was prohibitive. Colonies also appeared less necessary in defence terms, not least because, in 1957, Britain had added the hydrogen bomb to the atom bomb. Meanwhile, the US administration encouraged decolonization and also sought to manage it as a means of increasing informal American control.

The military dimension of decolonization included not only the containment of independence movements, but also a process of chang-ing the character of locally raised forces. Prior to independence these were developed in the hope that imperial influence, or at least an order beneficial to Western interests, would continue. In 1960, Lord Louis Mountbatten, the Chief of the British Defence Staff, noted:

> The East African Governors are concerned at the slow rate of african-ization of the King's African Rifles, and in particular with the problem of providing African officers quickly . . . With the example of the Congo disaster before them, African politicians are pressing

strongly for the early provision of African officers, and it would appear only sensible to support them by producing officers of known reliability.[12]

Belgium had abandoned the Belgian Congo that year, leading to a situation of great chaos. France also gave most of its sub-Saharan colonies independence in 1960, although it maintained considerable political, economic and military influence over them.

The British and, even more so, the Portuguese and Spanish were still ready to fight to retain their colonies. However, the major British conflict in the early 1960s was not in a colony, but, in 1963–5, on behalf of a state composed of former colonies, Malaysia, that was attacked by neighbouring Indonesia. The crisis began in 1962 with the Indonesian-supported Brunei revolt, which was suppressed by British forces from the Singapore garrison. President Sukarno of Indonesia then turned on Sabah and Sarawak, colonies in Borneo, which the British had transferred to Malaysia. The Indonesians had good weapons, especially anti-personnel mines and rocket launchers, but the British and Commonwealth forces, who deployed up to 17,000 men (more than the US had in Vietnam in 1963), were well led, had well-trained, versatile troops, and benefited from complete command of air and sea. The British made effective use of helicopters and had a good nearby base at Singapore; they had an excellent intelligence network and were helped by an absence of significant domestic opposition to the commitment. The British used a flexible response system to counter Indonesian incursions, and, eventually, followed up with cross-border operations of their own, putting the Indonesians on the defensive. Indonesian attempts to exploit tensions within Malaya by landing forces by sea and sending parachutists there failed. Anglo-Malaysian firmness prevented the situation deteriorating, and a change of government in Indonesia in the winter of 1965–6 led to negotiations.[13]

There was also tension in the Middle East, where the British acted to protect allies and their surviving colony. In 1958 there was an intervention to support Jordan, while in 1961 British and Saudi Arabian troops were moved to Kuwait to thwart a threatened Iraqi attack. More seriously, in Britain's colony of Aden, nationalist agitation, which had been increasingly strident since 1956, turned into revolt in 1963. The resulting war, which continued until independence was granted in November 1967, involved hostilities both in the city of Aden and in the mountainous hinterland. The British deployed 19,000 troops, as well as tanks and helicopters, but their position was undermined by their failure to sustain local support. The British-officered Federal Reserve Army proved unreliable, and, in June 1967, the South Arabian Police and the Aden Armed Police rebelled in the city of Aden. Furthermore, the British were unable to support allied sheikhs in the interior against the guerrilla attacks of the National Liberation Front (NLF). The British used the scorched earth tactics and the resettlement policies seen in Malaya, but the NLF's inroads led them to abandon the interior in the early summer of 1967. In tactical terms, the NLF made effective use of snipers. Reduced to holding on to Aden, a base area that had also to be defended from internal disaffection and where the garrison itself had to be protected, the only initiative left to the British was to abandon the position, which they did in November 1967. Once the British were clearly on the way out, they found it hard to get effective intelligence, and this made mounting operations difficult.[14]

PORTUGAL AND DECOLONIZATION

There was no large-scale independence conflict in the Spanish Sahara and the death in 1975 of Franco, the longstanding Spanish dictator, was followed in 1976 by Spanish withdrawal. The situation was very differ-ent in Portugal's African colonies, and the most significant effort to retain a colonial empire after the French withdrawal from Algeria was made by Portugal. Guerrilla movements in Portugal's colonies began in Angola in 1961, Guinea-Bissau in 1963 and Mozambique in 1964. The Portuguese benefited from divisions among their opponents, espe-cially between the MPLA (Movimento Popular de Libertação de Angola) and UNITA (União Nacional para a Independência Total de Angola) in Angola; from their weaponry, including tactical air support and heli-copters; and from the support of South Africa, then a white-ruled state opposed to black liberation movements and viewing Angola and

Mozambique as its forward defences. Napalm and aggressive herbicides were also used by the Portuguese, who were able to retain control of the towns, for example crushing a rising in Angola's capital, Luanda, in 1961, but found it impossible to suppress rural opposition. Their opponents could also operate from neighbouring states that were hostile to Portugal, such as Tanzania to the north of Mozambique, and Angola's neighbours Zaire and Zambia. Guerrilla forces moved from attacks on border villages to a more extensive guerrilla war, which sought to win popular support and to develop liberated rural areas.

Nevertheless, the Portuguese were still able to control many key rural areas, especially the central highlands of Angola. Until 1974 the 70,000-strong army in Angola, supported by secret police, paramilitary forces, settler vigilantes, African units and informers, effectively restricted guerrilla operations there. More generally, they also protected the 350,000 white settlers in the colony, many of whom were recent immigrants, encouraged to settle in the 1950s as the Portuguese government sought to develop its colony.[15] However, a left-wing revolution in Portugal in April 1974 proved the catalyst to independence, demonstrating the crucial role of events in the metropole. In turn, these events were greatly affected by the war, for the revolution owed much to military dissatisfaction, and to civilian hostility to military service: in response to long tours of service in Africa, there was desertion and large-scale emigration by young men. The change of government led to the granting of independence to the colonies the following year.[16]

Native opposition to imperial rule in Africa looked back to earlier resistance to conquest, but post-1945 mass nationalism was also affected by political movements current in that period, not least Socialism. Indeed, it is possible to identify a development in post-war decolonization struggles with a growing politicization in terms of more 'modern' political ideologies, as well as their location in the Cold War. This was particularly the case in Africa from the mid-1960s. Some earlier uprisings, such as the Mau-Mau in Kenya and that among the Bakongo in northern Angola, displayed many facets of old-style peasant uprisings or militant tribal identity. Although these elements still played a part, the uprisings from the mid-1960s were more explicitly located in a different ideological context, that of revolutionary Socialism. There was direct reference to the revolutionary war principles of Mao Zedong, as well as training by foreign advisers, especially from the Soviet Union, China and Cuba, and a provision of more advanced weapons, although many did not arrive in any quantity until the early 1970s. Anti-personnel and anti-vehicle mines restricted the mobility of counter-insurgency forces on land, and Soviet surface-to-air SAM-7 missiles hit their low-flying aircraft and helicopters. In addition, the guerrillas benefited from Soviet rocket-propelled grenade launchers, and from the durable Kalashnikov AK-47 self-loading rifle, which became the guerrilla weapon of preference.

The impact of these shifts was seen in the struggles in Portuguese Africa. In Angola, the MPLA's military wing, the EPLA (Exército Popular de Libertação de Angola), received weaponry and training from Communist powers, including Cuba, and sought to follow Maoist principles (although the Portuguese were still able to inflict heavy casualties on it). The sense of a wider struggle was captured in the name of two forward bases: Hanoi I and II. Also in Angola, the FNLA (Frente Nacional de Libertação de Angola), a rival guerrilla movement, received Chinese weaponry. In Mozambique, FRELIMO (Frente de Libertação de Mocambique), formed in 1962, was steadily able to widen its sphere of operations, not least because the Portuguese forces did not receive adequate reinforcements. A wider economic strategy was seen in FRELIMO operations, from 1968, against the Cabora Bassa dam project on the Zambezi, a project that linked South Africa, which was to receive electricity from the dam, to Portugal. By 1972, FRELIMO was operating further south, near Beira. Militarily, Soviet and Chinese rocket launchers and, from 1974, SAM-7 anti-aircraft missiles shifted the balance of military advantage, and it was clear that Portugal could not win. In Guinea-Bissau PALEC had SAM-7 missiles, from 1973, and Cuban instructors. The missiles challenged Portuguese air superiority and powerfully contributed to the sense that the Portuguese had lost the initiative. Although they were reasonably successful in Angola, failure elsewhere sapped support for the war in the army and in Portugal.[17]

The end of the Portuguese empire was the last of the 'classic' wars of decolonization. The dissolution of the European colonial empires continued as remnants were given independence or surrendered. In 1977, when Djibouti became an independent state, France withdrew from its last African territory, although it retained rights to maintain forces and use bases in former colonies such as Djibouti. Defence and military cooperation agreements were also the basis for a system of military advisers, and the French maintained their influence in Africa through fiscal support and military intervention. In June 2003, when the French sent troops to eastern Congo as part of a multinational peacekeeping force, they were supported by French aircraft from French bases at Ndjamena in Chad and Libreville in Gabon. This military presence was seen as an important aspect of France's great-power status.[18]

In southern Africa, anti-Western decolonization struggles continued. In South-African ruled South West Africa (now Namibia), SWAPO (the South West Africa People's Organization) had begun guerrilla attacks in 1966. SWAPO received Soviet assistance, and Soviet and Chinese assistance were also sent to guerrilla organizations that sought to overthrow the minority white governments of Southern Rhodesia (now Zimbabwe) and South Africa. The Communist powers believed that the overthrow of Western colonies and pro-Western states would weaken the capitalist economies by depriving them of raw materials and markets, and would also challenge their geo-political position and strategic advantages. In the event, with the exception of Mugabe's Zimbabwe, the successor governments found it economically necessary to trade with the West and actively sought Western investment.

In order to maintain control by its minority white settler population, Southern Rhodesia unilaterally declared independence from Britain in 1965. Initial African guerrilla opposition, which began in 1966, suffered from the extent to which the Zambezi valley offered a difficult approach route, in terms of both support and terrain. From late 1972, however, it proved possible to operate through Mozambique as Portuguese control there was slackening. Full-scale guerrilla warfare was waged from then until 1979. The African opponents of the government were largely divided on tribal lines, and this was also linked to contrasts in their foreign bases and support, and in military strategy: the Ndebele-based ZAPU (Zimbabwe African People's Union) sought to apply Maoist concepts of guerrilla operations, while the Shona-based ZANU (Zimbabwe African National Union) preferred more conventional operations. The Rhodesian military proved better at attacking infiltrating guerrillas than its government was successful in winning 'hearts and minds'. The burden of the war was accentuated when South African military support was withdrawn in 1975. Increasingly isolated, the Rhodesian government conceded majority (African) rule, and Southern Rhodesia briefly returned to British control before, in 1980, becoming an independent state as Zimbabwe.[19]

Meanwhile, opposition had become more vigorous in South Africa, with the Soweto rising of 1976 spreading to major cities. The government responded with a mixture of firmness and concessions, and, eventually, white-minority rule was abandoned. As part of an agreement to limit the conflict in Angola, South Africa withdrew from South West Africa in 1990. The first majority-franchise election followed in South Africa in 1994, and led to the African National Congress peacefully gaining power.

In 1997 Britain returned Hong Kong, its last colony with a large population, to China. This was a peaceful event, although the combination of Chinese strength and the vulnerability of Hong Kong was such that, had the British government wished to, it would have found it difficult to cede control to the local population.

DECOLONIZATION REVIEWED

Decolonization was an important aspect of Western Europe's relative decline, and this was linked to US hegemony. The relationship was not simple, as the diminished range of global political interests that stemmed from decolonization was matched by a period of rapid economic growth in the 1950s and '60s, particularly in Germany and Italy, neither of which needed to defend empires, but also in France. However, as this growth, like that of Japan, was not applied to military force-projection, it did not challenge the impression of American dominance of the West.

The conventional list of wars of decolonization is not, however, necessarily a full one. There are two other categories to be considered. The first is decolonization struggles against non-Western states. These reflect the extent to which, whatever their political structure, whether democratic (India, post-Communist Russia), or autocratic (China, Burma, Ethiopia, Iraq), or both (Israel, a democracy which acts in an autocratic fashion in occupied territory), many states, both large and small, were, or indeed still are, at least as far as part of their population is concerned, imperial and colonial. This is the case, for example, with India in Kashmir, China in Tibet and Xinkiang, and previously with Ethiopia in Eritrea. Thus what, in one perspective, were, or are, regional separatist struggles can also be seen as wars of decolonization or of nationalism.

Secondly, there were decolonization issues involving Western powers after 1975. These took, and take, two forms: the first, regional separatist struggles that employ the language of decolonization and anti-imperialism, for example by Catholic Nationalists in Northern Ireland rejecting the link with Britain, and by Corsican separatists angry with being part of France; and, the second, attempts to claim the colonies of Western powers even if colonial rule is supported by the local population. The Spanish refusal to accept the views of the population of Gibraltar is a good instance of this, although the subsequent blockade, when applied, could best be described in terms of police and customs harassment, rather than as a military operation: it was truly war by other means, a low-intensity operation that precluded conflict.

THE FALKLANDS WAR, 1982

The Argentine invasion of the Falkland Islands in the South Atlantic in 1982 was a different matter. That Britain was to fight a last imperial war then was totally unexpected. The Falklands had been under British control from 1833, but were claimed, as the Malvinas, by the Argentines, whose new ruling military junta was convinced that because the British government was uncertain of the desirability of holding onto the colony, it would accept its seizure by the Argentines. Already, in 1976, after a military junta had seized power from the civilian government of Isabelita Peron, the Argentine navy had raised the Argentine flag on South Thule in the South Sandwich Islands. However, the following year, threatening Argentine manoeuvres were countered with the British response of a task force of two frigates and a submarine. In December 1981 a new junta seized power in Argentina. Its naval member, Admiral Jorge Anaya, insisted that the navy's plan for seizing Britain's territories be implemented. The British decision earlier that same year to withdraw the Antarctic patrol ship *Endurance* was seen as a sign of Britain's lack of interest in the South Atlantic, and, on 2 April 1982, in Operation Rosario, the virtually undefended islands were successfully invaded.[20]

Britain's Prime Minister, Margaret Thatcher, was assured by the Royal Navy that a successful operation could be launched (indeed its leadership was anxious to assert its indispensability), and, determined to act firmly in what was seen as a make-or-break moment for the government, she decided to respond with Operation Corporate, an expeditionary force dispatched from 5 April that included most of the navy: 51 warships were to take part in the operation. As another sign of British maritime strength, 68 ships were contracted and requisitioned, including the cruise ships *Queen Elizabeth II* and *Canberra*, which were used to transport troops, and the container ship *Atlantic Conveyor*, which was sunk by an Exocet missile, taking a large amount of stores to the bottom. The speed with which the operation was mounted contrasted markedly with the time taken for the Suez expedition in 1956.

Concerned that Argentina might go Communist, and anxious about the impact on NATO of British warship losses, the US attempted mediation which would have left the Falklands under Argentine control: Thatcher rejected these attempts. Thanks, in part, to the cancellation of the CVA-01 project in 1966, the British lacked a large aircraft carrier, and therefore airborne early warning of attacks, but they did have two anti-submarine carriers equipped with Sea Harrier short take-off fighter-bombers, which enabled them both to contest Argentine air assaults on the task force and to attack the Argentines on the Falklands.

On 25–6 April, the British recaptured the subsidiary territory of South Georgia, and on 1 May large-scale hostilities began when Port Stanley, the capital of the Falklands, was attacked, with an attempt made to disable its runway. The following day, HMS *Conqueror*, a nuclear-powered submarine, sank the Argentine cruiser *General Belgrano*, with the loss of over 300 Argentines. This was crucial to the struggle for command of the sea as it discouraged subsequent action by the Argentine navy.

French-supplied Argentine Exocet missiles, and other bombs, led to the loss of a number of British warships, including HMS *Sheffield* on 4 May and HMS *Coventry* on 25 May, showing that anti-aircraft missile systems – in this case Sea Darts and Sea Wolfs – were not necessarily a match for manned aircraft, and revealing a lack of adequate preparedness on the part of the British navy, which had had to rely on missile systems not hitherto tested in war. However, the Argentines did not sink the two carriers which provided vital air support (but not superiority) for both sea and land operations. The twenty Sea Harriers were armed with Sidewinder A1M-L missiles which offered an important edge in aerial combat. US logistical and intelligence support aided the British, particularly 12.5 million gallons of highly refined aviation fuel.

The Argentines on the Falklands outnumbered the British force, and had both aircraft and helicopters, while the British were short of ammunition, having underestimated requirements, and were operating at the end of a very long supply line. Landing from 21 May at San Carlos, British troops advanced on Port Stanley, fighting some bitter engagements on the nearby hills, and forcing 11,400 isolated and demoralized Argentines to surrender on 14 June. By landing, the British had not ensured success, as the Argentine plan rested on fighting on from fixed positions in order to wear down British numbers and supplies and take advantage of the forthcoming grim South Atlantic winter. In the end, it was a matter of bravely executed attacks, the careful integration of infantry with artillery support, and the ability to continue without air control. The Argentine will to fight on had been destroyed, and this was crucial as the Argentines still had plentiful troops, artillery and supplies.[21]

All systems of classification invite debate. The decision to consider opposition to non-Western states/empires in later chapters does not reflect a view that imperial or colonial rule by such states is in some way better than, or necessarily different in character from, that by Western states. It is simply organizational, not least because, chronologically, the focus on Western decolonization ended in 1975, whereas elsewhere the process has not ceased.

Chapter 4

Cold War Conflicts

The most prominent Cold War conflict was that in Vietnam. Its classification is a matter of controversy, as the US presence in Indo-China was castigated by critics as another aspect of Western imperialism, and the Vietnam war has been presented as one of the wars of decolonization, especially as the second stage of the war, involving the Americans, followed that in which the Viet Minh fought the French. This approach, however, misrepresents the reasons for US intervention, and the motives of the Communist powers that assisted North Vietnam, reasons that are located centrally in the Cold War. This term for the struggle between the USA, with its allies, and the Communist powers and their supporters, captures its essential feature: that it did not become a full-blown war. However, the use of the term Cold War underplays the extent to which it repeatedly became 'hot'. This was true not only of what were readily discerned as wars, particularly those in Korea, Indo-China and, increasingly, the Arab–Israeli conflicts, but also less widely considered struggles, including many civil conflicts in Latin America and sub-Saharan Africa.

The issue of classification is again a problem, as there is an overlap both with the World War II aftermath wars and the wars of decolonization discussed in earlier chapters, and with the conflicts between non-Western powers considered in chapter six, not least because the Vietnam War can be seen in part as a civil war. This chapter begins with the Vietnam war, because it is the one most frequently considered in discussion of this topic, and then continues by discussing warfare elsewhere that can be readily classified in terms of the Cold War.

Concern about spreading Communist power, especially as, and after, China fell in 1948–9, helped lead to US interest in South-East Asia. In 1948, the British encouraged the Americans to become involved in resisting Communist expansion in South-East Asia: the French were under pressure in Indo-China, and the British in Malaya. Although nationalism was crucial to these 'liberation struggles', they were also characterized by Communist exploitation as the Soviet Union and China sought to challenge the USA indirectly by encouraging supporters to attack US allies. These attacks brought together notions of popular warfare, nationalism and revolutionary Communism in a programme of revolutionary struggle in which success was believed to be inevitable. Conversely, Western governments feared that Third World anti-colonial movements and nationalism would be exploited by the Communist powers, and this encouraged a view that the West's front line ran round the world, and that Communism had to be contained.

The USA was determined to keep the front line not only away from the Western hemisphere but also as close to the Communist bloc as possible. This entailed a variety of strategies including: membership of, and support for, NATO in Western Europe – the most important of a number of regional defence agreements; an American hegemony in the Pacific that rested on naval power and on bases, including those obtained under the peace treaty with Japan, as well as the former Japanese colonies now administered under UN trusteeship as the Trust Territory of The Pacific Islands;[1] military assistance to allied countries; pro-active covert operations, some of which can scarcely be defined in terms of containment; and an active engagement to resist the Communist advance in the Third World, particularly by contesting the consequences of the Communist use of liberation struggles; this latter strategy brought the Americans to Vietnam.

THE VIETNAM WAR

Vietnam had been partitioned after the defeat of the French in 1954. The Communist Viet Minh were left in control of North Vietnam, and a US-supported government was established in South Vietnam, where, from 1957, it faced a Communist rebellion by the Viet Cong, which led to more overt and widespread US intervention. The South Vietnamese government was corrupt and unpopular. It had won the 1955 election using fraud, and it represented best the landowning élite that composed it. The Catholic identity of the regime further compromised its popularity in what was a largely Buddhist country. The Viet Cong offered an attractive programme of socio-economic transformation, including land reform, and won considerable support, providing a basis for military action.

From 1959, forces from North Vietnam were infiltrated into South Vietnam in support of the Viet Cong. The US were concerned that a failure to support South Vietnam would lead to the further spread of Communism in South-East Asia. In response, the commitment of US 'advisers' to South Vietnam, including the foundation in February 1962 of Military Assistance Command, Vietnam, encouraged pressure for increased support, and by 1963 there were 16,000 US military advisers. American intervention helped limit Viet Cong advances in 1962, but the combination of the lack of fighting quality of much of the South Vietnamese army (which grew in size from 150,000 men in 1960 to 250,000 in 1964), and flawed advice from the Americans, in particular an emphasis on firepower, failed to win victory.[2] Meanwhile, invalidating notions, supported by France in particular, that South Vietnam could have been neutralized through negotiation, the North Vietnamese were determined to maintain the struggle. Meeting in December 1963, the ninth plenary session of their Communist Party's Central Committee criticized the Soviet notion of 'peaceful existence', decided to step up the war in South Vietnam, and pushed forward more militant politicians.

Apparent attacks on American warships (and certainly an attack, however much provoked by American support for South Vietnamese commando raids) by the North Vietnamese in the Gulf of Tonkin off Vietnam in August 1964 led Congress to pass a resolution permitting President Johnson 'to take all necessary measures to repel any armed attack against the forces of the United States and to prevent further aggression', in short to wage war without proclaiming it. This was the preferred US option because Johnson wanted to avoid an explicit choice between war and disengagement, as well as to apply more easily the strategic concept of graduated pressure. In a general sense, the credibility of US power seemed at issue, and there was a belief in Washington that the line against further Communist expansion had to be drawn somewhere, and that this was it. The Americans were concerned about the impact of developments in South Vietnam for those elsewhere in Indo-China, especially Laos, where Communist moves greatly concerned its neighbour Thailand, as well as their more general implications throughout South Asia and the West Pacific. The Vietnam struggle could be put alongside China's 1962 war with India, and Indonesian attacks on Malaysia (Sukarno was close to China), to indicate a widespread threat as part of a crisis that the US could respond to and affect by acting in South Vietnam. The power in the USA of the 'China Lobby', namely the supporters of Taiwan, was also significant. In late 1964, regular units of the North Vietnamese army were sent south in strength, and by 1965, the South Vietnamese army was on the verge of collapse.[3]

The US response was delayed by Johnson's wish to avoid anything that might compromise his chance of re-election in November 1964, but, by the end of 1964, US forces in South Vietnam had reached 23,000; they shot up to 181,000 in 1965, 385,000 in 1966, and peaked at 541,000 in January 1969. Aside from the important contribution by the South Vietnamese, massive American involvement was supplemented by troops from South Korea, the second largest international contingent with 48,000 troops,[4] Australia, New Zealand, Thailand and the Philippines. The South Koreans were largely paid for by the USA, which regarded them as good troops that cost less than Americans. Although the war effort was less international than the US had wished, and than had been the case in the Korean War, it reflected a widespread concern about the strategic position in South-East Asia and the Communist advance, as well as a need to support the USA. Thus Australia, which kept troops in Vietnam until 1972, was anxious to secure US support in the event of confrontation with Indonesia.

The Communists were well led and organized, and their political system and culture enabled them to mobilize and direct resources efficiently and to maintain a persistent effort. American involvement permitted the North to promote the war as a national crusade against Western imperialism. Military struggle and political indoctrination were seen to act in symbiosis, and the North Vietnamese and Viet Cong were more willing to suffer losses than the US. 'Limited War' theory was (and is) a Western concept that was not shared by the Vietnamese, and American strategy was wrongly based on the assumption that unacceptable losses could be inflicted on the North Vietnamese in the way that they could on the Americans:[5]

> Early in the war, US policymakers opted for a war of attrition based in part on an imperfect understanding and unrealistic expectations of the ability of American firepower to send a persuasive message. The Communist forces never did crack, despite the ever-increasing levels of destruction. In the end it came down to a classic Clausewitzian test of wills and national resolve,[6]

and, in the face of North Vietnamese and Viet Cong determination and morale, the Americans cracked first, after attrition had led to stalemate. Looked at differently, the US came to appreciate the consequences of Limited War: that it could lead to failure, and did so rapidly once their initial hopes for success had been thwarted. Subsequent debate as to whether total war (which, with the technology of the period, would have encompassed nuclear weapons) would have led to US victory can only go so far, as the intention was not to fight such a war.

Viet Cong morale was sustained despite heavy casualties. This morale, which owed much to coercion and indoctrination, extended throughout the army: the soldiers who built the Ho Chi Minh trail, down which supplies moved from North Vietnam to Communist forces in the South, were inferior troops in military terms, but they believed that they could attain status by doing these menial tasks. They were also taught to believe that if they died – as most did – their descendants would be rewarded, for instance in the distribution of land. In contrast, US morale suffered once success proved elusive, and serious drug use and indiscipline grew, affecting unit cohesion and operations. The political context had a more direct impact on US grand strategy. Concern that China might intervene, as in the Korean War, discouraged any US invasion of North Vietnam, and thus dramatically reduced their options. The Chinese also provided North Vietnam with large quantities of *matériel* and substantial numbers of support troops.

When the US intervened in force in 1965, their opponents were already operating in sizeable units and this led, in 1965-8, to battles that were won by the Americans. Initially, the Americans focused on defending coastal areas that were strongholds of South Vietnamese power and essential for US deployment, but gradually they moved into the interior. They were able to advance into parts of South Vietnam which had been outside the control of Saigon and to inflict serious blows on the Viet Cong in the Mekong delta. In addition, direct mass Viet Cong attacks on US positions were generally repulsed with heavy casualties, for example at the siege of Plei Me in the Central Highlands in 1965. Under General William Westmoreland, commander of the US Military Assistance Command, the Americans sought to advance throughout South Vietnam, establishing 'firebases' from which operations would be mounted, in order to inflict casualties on their opponents and erode their strength. The helicopter played a major role in this extension of activity, particularly with the use of the new 1st Cavalry Division (Airmobile).

Yet the activity only brought so much advantage. Although heavy casualties were inflicted, opposing numbers rose, as North Vietnam responded to the US build-up by sending troops down the Ho Chi Minh Trail. Furthermore, there was no concentration of opposing power that could be rapidly fixed and readily destroyed as, in very different circumstances, the Israelis were to do against Egypt, Jordan and Syria in 1967. American advances concealed the extent to which they shared the initiative with their opponents, while the need to devote significant resources to building up forces, logistics and security limited US combat strength.

By the end of 1967 the situation, nevertheless, appeared promising, and Westmoreland felt that he was winning. This was inaccurate, and the Tet offensive of 1968, which involved Viet Cong and North Vietnamese attacks on cities and military bases across South Vietnam, indicated the resilience of the opposition. These assaults, mounted under cover of the Lunar New Year celebrations of Tet, were launched in the belief that they would engender a popular uprising, but none followed, and the attacks were beaten off with heavy losses, hitting Viet Cong morale. The US benefited from a pre-Tet decision to move some combat units back from near the border, where they had been concentrated. This decision, taken on 10 January, was in response to indications that Viet Cong and North Vietnamese forces were being built up near the cities. However, the Americans failed to anticipate the timing and, more particularly, scale and character of the attack: over-optimistic assumptions about enemy casualties in the border battles of late 1967 were matched by an inability to believe that a full-scale attack on the cities would be mounted.

About 85,000 Viet Cong and North Vietnamese forces attacked from 30 January 1968, with 36 of the 44 provincial capitals and five of the six autonomous cities being among the targets. Attacks also on 23 airfields were a testament to the role of airpower. Over two divisions were used for the attacks in and close to Saigon, but these attacks were largely contained and overcome within several days. The most serious and longest battle was waged for control of the city of Hué, the former imperial capital, much of which fell on 31 January. The city was not regained until 25 February, after both difficult house-to-house struggles within its walls, and an eventually successful cutting off of supply routes into the city: the US lost 216 dead, the South Vietnamese forces 384 dead, and their opponents over 5,000. Part of the nature of the conflict, as well as its brutality, was shown by the slaughter or 'disappearance' of about 5,000 South Vietnamese civilians by the Viet Cong during their occupation: their crime was that they came from social categories judged unacceptable in the Maoist society that the Communists were trying to create. The massive use of air and artillery power during the recapture of Hué destroyed about half of the city, making over 100,000 people homeless. By the end of February it was clear that the North Vietnamese/Viet Cong offensive had failed to achieve its goals. There was no popular uprising, and the US and South Vietnamese had not been defeated, although their losses were heavier than in earlier battles.

While the Americans could repel mass attacks on their strong points and drop thousands of bombs from a great height without opposition, their will for the war was worn down by its continuation, while they could not deny control of the countryside to their opponents. American units suffered from a lack of accurate intelligence, and this helped to lead them into ambushes. General Vo Nguyen Giap, the North Vietnamese commander, was an effective leader who developed logistical capability to give effect to his strategy of denying his opponents (first France, and then South Vietnam and the USA) control over territory while maintaining operational pressure on them. Giap was less successful when he turned to positional warfare and to mass attacks against opposing forces in reasonable positions, as in 1951 against the French, and in 1968 and 1972 against the South Vietnamese and Americans, but his military strategy and the political determination of the North Vietnamese government did not depend on continual success.

The jungle nature of the Vietnamese terrain limited the options for US airpower, which was applied for strategic, operational and tactical goals and, in the last case, played an important role in helping army and marine units under attack, as at Khe Sanh in 1968, complementing artillery support in this valuable role. Over half the $200 billion the USA spent on the war, a sum far greater than that spent by other Western powers on decolonization struggles, went on air operations, and nearly eight million tons of bombs were dropped on Vietnam, Laos and Cambodia: South Vietnam became the most heavily bombed country in the history of warfare. There were also major US bombing offensives against North Vietnam, which were designed both to limit support for the war in the South and to affect policy in the North by driving the North Vietnamese to negotiate. These attacks faced serious opposition from Soviet surface-to-air missiles, supplied from April 1965, as well as from Soviet MiG-17 and MiG -21 aircraft. The use of electronic jamming in order to limit attacks by missiles and radar-controlled guns had considerable success for the US, but the North Vietnamese learned, in part, to counter this by aiming at the jamming signals.[7] Prisoners taken from US planes that were shot down gave the North Vietnamese a valuable negotiating card that they could also use in their struggle to influence US domestic opinion.

More seriously, in operational terms, the failure of the Marines and the Navy to accept Air Force pressure for operational cooperation, in the shape of a single airpower manager, had major consequences, not only in inhibiting a consistent level of attack and thus maximizing US capabilities, but also in preventing the sharing of lessons. This was but part of a more general failure of preparedness which encompassed inappropriate doctrine and aircraft, as well as inadequate command and training.[8]

As an example of the difficulty of assessing military history, controversy continues over the extent to which, among other options,[9] a more determined (less reluctant and restricted) and persistent air assault on North Vietnam would have ensured US victory. American policymakers seeking to contain the struggle were reluctant to use an all-out non-nuclear air attack with unrestricted targeting and were affected by the idea that, by means of gradual escalation, they could send appropriate messages and affect their opponents' decisions,[10] an idea that was not vindicated by the Vietnam War. Conversely, the proponents of airpower claim that had Operation Rolling Thunder (the unrestricted bombing of the North) continued, instead of ending in 1968, it would have led the North to yield; although it had certainly not stopped the Tet Offensive.[11] A drive west of the Demilitarized Zone to cut the Ho Chi Minh trail, a policy rejected during the war, has also been hotly debated subsequently, as has a 'northern' hook landing (similar to Inchon in 1950) around the port of Vinh and west into the entrances to the trail.

Airpower also played a major role in the unsuccessful attempt to block Viet Cong supply routes, as well as the more successful endeavour to provide tactical and supply support for US troops on the ground. Tactical support led to the use of slow flying gunships with massive firepower capability, although the Viet Cong were proficient in entrenching in order to minimize their losses. Helicopters were extensively used, not least in supplying positions and in applying the doctrine of air mobility: airlifted troops brought mobility and helped take the war to the enemy.

As an instance of the scale of conflict, the US flew about 36,125,000 helicopter sorties during the war, including 7,547,000 assault sorties, in which machine-guns and rockets were used, plus 3,932,000 attack sorties. Over 2,000 helicopters were lost to hostile causes (and many others to accidents), but heavier losses had been anticipated. Helicopters had become more reliable, more powerful, and faster than in the 1950s, and their use helped to overcome guerrilla challenges to land supply and communication routes.

The Americans had to adapt to fight in a variety of unfamiliar terrains, including dense jungle and rice paddies. The jungle nature of much of the terrain gave the Viet Cong ideal cover, and ensured that superior us technology had little to aim at. Partly as a result, both Westmoreland's quest for battle, in which us firepower could be applied in order to ensure successful attrition, and the search-and-destroy operations, pursued until 1968 in order to build up a 'body count' of dead Viet Cong, were each of limited effectiveness, not least because it was difficult to 'fix' the Viet Cong. The Americans lacked adequate intelligence of their opponents' moves, and, instead, the Viet Cong tended to control the tempo of much of the fighting, mounting ambushes that caused heavy casualties, and then ambushing relief units in their turn.

As with the air offensive against supply lines, the us displayed a preference for seeing the Viet Cong as a regular force that could be beaten by conventional means, rather than an understanding of their doctrine and operational methods. Furthermore, the creation of a political organization by the Viet Cong ensured that more than the defeat of the guerrillas was required. The us army, however, bereft of an adequate counter-insurgency doctrine,[12] and lacking a reliable political base in South Vietnam, preferred to seek a military solution, and to emphasize big-unit operations, not pacification. However, without the latter, its operations were of limited value and, instead, alienated civilian support. Many Americans found it difficult to understand the nature of the war they were engaged in, and to appreciate the extent to which their opponents, by refusing to fight on American terms, nullified American advantages, and thus multiplied the difficulties posed by the terrain. The Americans failed to appreciate that, although they had more firepower and mobility than the French had done, they were faced with the same problems of Communist determination, and that even if it was achieved, victory in battle would not change this.[13]

Creighton Abrams, who became US commander (of Military Assistance Command) in June 1968, preferred instead to rely on small-scale patrols and ambushes, which, he argued, provided less of a target for his opponents than large-scale sweeps. Abrams set out to contest the village-level support the Viet Cong enjoyed and to counter the impact of Tet, which had led to a regrouping of US and South Vietnamese troops as units were pulled back to defend the cities. The US also tried to lure the Communists onto killing grounds by establishing 'firebases': positions supported by artillery and infantry. In 1969, the Americans inflicted serious blows on the Viet Cong, whose capability had already been badly compromised by the failure of the Tet Offensive in which the Viet Cong and the North Vietnamese had lost close to half the troops used. Viet Cong attacks in 1969 suffered heavy casualties and achieved little.[14]

Conversely, in the 1970s, the Communists came to rely more heavily on conventional operations mounted by the North Vietnamese. This was a consequence not only of the casualties and damage that Tet had inflicted on the Viet Cong, but also of the failure of Rolling Thunder, the bombing of North Vietnam launched in March 1965, to destroy the war-supporting capability of North Vietnam, and, also, of the failure of the air offensives launched against the Ho Chi Minh trail. The latter was crucial to North Vietnamese logistics, and the failure to cut it on the ground was a major limitation in American war making.

Although US and South Vietnamese counter-insurgency policies worked in some parts of Vietnam, they were generally unsuccessful; although, conversely, there was no general pro-Viet Cong uprising in response to the Tet offensive. The pacification programme entailed a 'battle for hearts and minds', involving American-backed economic and political reforms, but these were difficult to implement, not only due to Viet Cong opposition and intimidation, and the effectiveness of their guerrilla and small-unit operations, but also because the South Vietnamese government was half-hearted, corrupt and weak, and thus unable to take advantage of military success.[15] The US could not find or create a popular alternative to the Viet Cong. As the Americans also brought much disruption, including high inflation, and devastation through the use of firepower, pacification faced additional problems, while the culture-clash between the US and their South Vietnamese allies hindered cooperation.[16]

Domestic economic problems as well as political opposition, and his own disillusionment at continued signs of North Vietnamese vitality, led President Johnson, his views confirmed by a policy review by a group of senior outside advisers, the 'Wise Men', to reject, in March 1968, Westmoreland's request for an additional 206,000 men in Vietnam instead, he authorized only 13,500 more troops.[17] Military difficulties combined with political pressures within the USA resulted in an attempt to shift more of the burden back on the South Vietnamese army by improving its capability, and some success was achieved. Indeed, Vietnamese units fought better in response to the Tet offensive than had been anticipated. Yet the context was very different to the use of large numbers of native troops in European imperial forces earlier in the century, for example the contribution by Indian troops to British hegemony in South Asia.

Domestic opposition in America to involvement in Vietnam rose because of the duration of the conflict and because the goals seemed ill defined. Their leadership divided on policy, the Americans had lost the strategic initiative, but there was already a lack of deep commitment. Dean Rusk, the Secretary of State, later commented:

we never made any effort to create a war psychology in the United States during the Vietnam affair. We didn't have military parades through cities. We didn't have beautiful movie stars out selling war bonds in factories and things like that as we did during World War II. We felt that in a nuclear world it is just too dangerous for an entire people to get too angry and we deliberately played this down. We tried to do in cold blood perhaps what can only be done in hot blood.[18]

By denying the US victory in the field, and, instead, continuing to inflict casualties, the North Vietnamese and Viet Cong helped to create political pressures within America and to sap the will to fight, although their objectives were focused on success in South Vietnam: affecting American public opinion was only a side-issue. In the USA, the absence of victory led many to see the continuing casualties as futile, especially when the Tet Offensive led to questioning of Pentagon pronouncements about the course of the conflict.

The conscription necessary to sustain a large-scale American presence in an increasingly unpopular war played a major role in the growth of disenchantment. A majority of the Americans who went to Vietnam were volunteers, not draftees, but, in 1965-73, about two million Americans were drafted, and draftees accounted for a third of American deaths in Vietnam by 1969. The draft led to a massive increase in anti-war sentiment. Opposition was widely voiced and 'draft dodging' common, with many Americans taking refuge in Canada. Johnson abandoned his re-election bid on 31 March 1968 because he had failed to end the war, and, once elected, his successor, Richard Nixon, who had promised peace with honour, pressed ahead with substituting Vietnamese for US troops, so that he could bring the men back home and end the draft.[19]

American disengagement under Nixon, which led to a fall in the military commitment from 536,000 men when he came to office at the start of 1970, to 335,000 men at the close of the year, and 156,000 a year later, was not, however, to be an easy process. In 1969 knowledge that withdrawal was beginning and a sense that the conflict was pointless led to a marked, cumulative and escalating decline in morale and discipline among the troops, with negative effects on fighting quality and sense of purpose. Nixon's policies had only limited success. Although he planned to move the burden of the ground war onto the South Vietnamese army, which was over a million strong at the close of 1971, there were to be more US casualties after 1968 than earlier in the conflict, and 1972 was to see a North Vietnamese offensive greater in scale than that in 1968.

Although seen as realists, beginning negotiations with the North Vietnamese in Paris in January 1969, Nixon and his Secretary of State, Dr. Henry Kissinger, stuck with Vietnam, extending the war. In April 1970, Nixon widened its scope by launching an American–South Vietnamese ground invasion of neutral, neighbouring Cambodia to destroy Communist bases there, after bombing had failed to do so. This 'incursion' succeeded in the short term, helping to strengthen the Allied position in South Vietnam, while, in Cambodia, the USA provided military aid and air support for the government of General Lon Nol which had seized power in March 1970. In turn, the North Vietnamese provided help to the Khmer Rouge, the Cambodian Communist movement let by Pol Pot.

However, the 'incursion', which was of dubious legality, further lessened support for the war in the USA, and helped the Communists to seize power in Cambodia in 1975. In 1971, Lamson 719, a comparable invasion of Laos by the South Vietnamese without US support (apart from air and logistical help), failed with heavy losses in fighting with North Vietnamese units. The US commitment to Cambodia and Laos took a variety of forms, including the establishment, in 1967, of a long-range radar control station at Pha Thi in Laos to assist US air attacks in North Vietnam,[20] the attacks on Communist supply lines through Laos, particularly from 1968, and air operations over Cambodia in 1970–73.[21]

In March 1972, the North Vietnamese launched the Nguyen Hue campaign (or the Easter Offensive), a conventional invasion of South Vietnam across the Demilitarized Zone, which led to the fall of Quang Tri, a provincial capital, and to the siege of another, An Loc. This led to a heavy US air response, in the Linebacker I air campaign of May to October 1972, which hit the North Vietnamese supply system, cutting the movement of supplies to their forces. The conventional nature of the force that had invaded the South – fourteen divisions including tanks and trucks that required fuel – made the air attacks more devastating than those directed against the Viet Cong had been; this had a major impact on the conflict on the ground.

The enhanced effectiveness of US airpower was due not only to North Vietnamese operational goals and methods, but also to a marked improvement in US air capability that reflected both the displacement of earlier doctrine, stemming from adjustment to the varied needs of the Vietnam War, and the use of laser-guided bombs. These precision weapons hit North Vietnamese logistics by destroying bridges, and were also very useful in close air support, for example against tanks. Furthermore, advances in ground-based radar technology helped in the direction of B-52 strikes.[22]

After initial North Vietnamese success in March, April and May 1972, that, in part, reflected the surprise nature of the attack and the forces deployed, the invading force was held off by the South Vietnamese, and territory was regained. The North Vietnamese suffered in 1972 from their inability to master high tempo manoeuvrist warfare, a theme that repeatedly emerges in defeats covered by this book. In particular, there was a failure to make the best use of tanks, which reflected both an operational inability to use them in a manoeuvrist capacity, in order to gain mobility and achieve particular objectives, and a tactical failure to achieve infantry–armour coordination. Instead, the tanks were used as an assault force on South Vietnamese positions, indeed essentially as mobile artillery. Losing mobility meant not only squandering the initiative in operational terms, but also the tactical problem of providing ready targets for US airpower, and reflected a degree of inflexibility that suggested that determination was far less of an advantage in conventional style offensive operations than in guerrilla warfare.[23]

The USA had meanwhile strengthened its diplomatic position by a *rapprochement* with China in 1972, a step that made it less serious to abandon South Vietnam. Using the pressure of further heavy air attacks on North Vietnam, the B-52 raids in the Linebacker II campaign of December 1972 (the effectiveness of which, in the face of strong North Vietnamese air defences, has been doubted[24]), Nixon was able to negotiate a peace settlement, the Paris Peace Agreements, which were signed on 27 January 1973. That month, he announced the end of all hostile acts by US forces in Vietnam.

The US withdrawal, completed in March 1973, left South Vietnam vulnerable; the war continued, with heavy South Vietnamese casualties, and, in April 1975, South Vietnam was overrun, in the Ho Chi Minh campaign, by a renewed invasion from the north. Conventional North Vietnamese divisions achieved what the Viet Cong fighting in more adverse conditions in 1968, and the earlier conventional attack in 1972, had failed to do. The North Vietnamese made good use of tanks in 1975, and ably integrated them with infantry and artillery. In contrast, when used against An Loc in 1972, they had fallen victim to US helicopter-fired wire-guided missiles and anti-tank weapons. The South Vietnamese showed in 1975 that, on their own, they were not a match for their opponents, which, in part, was an aspect of the failure of US intervention. Unlike the North Vietnamese, the South Vietnamese military was politicized without equivalent gains in motivation, while there were also important operational and doctrinal problems, including a failure to take, and use, the initiative that amounted to a widespread reluctance to take combat to their opponents. Moreover, in 1975 the South Vietnamese followed an unwise strategy with an abandonment of the Central Highlands, where the North had launched its attack, and a focus on defending the south that gave their opponents a powerful impetus and gravely weakened their own morale. Although some units fought bravely, resistance crumbled and, on 30 April, Saigon fell.[25]

It is possible to argue that had the US continued to provide the aid they had promised, but that Congress cut off, then the South Vietnamese forces would have gone on fighting successfully. American airpower could have made a major impact, as it had done in 1972. However, South Vietnam was no South Korea: geographically, South Vietnam, and the areas within it held by the government, were far more exposed, while the regime was weaker, and its weaknesses were exacerbated by the poor policy followed in 1975. It is instructive to consider the stress on how continued US intervention might have altered the situation, as it is part of a longstanding American tendency to see the conflict in their own terms, and to underrate the extent to which the Vietnam War was an Asian civil war. In 1976, the two halves of Vietnam were reunited as the Socialist Republic of Vietnam. In April of the previous year the guerrillas of the Khmer Rouge, the Cambodian Communist Party, had overcome the pro-American Lon Nol government; while the US abandonment of support for the Royal Lao armed forces was followed by the triumph of the Communists in the struggle for dominance of Laos.

The Vietnam War demonstrated that being the foremost world power did not necessarily mean that less powerful states could be defeated, because power existed in particular spheres and its use was conditioned by wider political circumstances,[26] especially, in this case, the danger of a confrontation with other Communist powers and growing opposition to the war in the USA. The Americans themselves suffered more than 58,000 dead, while large numbers were wounded physically or mentally, the last leading to a considerable number of suicides. In addition a sense of defeat and division had a major impact on US society.

Aside from the personal traumas which, collectively, were also a major social issue, indeed crisis (although of course far, far less than the casualties and damage suffered by the Vietnamese), the Vietnam War also led in the USA to a major rethinking of the political context of force projection. The War Powers resolution passed by a Democrat dominated Congress, in November 1973, over Nixon's veto, stipulated consultation with Congress before US forces were sent into conflict and a system of regular presidential report and congressional authorization thereafter. This law was to be evaded by successive presidents and was not to be enforced by Congress, but it symbolized a post-Vietnam restraint that discouraged military interventionism in the 1970s, and helped ensure that, in the 1980s, the more bellicose Reagan administration did not commit ground forces in El Salvador or Nicaragua, let alone Angola. In March 1991, in the aftermath of the first defeat of Iraq, President George H. Bush stated 'By God, we've kicked the Vietnam syndrome once and for all', but the legacy of the conflict continued to influence not only civilian attitudes but also attitudes among military leaders, leading to a reluctance to get involved in counter-insurgency operations, and an emphasis on a clear mission, and an obvious exit-strategy.

THE SOVIET UNION AND AFGHANISTAN

In the 1980s, the Soviet Union was also involved in an unsuccessful counter-insurgency campaign, although there were important differences alongside the similarities. A major contrast was that Afghanistan bordered the Soviet Union, helping to increase Soviet concern and to ensure that the Soviet government did not feel that it had an easy exit strategy. The Soviets had been major aid donors to Afghanistan from the 1950s, taking its side in a frontier dispute with US backed Pakistan. In 1973, the monarchy was overthrown in a coup and an authoritarian strongman, Mohammed Daoud Khan, took power. In turn, in the Saur

Revolution on 27/28 April 1978, Daoud was overthrown and killed in a coup mounted by the Soviet backed People's Democratic Party of Afghanistan.

Bitterly divided, the new government responded to opposition with repression, and its attempts to reform society (particularly with land reform and equality for women) led to rebellions, from late 1978, including a serious rising in Herat in May 1979. The government met these with considerable brutality, not least with the colonial era remedy of 'pacification' by bombing. After a coup from within the regime, on 16 September 1979, did nothing to stem the tide of chaos, the Soviets intervened from 27 December 1979, overthrowing the government and installing Babrak Karmal as president. The Soviet intervention appears to have resulted from concern about the stability of their position in Central Asia and from their unwillingness to see a client state collapse. Contemporary suggestions that the Soviet Union was seeking to advance to the Indian Ocean appear overstated.

The Soviets were able to overthrow the Afghan government in 1979, in part by the use of airborne troops, and to seize the cities. Thereafter, however, they found it impossible to crush guerrilla resistance, in a conflict that lasted far longer than anticipated, and finally withdrew in 1989. The bellicose nature of its society, and the fragmented nature of its politics, made Afghanistan difficult to control, and the Soviets and their Afghan allies held little more than the cities.

The Soviet forces were poorly trained, especially in counter-insurgency warfare, for which they lacked experience; their doctrine and tactics were designed for high-tech conflict with NATO in Europe; and they had inadequate air support. Without that, the infantry was vulnerable. The Soviets had to confront an intractable military environment; they faced obdurate opponents, harsh terrain, disease, and the difficulty of translating operational success into lasting advantage. In addition, relations between the Soviet and Afghan armies were poor, while the initial inclusion in the invasion force of a large percentage of Uzbeks, Tajiks and Turkmen led to tension with the Pushtuns in Afghanistan. In turn, the opposing guerrillas were seriously divided.

The Soviets failed to understand both their opponents and the nature of Afghan politics and society, and their belief that insurgency movements were the characteristic of progressive forces, and that conservative systems lacked popularity, ensured that they lacked both the necessary military doctrine and an understanding of the relationship between military moves and political outcomes. As in the Vietnam War, 'hearts and mind' did not work, and the Soviets suffered from the lack of effective counter-insurgency doctrine, strategy and tactics. The block and sweep was a new operation for the Soviet military, but it further alienated Afghan opinion. Driving the population off land that could not be controlled was the strategy followed from 1983, but this did not win support, and was further compromised by indiscipline and atrocities. Soviet sweeps or operations, such as the relief of Khost in late 1987, were followed by a return to base that brought no permanent benefit. The Soviets were unable to force large-scale battle on their opponents, who generally proved able to avoid Soviet advances; and, although the airborne special forces were able to carry the fight to opposing Afghans, they were not employed with sufficient frequency.

The Soviets also deployed too few forces, 120,000 troops at the peak, in a country much bigger than South Vietnam, in large part for political and logistical reasons, and, therefore, lacked the numbers required for the concurrent and consecutive operations that Soviet war-fighting envisioned, while, to maintain the operational dynamic, the Soviet commanders conducted operations with smaller forces than they were trained for. In addition, convoy escort engaged a large portion of the Soviet combat forces, necessarily so because the Soviets were totally dependent on supplies from the Soviet Union. The pro-Soviet Afghan army contributed little to operational effectiveness.

The guerrillas benefited from ample foreign support, including, from 1986, American ground-to-air Stinger missiles and their British counterpart, the Blowpipe, which brought down Soviet helicopter gunships, forcing them and aircraft to fly higher, which cut the effectiveness both of their ground support and of their bombing. The guerrillas made extensive use of the Soviet RPG-7 anti-tank grenade launcher, which proved effective against all Soviet vehicles. The supply of the guerrillas through Pakistan helped make it more important strategically to the West, and also increased US interest in its stability.

Technology was useful to the Soviets, particularly with aerial resupply, but it could not bring victory. The Russian General Staff Study of the war noted that it posed unfamiliar problems:

> combat was conducted throughout the country, since there were no clearly defined frontlines . . . The war in Afghanistan gave the Soviet forces their first significant experience in the preparation and conduct of operations and combat against irregular guerrilla formations on mountain–desert terrain . . . the peculiarities of counter-guerrilla war and the rugged terrain determined the Soviet tactics in Afghanistan, where it was impossible to conduct classic offensive and defensive warfare. In Afghanistan, the principal forms of combat were the raid, block and sweep, ambush and those actions connected with convoy escort and convoy security'.[27]

Although the Soviets could afford their manpower losses in Afghanistan, Mikhail Gorbachev, who became General Secretary of the Soviet Communist Party in 1985, decided to end the commitment, which he saw as detrimental to the Soviet Union's international position, particularly his wish to improve relations with the West, as well as domestically unpopular. The Geneva Accords of 14 April 1988 led to a Soviet withdrawal, completed by February 1989, although Soviet military and financial aid to the Afghan government continued. It held out against the guerrillas, who were weakened by serious divisions; while their murderous treatment of prisoners did not encourage defections. As in South Vietnam, the departure of the supporting outsiders did not lead to the fall of the regime at once, but this departure was eventually followed by its collapse. Failure in Afghanistan also hit the morale of the Soviet military, and had an impact on its response to the crises of the collapse of Soviet dominance in Eastern Europe and of the Soviet Union itself. In turn, these crises led to the demoralized character of the Russian military in the 1990s.

The Cold War also saw intervention by the major powers in regional struggles, as well as a rush to arm and train allies and protégés. The arms trade indeed ensured that much conflict around the world was an aspect of the Cold War. The USA and the Soviet Union were the biggest providers of arms. The provision, as a result, of large quantities of modern arms, albeit not always cutting-edge weapons, added to the destructiveness of regional conflicts. This trend was particularly apparent in the Middle East. There and elsewhere, states that saw their rivals armed by foreign powers sought arms from the rivals of the latter. In 1955, in the first Soviet–Egyptian arms agreement, the Soviets agreed to provide 200 MIG -15 fighters, 50 Ilyushin-28 bombers and hundreds of tanks. The following year, an agreement led to the dispatch of 800 Soviet advisers. These agreements led Israel to turn to France, which was opposed to Egyptian president Nasser's support for Algerian rebels, and the French armed Israel until 1967. From the late 1960s, the USA armed Israel; it decided, in 1968, to provide Israel with Phantom F4 jets,[28] while the Soviet Union armed Egypt and Syria. During the 1973 war, the US rushed supplies to the Israelis by air, in C-141s and C5s, via their air base in the Azores. In the 1980s, India was armed by the Soviet Union and its Pakistani opponent by the USA and China. By spending over $20 billion on Soviet arms, Colonel Qaddafi, the dictator of Libya since 1969, had by the mid-1980s built up a military that included 535 combat planes and over 2,800 tanks.

AFRICA

The extent to which regional struggles were drawn into the Cold War varied greatly. In East Africa, a secessionist dispute became a violent part of the Cold War, as Somalia's support for secession from Ethiopia of the Somali-populated Ogaden region ensured that the conflict involving the Western Somali Liberation Front became a war between two states. When Soviet armed Somalia attacked Ethiopia in 1977 with weapons including MIG fighters and Iluyshin-28 bombers, the Soviet

Union offered arms to Ethiopia if it abandoned its US alliance, which it did. As a result, by March 1978, 11,000 Cuban and 4,000 South Yemeni soldiers had arrived to help Ethiopia. The Cubans were necessary in order to man the tanks, armoured personnel carriers and artillery provided by the Soviets, and more generally, the Cubans provided a valuable level of competence in supporting indigenous armies in Africa, although, in Angola, they displayed poor training and inadequate use of airpower and were eventually affected by war weariness and low morale.

Helping Ethiopia against their former Somali allies, the Soviets also provided air reconnaissance, airlift, signal intercepts, and a commander, General Petrov, who ably adapted cutting-edge weaponry and operational systems devised for war in Europe to the exigencies of Africa, although he was helped by the nature of the terrain, much of which was relatively flat and lacking dense vegetation. Having gained air dominance and used it, in January 1978, to attack Somali supply routes, Petrov launched assaults, spearheaded by tanks and rocket-launchers, and supported by air attacks. Firm resistance near Jijiga led to the use of airborne attacks with parachutists assisted by helicopter troops, which enabled the attackers to overcome the tactical strengths of the Somali position. Victory at Jijiga was followed by the reoccupation of the disputed Ogaden region. This campaign was one of the most impressive of the decade and showed how what the US termed AirLand battle could be waged and won.

Cuban forces (up to 50,000 troops), and Soviet money, arms and advisers, were also sent to Angola to help thwart US backed South African intervention in the civil war between MPLA and UNITA that followed Portuguese withdrawal in 1975. The initial South African advance on the capital, Luanda, was blocked by the Cubans, and left in the lurch by the US. The South Africans had to withdraw, but South African support for UNITA continued,[29] helping UNITA to consolidate its position in southern Angola, and thus helping cover the South African position in South West Africa. The MPLA, which had seized control of the government in 1975, was unable to overrun the south, but UNITA failed to capture the major cities and, in the winter of 1987–8, a UNITA and South African siege of the southern city of Cuito Cuanavale failed.

The South African inability to maintain air superiority during the siege was a major development.

African states that received Soviet military aid in the mid-1970s also included Guinea, Mali, Mauritania, Nigeria and Uganda, while Western powers were willing to provide aid to their own allies. Faced with guerrilla opposition in 1964 the Congolese army received US and Belgian aid and, eventually, help from Belgian paratroopers transported by US aircraft. In 1978, also in Congo, Belgian and French paratroopers supported by US and French air transport helped suppress a Cuban-backed invasion of the province of Shaba.

THE MIDDLE EAST

In the Middle East, the wars between Israel and, in each case, some of its Arab neighbours (1948–9, 1956, 1967, 1973 and 1982) were subsumed into the Cold War as Soviet support for Egypt and Syria, and US for Israel, became more pronounced from the 1960s. Equally, the USA devoted major efforts from the mid-1970s to lessening tension, and the Camp David Accords of 1978 were consolidated with the deployment of US troops to monitor the Sinai frontier, although massive quantities of financial aid to Egypt and Israel were more important.

Furthermore, the superpowers played a major role elsewhere in the Middle East, as with the commitment of US forces to Lebanon in 1958 and 1983. The latter episode indicated the limitations of modern militaries. Thus, the Americans were hit not only by a suicide bombing, but also by the shooting down of two carrier aircraft by Soviet surface-to-air missiles fired by the Syrians. In addition, terrorism was intertwined with the Cold War in the region, as elsewhere. Libya was bombed by the US on 15 April 1986 in response to its large-scale sponsorship of terrorism: the bombing demonstrated Libyan vulnerability, but, if its intention was to kill the Libyan leader, Colonel Qaddifi, it failed, although in the long term the bombing seems to have restrained him at least in part.[30]

Struggles throughout the Middle East were regarded as aspects of the Cold War. When Syria unsuccessfully invaded Jordan in 1970 in support of Palestinian guerrilla forces this was seen as a threat to US interests. Further east, Iraq's move towards the Soviet Union in 1972, which included an agreement for military cooperation, led that year to closer ties between the USA and Iran: Nixon announced that Iran could purchase any non-nuclear American weapons it wanted and that the two states would jointly support the Kurds in their struggle with Iraq. However, when the Iranian revolution of 1979 led, that November, to the imprisonment of the staff of the American Embassy at Teheran, the US, in April 1980, tried to mount a helicopter borne rescue operation. This failed as a result of problems with some of the helicopters, as well as poor communications.[31]

LATIN AMERICA

Conflict across much of Latin America also involved the intervention of the major powers, or at least American action against left-wing movements, and can therefore be located, at least in part, in the context of the Cold War.[32] This was particularly the case with Cuba and Nicaragua, each of which led to major episodes in the US covert operations that were an important aspect of the Cold War.[31] The seizure of power by Fidel Castro had initially been acceptable to the USA, but his leftward move led to support for an *émigré* attempt to seize power that miscarried in the Bay of Pigs invasion in 1961, in part because the absence of US air support left the invaders vulnerable, although their assessment of the political situation inside Cuba was also overly optimistic. Cuba then became more prominent when the stationing of Soviet missiles there in 1962 led to a US blockade that threatened to lead to conflict between the USA and the Soviet Union.

After the Soviets had backed down, the US demonstrated their strength in the Caribbean by successfully intervening in the Dominican Republic in 1965, sending in nearly 23,000 troops to prevent it from becoming a second Cuba, a misreading of the risks posed by a rebellion against a conservative regime. The US enforced peace and oversaw an election in 1966 that produced another conservative government, that under Joaquin Videla Balaguer, before withdrawing, while leaving a Military Advisory and Assistance Group that helped the US administration to oversee developments by maintaining close links with the army. The USA also became concerned about Cuban support for Latin American radical movements, although attempts to repeat Castro's success were unsuccessful: Che Guevara dismally failed when he tried to mount a revolution in Bolivia in 1967. In the 1970s, the commitment of Cuban forces to conflicts in Africa became an important aspect of the Cold War.

The US who, like the Soviets, were major trainers of foreign military personnel, devoted particular effort to training the Latin American military. Combined with higher morale and greater determination than was shown by the Cuban army in 1956–9, this helped lead to the defeat of radical insurrections. From the mid-1950s, and particularly after Castro's success in Cuba, Latin American military establishments were restructured in accordance with American views;[33] the first Latin American counter-insurgency school being founded, with US aid, in Colombia, and a US trained unit helped crush Guevara's revolution in Bolivia. As a result, military help was seen as part of a programme that included economic aid and political support for the development of democratic regimes that were considered necessary in order to secure pro-US societies.[34] The emphasis on these respective goals varied, with a particular ambivalence when political developments did not match geo-strategic aspirations. This ambivalence had existed from the outset of the Cold War, with aid to Greece and Turkey from 1947 being primarily military and with scant emphasis on the democratic reforms that were proclaimed.

The Communist challenge in Latin America was seen by the USA as more insidious than that of the Germans there during World War II, because Communism was seen both as geo-strategic threat to the USA itself, directed by the Soviet Union, and as a diffuse social challenge to the coherence and stability of Latin American regimes. Following the 1951 Military Security Act, the USA signed bilateral agreements with twelve Latin American states, the latter agreeing in return for military assistance to focus their production of strategic materials on the USA and not to trade with hostile states. Concern about radicalism encouraged the CIA to oppose the government of President Jacobo Arbenz Guzmán in Guatemala and, finally, in 1954, to instigate a successful coup.[35] The US administration also supported the Chilean army under

General Pinochet when it overthrew the Marxist Allende government in 1973.

Nicaragua was seen as a threat after 1979 when the Sandinista National Liberation Front overthrew the dictatorship of Anastasio Somoza Debayle. The left-wing Sandinistas drew inspiration and support from Cuba, and also provided support for left-wing rebels in El Salvador. Concerned about the risk of instability throughout Central America, and determined to mount a robust response, the Reagan administration, which came to power in 1981, applied economic, political and military pressure on the Sandinistas, providing funds from 1981 to train and equip the Contras, a counter-revolutionary force that was based in neighbouring Honduras. Although the Contras helped to destabilize Nicaragua, they could not overthrow the Sandinistas. Instead, diplomatic pressure from the international community led to free elections in 1989 that led to the replacement of the Sandinista government.

In El Salvador, the Reagan administration provided advisers, arms, including helicopter gunships, and massive funds to help the right-wing junta resist the Farabundo Marti National Liberation Front (FMLN); although the commitment of numerous advisers was not followed by ground troops. This enabled the US to define the struggle as low-intensity conflict, although it did not appear so to the population of El Salvador as they were caught between guerrillas and brutal counter-insurgency action, which frequently took the form of terror. The American hope that the election of the moderate José Napoleon Duarte as President in 1984 would lead to peace proved abortive, while the war revealed the classic weaknesses of guerrilla operations, not least the difficulty of moving from rural power and harrassing attacks, to dominance and control of the towns and an ability to achieve victory. The war also revealed some of the weaknesses of counter-insurgency strategies, including the problems of using military strength, especially air attacks, to ensure civil peace. While the Cold War was fading in Europe, it continued in El Salvador, with a large-scale FMLN offensive in November 1989. This took over part of the capital, San Salvador, for a week, but could not incite a popular uprising. Equally, the failure of the government to prevent the offensive led its US sponsors to press for negotiations which eventually led, in 1992, to a settlement under which the FMLN translated its activism to civilian politics.

To consider warfare, the role of armed forces, and military developments in many parts of the world in relation to the Cold War is not to neglect the role of indigenous traditions, interests, issues and pressures in events, but it captures their wider interactions and relevance.

Chapter 5

Cold War Confrontations

Although there was no conflict to match World War II, the Cold War involved a massive and dangerous confrontation of conventional forces between the Western and the Communist powers, backed by intercontinental nuclear forces capable of destroying the planet. This 'superpower' stand-off lasted 45 years until the collapse of the Soviet Union at the start of the 1990s.[1]

COLD WAR: EARLY STAGES

The origins of the Cold War lay in the long tension between democratic capitalism and radical socialism that stemmed from the Russian Revolution of 1917 and its international sequel. Cooperation against Fascism in World War II was only a temporary truce, and the post-World War II Cold War began with the tension within the anti-Axis alliance. Wartime alliances frequently do not survive peace, and this was particularly true of World War II, because of the ideological division between the Soviets and the Western powers. Even in 1942–3, Stalin suspected that a second front in Western Europe was being delayed deliberately in order to drain Soviet resources, while by 1944 differences within the alliance over the fate of Eastern Europe, especially the future of Poland, were readily apparent. Ideologically and culturally, each side felt threatened by the other, and this conditioned

84

their response to the events that followed the war.

In 1945, the creation of occupation zones in Germany and Austria involved the military of Britain, France, the USA and the Soviet Union in a number of tasks for which they were poorly prepared, including controlling large numbers of refugees and prisoners of war, seeking to run a devastated economy, and maintaining law and order, not least trying to tackle smuggling, counterfeiting and black marketeering. These tasks were increasingly undertaken within a context of confrontation.[2] The *de facto* partition of Germany, between the Soviets and the Western powers, ensured that Germany was on the front line of the Cold War, while the breakdown of cooperation over occupied Germany and the imposition of Communist governments in Eastern Europe, which culminated with the Communist coup in Prague in 1948, led to pressure for a response. Soviet actions appeared to vindicate Churchill's claim in March 1946 that an 'Iron Curtain' was descending from the Baltic to the Adriatic, and there was a growing conviction that expansion was inherent in Soviet planning.

The debacle of 1940, when Denmark, Norway, Belgium and France had rapidly fallen to German attack and Britain had been threatened with invasion, had revealed that guarantees by Britain and other European powers of each other's territorial integrity were of limited effectiveness. Nevertheless, after the war there was interest in the idea of a Western European 'Third Force', independent of the USA and the Soviet Union, and Britain and France signed the Treaty of Dunkirk in 1947, followed, with the addition of the Benelux States, in 1948 with the Treaty of Brussels which created a Western European Union. However, in response to fears about Soviet strength, an alliance with the USA appeared essential. The Soviet Union lacked the atom bomb, but its numerous army appeared well placed to overrun Western Europe. In addition, in February 1947, the British had acknowledged that they could no longer provide the military and economic assistance deemed necessary to keep Greece and Turkey out of Communist hands. Instead, the British successfully sought US intervention. Concerned about Communism, the Americans did not intend to repeat their inter-war isolationism. The Marshall Plan of 1947 was intended to stabilize Europe's economy, and indeed strongly contributed to this, and was a powerful pledge of commitment. The US economy had expanded greatly during the war, both in absolute and in relative terms, and it had the manufacturing capacity, organizational capability, and financial resources to meet the costs of post-war military commitments.

As the Soviet Union became increasingly assertive in Europe, so the US became more committed to its defence of European democracy. The Berlin Crisis of 1948, in which the Soviets blockaded West Berlin only to be met by an Anglo-American airlift of supplies into the city, led to the stationing in Britain of US B-29 long-range bombers which were intended to attack the Soviet Union in the event of war. The threat of the use of the atom bomb helped bring a solution to the crisis, but the bombers remained.

NATO

In 1949, the foundation of the North Atlantic Treaty Organization (NATO) created a security framework for Western Europe, at the same time that Communist success in China apparently increased Soviet options, while the first successful Soviet nuclear test seemed to remove the power of the US nuclear deterrent. Totally abandoning its pre-war tradition of isolationism, the USA played a crucial role in the formation of the new alliance, and was thus anchored to the defence of Western Europe. An analysis of World War II that attributed the war and Hitler's initial successes to appeasement in the 1930s led to a determination to contain the Soviet Union, and, in 1949, the Senate ratified the North Atlantic Treaty establishing NATO by 82 votes to 13, a clear contrast with their predecessors' failure to support the League of Nations after World War I. From 1950, substantial US forces were stationed in Europe,[3] thus increasing US commitment to the region and spreading their logistical system.[4] That December, General Eisenhower, an American, was appointed NATO's Supreme Allied Commander. The establishment of NATO was followed by the creation of a military structure, including a central command, by the provision of American munitions and surplus commodities, such as fuel, to NATO allies, and, eventually, by West German rearmament. The original members of NATO, the USA, Canada,

Norway, Denmark, the UK, Netherlands, Belgium, France, Luxembourg, Italy and Portugal, were joined by Greece and Turkey in 1952.

The Korean War led to a major increase in Western military spending, particularly in the USA, but also among its allies. Thus, in Canada, which played an active role in NATO and sent troops to Korea, defence spending rose from $196 million in 1947 to $1.5 billion in 1951. Under American pressure, Britain embarked in 1950 on a costly rearmament programme, which undid recent economic gains and strengthened the military commitment that was to be such a heavy post-war economic burden. Western policy had been militarized, the USA had become a national security state, and the division of Europe had been cemented; but such remarks pay insufficient attention to the threatening character of Stalin's policy. The threat from the Soviet Union was also crucial to the development of Western intelligence agencies and of the practice of surveillance against both domestic and foreign opponents. In the USA, the Central Intelligence Agency was created under the National Security Act of 1947. Intelligence operations involved conflict, as with attempts to intercept aerial reconnaissance missions, which included the Soviet shooting down of the U2 spyplane, and also with the use of covert operations.[5]

The threat of Soviet attack in Europe while the US were committed in Korea, led from 1950 to US pressure for German rearmament. The British Chiefs of Staff who, in June 1950, had argued that the Soviets were essentially cautious and opportunistic, were more worried a year later. West Germany was finally admitted to NATO in 1955, when the Allied High Commission came to an end, laying the basis for German rearmament within an alliance system, a rearmament that was seen as necessary in order to provide the forces required to defend Western Europe, not least because of the heavy imperial commitments of Britain and France.[6]

There had been major differences among US policymakers and politicians over the strategy that should be followed, not least the degree to which there would be a policy of global containment of Communism and a reliance on nuclear weaponry. By the early 1950s, however, the requirement and strategy for atomic defence and war were in place: the US forces in Western Europe had to be protected.

Whereas initially the American Joint Chiefs of Staff had assumed that the defence of Western Europe would be the responsibility of the Europeans, with the US providing help from the Strategic Air Command and being most concerned about its air bases in Britain, membership in NATO ultimately led to a full-scale US ground commitment to the defence of Western Europe. On 18 December 1950, the NATO Council agreed to a strategy of forward defence which meant holding West Germany.[7] This affected US, British and French planning and force requirements. Particularly after the Communist takeover in Czechoslovakia, which considerably extended the frontier between Communism and West Germany, the linear defence of the latter had become a formidable and costly[8] task across a very broad front. NATO, conversely, did not encompass European colonies, and, despite French arguments, the exclusion extended to Algeria, which, legally, was part of metropolitan France.

A clear front line was also in place across Europe. The Communists had been defeated in Greece, while, thanks to its anti-Communism, Franco's Spain, a Fascist dictatorship, was brought into the Western alliance. In 1953, the USA and Spain signed an agreement giving the Americans the right to establish air bases in Spain, although Spain did not join NATO until 1983, by which time it was a democracy. Behind the front line, the US encouraged political, economic and cultural measures across Western Europe to limit support for Communism; and saw this as a crucial aspect of defence.

Thanks to the geo-politics of the Cold War, the Americans were able to preside over and organize the most powerful part of the global economy, and to benefit from its growth. There was a positive synergy, with the expansion of the global economy providing opportunities for the USA, while the introduction of American techniques and the availability of the US market provided opportunities for Japan and Western Europe. The economies of the non-Communist world benefited from the growing availability of capital and from a major growth in trade, which encouraged specialization and economies of scale, while the efficiency of the system was increased by structural reforms and by improved communications. Economic growth, in turn, helped provide the resources for a stronger military posture.

NATO and the rival Soviet-led Warsaw Pact, established in 1955, prepared and planned for conflict. A paranoid sense of vulnerability, which owed much to World War II and something to Communist ideology, encouraged a major emphasis on military expenditure in the Soviet Union: nearly a quarter of Soviet state expenditure went to military purposes in 1952. A feeling of uncertainty on both sides, and of the fragility of military strength, international links, political orders and ideological convictions, encouraged a sense of threat and fuelled an arms race that was central to the Cold War. Both sides claimed to be strong, but declared they required an edge to be secure; the inherent instability of an arms race where only the mutually assured destruction (MAD) threatened by massive nuclear stockpiles eventually brought a measure of stability. Aside from the competition between the USA and the Soviet Union to produce and deploy more and better weapons, there was also rivalry between the various services of the US armed forces, and comparable arms races between those of other countries.

The leading powers of the Cold War also tried to ensure that their allies were militarily effective, while the provision of arms helped to consolidate military cooperation, making training and joint exercises easier. In Eastern Europe the forces received Soviet equipment, uniforms and training, while in 1950, the Soviet Naval Advisory Mission to China was established: Soviet training, supplies and ship designs were important in the development of the Chinese navy.[9]

The outbreak of war in Korea in 1950 helped increase tension elsewhere, not least because it was seen as a stage in Soviet expansion; in particular, it was assumed that this would be a prelude to an invasion of Western Europe. Indeed, throughout the Cold War, the conflicts that did occur sustained attitudes of animosity, exacerbated fears and contributed to a high level of military preparedness. Just as nineteenth-century theorists of international relations had concentrated on conflict, so their Cold War successors focused on confrontation rather than conciliation, affecting both the public and political and military leaders. Planning for war, especially with the added factor of nuclear strength, led to an emphasis on strategic theory.

The premises behind Western planning were the need to repel Soviet attacks and resist Soviet advances across the world. Nevertheless, there were variations in the intensity of confrontation. The Soviets did apparently come close to attacking Western Europe in the early 1950s, particularly in 1951, but Stalin's death in 1953 led to a relaxation of tension, which was marked by the withdrawal of Soviet forces from their occupation zone in Austria in 1955. Austria became a buffer zone, outside NATO, very different from Germany, where the forces of NATO and the Warsaw Pact continued to be in close and hostile proximity. The Austrian Treaty was followed in July 1955 by the Geneva Summit; the first meeting of the leaders of the USA, the Soviet Union and Britain since 1945, and one that saw an attempt to take disarmament, or at least confidence building, forward. Similarly, there were variations in the intensity of confrontation with China, with aggressive Chinese moves in the Taiwan Strait area in 1954 and 1958 leading to serious crises.

NUCLEAR CONFRONTATION

Overhanging all else was the nuclear deterrent. America's nuclear monopoly, which appeared to offer a means to coerce the Soviet Union, had lasted only until 1949, when, thanks to successful spying on Western nuclear technology, the Soviet Union completed its development of an effective bomb that was very similar to the American one. This development had required a formidable effort, as the Soviet Union was devastated by the impact of World War II, and it was pursued because Stalin believed that only a position of nuclear equivalence would permit the Soviet Union to protect and advance its interests. However, such a policy was seriously harmful to the economy, as it led to the distortion of research and investment choices, and militarily questionable, as resources were used that might otherwise have developed conventional capability. Although the Communist governments that followed Stalin, after he died in 1953, introduced changes in some aspects of policy, they did not break free from his legacy of nuclear competition.[10]

Even when America alone had had the bomb, the value of the weapon was limited, as it was insufficiently flexible (in terms of military and political application or acceptance of its use) to meet challenges other than that of full-scale war. Thus the US did not use the atom bomb (of which they then indeed had very few) to help their Nationalist Chinese allies in the Chinese Civil War. Similarly, US possession of the bomb did not deter the Soviets from intimidating the West during the Berlin Crisis of 1948–9. Nevertheless, the availability of the bomb encouraged US reliance on a nuclear deterrent, which made it possible to hasten demobilization, leaving the USA more vulnerable when the Korean War broke out in 1950.[11]

The nuclear duopoly did not last long. Britain, France, China, India and Pakistan followed with their own atomic weapons in 1952, 1960, 1964, 1974 and 1988 respectively, while Israel and South Africa also developed a nuclear capability. Conversely, neither West Germany nor Japan developed such technology. This reflected the absence of any policy of *revanche* on the part of the post-war leaderships that gained control after Western occupation ceased, which spoke well of the post-war Allied rebuilding effort. It also accorded with US directed Western security policies.[12]

The destructive power of nuclear weapons increased when the atomic bomb was followed by the hydrogen bomb. This employed a nuclear explosion to heat hydrogen isotopes sufficiently to fuse them into helium atoms, a transformation that released an enormous amount of destructive energy. The USA first tested a hydrogen bomb in 1952, destroying the Pacific island of Elugelab. This was seen as a way to reconfirm nuclear superiority, but it was rapidly thwarted, as the USA was followed by the Soviet Union in 1954, Britain in 1957, China in 1967, and France in 1969.[13]

Delivery systems for nuclear weapons had, in the meantime, changed radically. In the late 1940s and early 1950s, the Soviet Union had been within range of US bombers based in Britain, but the USA had been out of range of Soviet nuclear attack. American doctrine focused on massive nuclear retaliation in response to any Soviet use of their larger non-nuclear forces in Europe or elsewhere, and the use of the atom bomb in 1945 ensured that there was a new impetus to airpower, one provided by the apparent ability of a small number of bombs to make a decisive difference. The major role of this in US strategy[14] was linked to the creation, in 1947, of an independent air service in the USA, the United States Air Force (USAF). In order to fulfil its independent role, and to take the leading part in the Cold War, US air force thinking was dominated by strategic nuclear bombing: the ability to strike at Soviet centres was seen as an effective deterrent, indeed as the sole counter to Soviet conventional strength and the vulnerability of America's allies and interests, as well as a war winning capability, and as the essential purpose of American airpower. This emphasis was given added force by the role of officers from Strategic Air Command in the senior ranks of the Air Staff; by a fascination with aerial self-sufficiency and big bombers; and by the absence of a powerful drive for integrated warfare, which would have encouraged the development of doctrines for cooperation with the army and navy.[15] Strategic nuclear bombing also played a major role in British air planning.[16]

In both countries the legacy of inter-war air doctrine and of the World War II 'strategic' (i.e., war winning) bombing campaigns, played a major role. In contrast, the value of close air support, shown by Allied air operations in 1944–5, was neglected and, in the USA, the Tactical Air Command that was founded in 1948 as an equal to Strategic Air Command was rapidly downgraded and swiftly lost most of its aircraft.[17]

During the Cold War the crucial strategic zone was defined as the North European Plain, and the Soviet Union had a great superiority in conventional forces there. This superiority was enhanced as Soviet forces were modernized and as the military effectiveness of their Eastern European allies was increased. This led to a series of responses in NATO planning (which was very much dominated by the USA), each of which focused on the degree to which nuclear weaponry would be involved, and when. The essential stages were: an immediate nuclear response to a conventional Soviet assault; the massive nuclear retaliation outlined in 1954 by John Foster Dulles, the US Secretary of State; the flexible response theory, outlined under the Kennedy administration, which was capable of many interpretations; and, eventually, US stress on an enhanced conventional response, albeit with the potential backing of strategic and tactical nuclear weaponry.

In the early 1950s it was feared that the Korean War might be the first stage of World War III, and/or that Western Europe might receive similar treatment to South Korea. In response to the threat of attack NATO developed as a defensive system, supporting its plans with the creation of airfields, radar stations, telecommunications and an oil pipeline system, as well as with the preparation of resistance networks able to operate if the Soviets occupied territory. There was also a major effort to develop opposition within the Soviet bloc in order to lessen the military potency of Eastern Europe in the event of war. Aside from support for resistance groups, the development of émigré forces, and a major propaganda offensive, there was a growing interest in trying to exploit divisions between the Soviet Union and its satellite regimes. Meanwhile, as NATO countries were unable to match the build-up their military planners called for, there was a growing emphasis, especially from 1952, on the possibilities of nuclear weaponry both as a deterrent and, in the event of war, as a counterweight to Soviet conventional superiority.[18] Nuclear strength was seen as a necessary support for conventional warfare in defence of West Germany.

Atomic weaponry was not employed during the Korean War, despite plans to do so and pressure from General MacArthur for its use to counteract Chinese numerical superiority. Instead, the war was fought with a strengthened conventional military, although in 1953 the use of the atom bomb was threatened by the US in order to secure an end to the conflict. This encouraged the view that nuclear strategy had a major role to play in future confrontations, as indeed did the cost of fighting the Korean War, and the extent to which it had revealed deficiencies in the US military;[19] although the war also caused a revival in the US army and led to its growing concern with 'readiness'.

The need to respond to Soviet conventional superiority on land and in the air, at least in terms of numbers, also encouraged an interest both in tactical nuclear weaponry and in the atom bomb as a weapon of first resort. The tactical nuclear weapons that were developed, such as bazookas firing atomic warheads with a range of one mile, were treated as a form of field artillery. The use of the atom bomb as a weapon of first resort was pushed by Eisenhower, NATO's first Supreme Allied Commander from 1950 until 1952 and US President from 1953 until 1961. Aware of NATO's vulnerability, he felt that strength must underpin diplomacy for it to be credible. In December 1955 the NATO Council authorized the employment of atomic weaponry against the Warsaw Pact, even if the latter did not use such weaponry.

The cost of raising conventional capability was a factor, as were the manpower implications in a period of very low unemployment, and, more specifically, the particular vulnerability of Western forces to Soviet attack in Western Europe. Thus, nuclear weaponry appeared less expensive and politically more acceptable, as well as militarily more effective, either as a deterrent or, in the event of deterrence failing, as a decisive combat weapon. Building up nuclear strength seemed the best way to increase capability in both respects.

This policy led to what was termed the 'New Look' strategy and, more particularly, to the enhancement of the American Strategic Air Command, which resulted in the USAF receiving much more money in defence allocations than either the army or the navy. Already, in 1949, the US navy had found its programme rejected and its major construction projects cancelled, in favour of the USAF's plans for strategic bombers. With the 'New Look', the number of army divisions fell from 18 in June 1956 to 14 by that December, and the number of naval vessels from 973 to 812.[20] The decline in conventional capability, which was resisted within the military,[21] both harmed the USA in the Vietnam War, and further ensured a reliance in planning on nuclear weaponry.

America's allies were also faced with difficult policy choices. Both in Western Europe and in the Far East, they relied on the US nuclear umbrella, but this made them heavily dependent on US policy choices. Part of the rationale behind the development of independent nuclear deterrents by Britain and France was the doubt that the USA would use its atomic weaponry if Europe alone was attacked; and there was also concern that the 'New Look' strategy might lead to a diminished commitment to Europe. Only an air force capable of dropping nuclear bombs seemed to offer a deterrent, but, as with the USA, the emphasis on this development affected conventional capability. In 1958, Lord Mountbatten, then the Chief of the British Defence Staff, observed:

there certainly isn't going to be enough money for a very large independent deterrent which can inflict unacceptable damage on Russia
as well as having the 88 [ship] Navy and the all-Regular Army with
adequate equipment.[22]

France's determination to develop a nuclear capability, achieved in
1960, represented a significant shift away from the emphasis on colonial defence. From the NATO perspective, however, the most worrying
feature of French policy had been the concentration of much of the
army in Algeria. Under de Gaulle, the emphasis on the nuclear *Force de
Frappe* (strike force) helped distract French military leaders from the
challenge to civilian authority in the *métropole* seen in the later stages
of the Algerian crisis, and lured them away from their psychologically
debilitating experiences of colonial defeats with promises of a more
prestigious and independent role in European and world affairs for
France's armed forces.

American focus on strategic airpower encouraged concern about the
Soviet counterpart, and in 1954–5 there was fear in the USA of a
'bomber gap', with Soviet intercontinental aircraft capable of dropping
atomic weapons on North America. This encouraged both a stepping
up of the US bomber programme and the construction of early-warn-
ing radar systems in Canada designed to warn of Soviet attacks over
the North Pole: the Pinetree Network in 1954, and the Distant Early
Warning and Mid-Canada Lines, both in 1957. The North American Air
Defence Command, established in 1958, was important to the development of joint air defence systems involving the USA and Canada.

The deployment of B-52 heavy bombers in 1955 upgraded US delivery capability, and a small number of aircraft appeared able, and
rapidly, to achieve more than the far larger Allied bomber force had
done against Germany in 1942–5. Thus, deterrence appeared both
realistic and affordable, and it was hoped that nuclear bombers would
serve to deter both conventional and atomic attack, although doubts
were expressed about the former.

The situation changed in 1957, when the Soviet Union launched Sputnik I, the first satellite, into orbit. The launch revealed a capability for intercontinental rockets that brought the entire world within striking range, and thus made the USA vulnerable to Soviet attack, both from first-strike and from counter-strike. In strategic terms, rockets threatened to give effect to the doctrine of airpower as a war-winning tool advanced in the 1920s and '30s, at the same time as they rendered obsolescent the nuclear capability of the American Strategic Air Command, which was already challenged by Soviet air defences. The development of intercontinental missiles also altered the parameters of vulnerability, and ensured that space was more than ever seen in terms of straight lines between launching site and target. As the major targets were in the USA and the Soviet Union, this led to concern with axes via the North Pole, and with the consequent mapping of these shorter routes. The threat to the USA from Soviet attack was highlighted by the 1957 secret report from the Gaither Committee.[23] The strategic possibilities offered by nuclear-tipped long-range ballistic missiles made investment in expensive rocket technology seem an essential course of action, since they could go so much faster than aeroplanes and, unlike them, could not be shot down. This altered the character of both anti-nuclear defence and nuclear deterrence, as the latter now apparently required an enhanced level of military readiness.

The wider significance of Sputnik was not restricted to military strategy. It also appeared to prove Soviet claims that it was overtaking the USA and Western Europe, not simply in military hardware, but also in technological capability and in standards of living. This public relations coup was totally misleading, in part because statistics were manipulated, but also because of a systemic Soviet failure to ensure that accurate figures were obtained and that proper balance sheets were produced. Nevertheless, Western concern about Soviet growth meant that anxiety about its apparent expansionism and military capability became ever more acute.

In fact, aside from high Western economic growth rates, the US army and air force (somewhat separately) had been developing long-range ballistic missiles after World War II, using captured German V-2 scientists; hence the so-called 'missile gap' of 1959–60 reflected more on domestic US politics than on reality. From 1957, there was a twofold Western response to the enhanced Soviet capability and to the crucial uncertainty about further developments. Notions of graduated nuclear retaliation through the use of 'tactical' (short-range) nuclear weapons in association with conventional forces, based in Western Europe, were complemented by a policy of developing an effective intercontinental retaliatory second-strike capability, in order to make it dangerous to risk attack on the USA. This attempt to give force to the notion of massive nuclear retaliation[24] entailed replacing vulnerable manned bombers with less vulnerable submarines equipped with Polaris missiles and, also, with land rockets based in reinforced silos. The invulnerability of US nuclear weaponry was thus enhanced.

The Americans fired their first intercontinental ballistic missile in 1958, and, in July 1960, off Cape Canaveral, the USS *George Washington* was responsible for the first successful underwater firing of a Polaris missile. The following year, the Americans commissioned the USS *Ethan Allen*, the first true fleet missile submarine. Submarines could be based near the coast of target states, and were highly mobile and hard to detect. They represented a major shift in force structure, away from the US air force and towards the navy, which argued that its invulnerable submarines could launch carefully controlled strikes, permitting a more sophisticated management of deterrence and retaliation. Other states followed. The first British Polaris test missile was fired from a submarine in 1968, while the French commissioned their first ballistic missile submarine in 1969.

The inhibiting effect of the destructive potential of intercontinental nuclear weaponry served as much to enhance the possibility of a nuclear war, by increasing interest in defining a sphere for tactical nuclear weapons and in planning an effective strategic nuclear first strike, as it did to lessen the chance of a great power war, or to increase the probability that such a conflict would be essentially conventional. The risk of nuclear destructiveness, nevertheless, made it important to prevent escalation to full-scale war, and thus encouraged interest in defining forms of warfare that could exist short of such escalation.

In the early 1960s, US concern about the nuclear balance increased. John F. Kennedy, US President in 1961–3, had fought the 1960 presidential election in part on the platform that the Republican administration under Eisenhower had failed to maintain America's defences. Kennedy aimed for a strategic superiority over the Soviet Union and increased defence spending. The Soviet leader, Khrushchev, however, deployed missiles in Cuba, a Communist state from which the USA was in close range and which, in turn, was being threatened by the USA. The ballistic missiles in Cuba had a range of 1040 nautical miles, which made Washington a potential target. This deployment brought the world close to nuclear war in 1962, although that very prospect may have helped prevent conventional military operations which would have begun with a US air attack on the Soviet bases on Cuba.

In the event, the USA imposed an air and naval quarantine to prevent the shipping of further Soviet supplies, considered an attack on Cuba, and threatened a full retaliatory nuclear strike. Cuba was successfully isolated, the Americans deploying a total of 183 warships, and the Soviet Union agreed to remove the missiles in return for the US withdrawing their Jupiter missiles (which carried nuclear warheads) from Turkey, and agreeing not to invade Cuba.[25] The previous year, during the Berlin Crisis, Kennedy had reaffirmed the willingness to use atomic weaponry even if the Soviets did not. This was because West Berlin was particularly vulnerable to Soviet conventional attack.

Kennedy, nevertheless, sought to move from the idea of 'massive retaliation' with nuclear weaponry to a policy that did not automatically assume escalation to nuclear war. This was an aspect of a more general strategy of 'Flexible Response' adopted in 1962 as an answer to Communist 'wars of national liberation'. Flexible Response postulated a spectrum of conflict from nuclear deterrence and conventional warfare at one end to guerrilla combat and non-military applications of national power at the other. Whatever the language, as it was unlikely that any conventional conflict between the two blocs would be anything less than devastating, and would rapidly become nuclear, the deterrent helped prevent the devastation of high-tech conventional warfare between well-resourced alliances.

The increase in US defence spending in the early 1960s, the rise of their number of nuclear warheads, the Soviet climbdown during the Cuban crisis, and the prospect of massive US nuclear retaliation, lessened the Soviet threat in Europe, although American preparations encouraged the KGB to report, inaccurately, that the USA was planning a nuclear first strike. In 1965, Robert McNamara, the US Secretary of Defense, felt able to state that the USA could rely on the threat of 'assured destruction' to deter a Soviet assault. Submarine-launched missiles provided the Americans with a secure second strike, as part of a triad that included bombers, ground-based missiles and sea-launched attacks.

Such strength did not, however, prevent further attempts by the nuclear powers to enhance their nuclear capabilities, for the logic of deterrence required matching any advance in the techniques of nuclear weaponry. For example having decided, in 1967, to proceed with the development of multiple independently targeted re-entry vehicles (MIRVs), first tested in 1968, in 1970, the US deployed Minuteman III missiles equipped with MIRVs, thus ensuring that the strike capacity of an individual rocket was greatly enhanced. As a consequence, warhead numbers, and thus the potential destructiveness of a nuclear exchange, rose greatly,[26] while the US cut the response time of their land-based intercontinental missiles by developing the Titan II, which had storable liquid propellants enabling in-silo launches and reducing the launch time, thus improving the reaction time of the missiles in a nuclear conflict.[27]

THE 1970S

The US position in the 1970s was challenged by the Soviet response, part of the action–reaction cycle of the missile race. After 1962 the Soviets had made major advances in comparative nuclear potency, especially in the development of land-based intercontinental missiles, producing a situation in which war was seen as likely to lead to MAD, as both sides appeared to have a secure second-strike capability, ensuring that a surprise attack would not wipe out the opposition. As a consequence, MAD-based strategies of deterrence and of graduated response were developed on the Western side, although it was never clear whether the Soviets agreed with this 'nuclear calculus', as it was called.[28]

In the 1970s, enhanced capability was matched by attempts to lessen the possibility of nuclear war. The USA–Soviet Union Anti-Ballistic Missile Treaty of 1972 (SALT I), which President Nixon felt able to conclude thanks to the MIRV programme, limited the construction of defensive shields against missile attack to two anti-ballistic missile complexes, one around a concentration of intercontinental ballistic missiles and the other around the capital. By leaving the USA and the Soviet Union vulnerable, the treaty was designed to discourage a first strike, as there would be no effective defence against a counterstrike. Thus, atomic weaponry was to be used to prevent, not to further, war. The treaty, which limited the two powers' nuclear arsenals, also served as the basis for further negotiations which led to the SALT II treaty in 1979.[29]

Despite Nixon's successful approach to China in 1972, which capitalized on the serious breakdown of relations between China and the Soviet Union, the West appeared weak in the 1970s. The left-wing Allende government in Chile was overthrown in 1973, and left-wing control of Portugal proved brief, but the Western colonial empires finally crumbled, the Vietnam conflict closed with the fall of Saigon to the Communists in 1975, and the overthrow of the Shah of Iran, in January 1979, was a major blow to Western influence and American prestige. The Soviet invasion of Afghanistan in December 1979 appeared to underline the weakness of the West in Central and South Asia.

At the same time, the economic strength of the West seemed compromised by inflationary pressures that owed much to the US decision to pay for the 1960s, not least the Vietnam War, by borrowing rather than taxation; by the difficulties of sustaining earlier rates of innovation and productivity growth; and, finally, by the economic strains following the oil price hike after the 1973 Yom Kippur (Arab–Israeli) war, from $3 per barrel to $18. Simultaneously, the West appeared to be suffering from poor leadership. The Watergate Scandal in the USA led not only to the fall of Nixon in 1974, but also to a crisis of confidence in American leadership. Western disunity was seen in growing French alienation from the USA, while Britain was faced in 1974 by a political upheaval stemming from a miners' strike, and then by a more general crisis, as high inflation and trade union power contributed to an acute sense of malaise and weakness. Apparent nuclear parity left the Soviet superiority in conventional forces a threat in Europe.

These problems were not to lead to a major world conflict, although the Cold War heated up in Angola in 1975, with the USA and South Africa supplying anti-Communist forces in the civil war there and Cuba and the Soviet Union helping the government. Instead, the mid-1970s saw a number of treaties, especially the Helsinki Treaty of 1975, that in recognizing the position and interests of the Eastern Bloc appeared to consolidate its position. This *détente* was a truce between rivals, and, although it suggested that the Cold War was now less intense, it did not signify any victory for the West. Whereas in 1990 it became clear that a major struggle had ended with the victory of the West, this was not apparent in 1975. Instead, it seemed that both East and West still had all to play for in a world adapting to the end of the European colonial empires: although Congress's prohibition on further involvement in Angola was a significant restraint on US interventionism.

Détente arose from the particular circumstances of the mid-1970s, and also from the military stalemate in Europe that was the product of nuclear confrontation. This stalemate permitted a registration of shifts of political alignment, as well as a measure of accommodation: thus, West Germany regularized its relations with the states of Eastern Europe, for example recognizing the Oder–Neisse frontier between East Germany and Poland in a treaty with the latter signed in December 1970. In East Asia, the improvement in American relations with China was followed, in 1979, by an American agreement to remove military personnel from Taiwan.

CHANGES IN WEAPONRY

While playing a major role in deterring war, the military were also preparing for it. In doing so there was adaptation to new technology and to the particular taskings of the period. The relationship between nuclear weapons, and force structure and doctrine was important. The development of new weaponry led to a major shift in the share of resources from armies towards, first, air forces, and then to submarines and land-based intercontinental missiles, capable of delivering atomic warheads. This contributed greatly to a sense of volatility in military structures and doctrines. At the same time, nuclear doctrine was framed by existing assumptions and was treated as an extension of already powerful military organizations and doctrines. Thus, it was used in 1945, and thereafter primarily envisaged as a form of strategic bombing.

As another sign of continuity, the weapons and the weapons systems of 1945, for example tanks, field artillery, specialized aircraft, aircraft carriers and submarines, remained dominant, suggesting a degree of continuity not apparent when contrasting, say, 1910 and 1945. Yet there were also major developments in armaments, especially in the enhancements of existing weapons systems, for example with armour-piercing warheads. The technology of warfare became more sophisticated, in part as weapons and techniques developed in the later stages of World War II – such as jet aircraft, rockets and the underwater recharging of submarine batteries – were refined. In submarines, for example, there were major advances in design, construction techniques, propulsion, communications, weaponry and surveillance. The range of weaponry also increased, as weapons, such as defoliation chemicals and infra-red viewing devices, were able to alter the physical environment of conflicts; the latter making effective night fighting more feasible. These devices were used by Syrian tanks against Israel in 1973. Competition, particularly but not exclusively focused on the Cold War, hastened the development and acquisition of weapons, such as jet fighters in the late 1940s and 1950s.

Sophisticated weaponry was expensive in both nominal and real terms. Advanced industrial mass-production capacity, and the ability to fund it, were crucial. Metal-bashing processes remained important, but a greater role than hitherto was played by electronic engineering, and in this the West had a major advantage, as it also did in higher growth rates and more flexible economic processes than those in the Soviet Union. However, the Soviet belief in the inevitably insoluble contradictions of Western capitalism ensured that they failed to appreciate the mounting crises their economy, society and political system were facing.

Meanwhile, skyrocketing defence budgets, especially for research and development and the production of new systems (as opposed to simple procurement), were a major driving force for widespread centralization of defence planning at all levels in Western democracies. This was particularly so with high-level civilian organizations (appointed defence ministers; legislators and their committees; private consultants and contractors) steadily usurping service autonomy and using budgetary authority and influence as the crucial means to control. A similar process took place within the individual military services.

THE SOVIET BLOC

The high costs of the Cold War placed a crippling burden on the Soviet Union and helped limit the appeal of Communism to its citizens, although economic problems stemming from the dominant role of state planning were more important, as was the inability to develop the consumer spending that was so important in the USA and Western Europe. This lack of popularity made it difficult for the Soviet government and those of their Communist allies to view change and reform with much confidence, and the maintenance of powerful armed forces by the Soviet Union was, in part, designed to prevent internal disaffection. Soviet willingness to use force to maintain its interests within its own bloc was displayed, most prominently, by invading Hungary in 1956 and Czechoslovakia in 1968. In both cases, and again later with the Polish Solidarity movement, the KGB presented nationalist opposition as ideological sabotage activity sponsored by Western intelligence agencies, and this sabotage was seen as a threat to the continuation of Communism.

In Hungary in 1956, the determined use of armour, supported by air attacks and helicopters, in Operation Whirlwind, crushed opposition, ending attempts to replace a Soviet client regime and create an independent Socialist state, which, it was feared, would be seen as a US triumph. In response, the Hungarians attacked tanks with Molotov cocktails (petrol bombs) and sniped at Soviet troops. Heavily outnumbered, the resistance was brutally crushed, with about 20,000 people killed and 200,000 going into exile, whereas of the Soviet forces 2,250 were either dead, missing or wounded. Affected by UN reluctance to act; the simultaneous Suez Crisis; the absence, due to Austrian neutrality, of direct land access; the fear of touching off a general war; the posture of NATO; and a lack of reliable information about options, the US were unwilling to intervene, while, to deter US intervention, the Soviet army deployed troops along the Austrian frontier.[30] Earlier that year, strikers in the streets of Poznan had been crushed by the Polish army, with 56 killed.

In 1968, about 250,000 Soviet troops, backed by Polish, Hungarian and Bulgarian forces, suppressed a liberalizing Communist regime in Czechoslovakia, although there was less fighting than in Hungary in 1956, because the government decided not to offer armed resistance, as it feared the consequences for the civilian population and knew that there was no prospect of Western support. Demonstrators relied on non-violent protest, for example throwing paint against tanks. Even so, 96 Soviet soldiers were killed, as well as about 200 Czechs and Slovaks. The protests had a major impact on international opinion, but failed to dislodge the Soviets, and Czechoslovakia remained under firm Communist control until the fall of the Soviet bloc.[31] The invasion of Czechoslovakia, nevertheless, probably undermined the capabilities and readiness of Warsaw Pact forces, as a lack of certainty about the loyalty of national contingents weakened the alliance, while the need to consider how best to respond to possible uprisings affected military planning. In another example of tension, the police were used to break student protests in Poland in 1968.

In December 1981, in response to Soviet pressure, the Polish army thwarted the liberalization offered by the Solidarity movement by imposing martial law. While the Soviet government was willing to allow a measure of independence to Romania, which was marginal to Warsaw Pact strategy and had refused to participate in military exercises after 1965, Poland was on its crucial axis from the Soviet Union to East Germany. However, by not intervening with its own forces, the Soviet Union ensured that the Polish crisis did not become more serious. The Soviets had been pressed to act by the Communist leaders in East Germany and Czechoslovakia, but warned not to do so by President Reagan.

While conventional weaponry could be used to suppress internal opposition, competition between the USA and USSR led to pressure for more sophisticated weapons. Weaponry in which machinery played a major role, including, for example, complex automatic systems for sighting, ensured that skill rather than physical strength became more important for soldiering. The force multiplier characteristics of weaponry was greatly enhanced and became more varied. Industrial age mass production was replaced by technological superiority as a key factor in weaponry and therefore in the economic capability of military powers. From the 1960s computers transformed operational horizons, and command and control options, and the American Defense Advanced Research Projects Agency took major steps to enhance computing, contributing in the process to the eventual creation of the Internet, and also developing a Strategic Computing Initiative that was responsible for advances in technologies such as computer vision and recognition, and the parallel processing useful for code-breaking.[32]

As a result of advances in weaponry and control systems, the notion that 'the navy mans equipment, while the army equips men', became an increasingly limited description of modern armies. The premium on skill led to greater military concern about the quality of both troops and training and encouraged military support for a professional volunteer force, rather than conscripts. A greater proportion of the civilian population was not suitable for military service, and certainly for skilled service. Furthermore, the logistical and financial burden of maintaining conscript forces, not least in the context of rising living standards and expectations, became an unacceptable burden. In 1968, Nixon, then a presidential candidate confronting the unpopularity of military service in the Vietnam War, announced that he would get rid of the draft, and he had done so by 1973.

Although a decision taken in response to disillusionment with the Vietnam War, this move was part of a more general shift in the social and political context of Western warfare, one that was to be dominated by small regular forces and to lack the cultural attributes expressed in the notion of the Nation in Arms. Many social currents were at issue, including individualism, hedonism, and the atomization of society, none of which proved conducive to nationalism, militarism or bellicosity. The military ceased to be a central symbol for state and society.

Britain phased out conscription in 1957–63, while in France, where discontent with national service grew in the late 1960s, conscription was cut to a year in 1970.[33] In the Soviet Union, conscription was cut from three to two years in 1967, although more men were drafted. This expansion of military service made it less popular, and led to an increase in desertion and in conscripts going absent without leave.

MOBILITY

Moves against conscription were also related to the dissemination of advanced weaponry to ordinary units, a major facet of post-war upgrading that was linked to changes in doctrine, planning and training. Armies became fully motorized and mechanized, as the character of infantry changed.[34] This permitted the development of infantry doctrine that focused on rapid mobility, rather than on advances on foot or essentially static position warfare. For example, in the early 1960s, the USA mass produced the M113 armoured personnel carrier, while in 1967 the Soviet Union introduced the high speed Boyevaya Mashina Pekhoty infantry vehicle, which was capable of carrying eight men as well as a crew of three, protected by an air filtration system and armed with an artillery piece, a machine gun, an anti-tank guided missile and rifle ports, and designed to give bite to the expansion in the number of Soviet motor vehicle divisions. The same process characterized logistics: the horses of World War II were replaced, but the role of rail was also minimized as the lorry came to dominate the supply system. Artillery also became more mobile.

Mobility was seen as necessary, as it was assumed, by both sides, that any war touched off by a Warsaw Pact invasion of Western Europe would be rapid. Although the defence of West Germany led to NATO forces preparing fixed defences, a flexible defence was called for by Western strategists, not least with counter-attacks to take advantage of the use of nuclear weaponry. Furthermore, only a flexible defence would allow the Western forces to regain, and exploit, the initiative. The Pentomic Division created by the US in the 1950s so as to fight on the nuclear battlefield was deemed too weak, and, in 1959–63, in a process termed ROAD (Reorganization of the Army Division), there was a reorganization and re-equipment of the US army, focused on a heightened flexibility that benefited from the provision of new tanks, helicopters, self-propelled artillery and armoured personnel carriers. In addition, the Israeli victory against Egyptian and Syrian defensive positions in the Six Day War of 1967 and, eventually, after initial Egyptian and Syrian successes, in the Yom Kippur War of 1973, showed the value of mobility, and the vulnerability of forces with a low rate of activity. The US military devoted considerable attention to the lessons learned from the Yom Kippur War.

Also putting an emphasis on mobility and tempo, the Soviets planned a rapid advance into NATO rear areas, which would compromise the use of Western nuclear weaponry. The Soviet emphasis on the offensive led to a stress on combined arms operations with a large contribution from armour. In Soviet conventional operational methods, lead divisions were to attack until they were fought out, and were then to be replaced by second and third echelon forces, taking full advantage of their numerical superiority over their NATO foes, and thereby sustaining the tempo of the offensive. In contrast to this emphasis on replacement, Western forces depended on reconstitution, with individual unit replacements, and battlefield repair and recovery, in order to sustain units in contact indefinitely.

Essentially building on the operational policy of their successes in the latter stage of World War II, with its penetration between German defensive hedgehogs, and the speedy overcoming of Japanese forces in Manchuria, the Red Army put a premium on a rapid advance. Thus, Plan Granite, which they helped produce for the Egyptians, included, in its last phase, the reconquest of the whole of the Sinai from Israel, although, in the event, in 1973, the Egyptians settled for far more limited goals. Under Marshal N. V. Ogarkov, who became Chief of the General Staff in 1977, the Soviets developed earlier concepts of Deep Battle, which had been enhanced by the spread of mechanization in their army and by the growth of airborne forces.[35]

In turn, the USA advanced the doctrine first of Active Defence and then of AirLand Battle, as their military reformulated its thinking and practice after the Vietnam War. They placed a renewed emphasis on protecting Western Europe, rather than planning for counter-insurgency operations elsewhere, an emphasis that responded to Soviet capability, but that was also doctrinally convenient for both the army and the air force.[36] AirLand Battle led to a stress on the integration of firepower with mobility in order to thwart the Soviet concept of Deep Battle,[37] and emphasized investment in the modernization of conventional weaponry to achieve these goals; it also matched the Soviets in recognizing a level of conflict in war between tactics and strategy (and thus planning): the operational level. Although untried in conflict in Germany, AirLand influenced notions of effective synergy between land and air, and suggested that NATO would be better placed than had been argued to repel a Soviet conventional attack in Europe. The AirLand strategy was designed to permit the engagement and destruction of the second and third echelon Warsaw Pact forces at the same time that the main ground battle was taking place along the front. This strategy also met the USAF's need for a clear role after the damage done by the Vietnam War to the doctrine of strategic airpower. Some of America's allies moved in a similar direction, the French creating a *Force d'Action Rapide* with five divisions designed to resist the Soviets in southern Germany.

NAVAL RIVALRY

The Cold War also took place at sea, where technology combined with economic resources to give the US fleet a strength and capability that the British navy had lacked even at the height of its power. The Americans dominated the oceans to a degree unmatched in history, and were also able to deploy a formidable amount of naval strength in the Korean and Vietnam wars, while the building of new ships and the upgrading of weaponry and communications kept them in a leading position. During the period of the so-called 'balanced navy', from 1949 to 1968, the US navy emphasized force projection, specifically an amphibious capability able to seize and hold forward bases and inter-vene throughout the world; an ability to protect sea lanes to critical theatres, especially Europe – a task that led to anti-submarine require-ments; and a role in aerial and, later, ballistic attack on the Soviet Union. Thus, the emphasis was not on a Mahanian focus on fleet engagements at sea.[38]

American naval strategy was challenged by the build-up of the Soviet navy that began in the 1950s under Admiral Sergei Gorshkov, which quickly made the Soviet Union the world's number two naval power, replacing Britain, the size of whose navy was greatly affected by financial stringency. The Canadian navy, which had been the world's third largest in 1945, continued thereafter to develop the anti-sub-marine capability it had rapidly expanded to provide during World War II, although now the focus was Soviet threats to Canadian sea routes. In the 1970s, however, Canadian military expenditure fell rapidly.[39] Wrecked in the war, the French navy and its infrastructure were revived in the early 1950s, in part with US help, but this was compromised by Franco-American differences, and French naval construction and deployment were reduced in the late 1950s. After de Gaulle withdrew the French fleet from NATO duties, it lacked a role.[40]

Naval force structure and doctrine changed greatly after 1945. The age of the battleship passed, as those built in the inter-war period were scrapped, to be followed by others launched in wartime. When the Korean War broke out, only USS *Missouri* of the American battleships was in commission, while the British *Vanguard* was, in 1946, the sole European battleship commissioned after the war, and was scrapped in 1960. In the Suez Crisis of 1956, the French *Jean Bart* became the last European battleship to fire a shot in anger. American battleships, however, remained in use, including off Lebanon in the 1980s and in the Gulf War of 1990–91 when the USS *Wisconsin*, whose guns had provided important fire support in Korea in 1951–2,[41] used both its guns and its cruise missiles; the former, which delivered 120 tons of high explosive, were particularly effective.

The decline of the battleship ensured that carriers were the big ships. The USA dominated carrier capability, and planned the use of its carrier strength for a variety of purposes. In the 1950s and early 1960s,

US carriers were assigned strategic bombing duties, not least the use of a nuclear strike capability,[42] but in the Korean and Vietnam Wars they were used extensively to provide ground support. The most extensive use of carriers was during the Vietnam War, when they provided a nearby safe base for operations over both North and South Vietnam. Improvements in supply methods since World War II, for example re-supply from other ships, ensured that carriers were able to stay at sea for longer. During most of 1972, no fewer than six US carriers were on station off Vietnam, and, that summer, an average of 4,000 sorties were flown monthly. The absence of hostile submarine attacks provided a mistaken impression of the general invulnerability of carriers.[43]

The USA was not unique in its use of carriers. Three French carriers had operated off Vietnam against the Viet Minh in the 1946–54 war, and two were used in the Suez Crisis. The British deployed carriers during the Korean War, and used three in the Suez Crisis; they also increased the capability of their carriers, with the introduction of the angled flight deck, the steam catapult, and, in 1960, the first vertical/ short takeoff and landing (V/STOL) aircraft based on carriers. These aircraft did not require fleet carriers, and financial problems led Britain in 1966 to the cancellation of the CVA-01, a planned fleet carrier, and, instead, to a reliance on smaller carriers with their shorter range V/STOL fighters.

The development of the Soviet fleet led to changes in US naval doctrine and force structure: the fleet was designed to support Soviet interests across the world, and to challenge the deployment of US and allied forces, and, more specifically, to threaten US carriers with their nuclear-strike aircraft. Traditional Soviet naval doctrine had emphasized support for land forces around the Baltic and Black Seas, and the quest for naval superiority in these areas, but Soviet forces could only gain access from these seas to larger waters through straits and shallow waters, where they were vulnerable; a similar problem affected the naval base of Vladivostok on the Sea of Japan. As a result, the Soviet navy developed their Northern Fleet based at Murmansk, and it became their largest fleet, with a particularly important submarine component – about 400 strong by 1956.

The development of the Northern fleet obliged NATO powers to develop nearby patrol areas for submarines, as well as underwater listening devices, and also to develop a similar capability in the waters through which Soviet submarines would have to travel *en route* to the Atlantic, both in the Denmark Strait between Iceland and Greenland and between Iceland and Britain. The USA feared that Soviet submarines would attack their trade routes, or launch missiles from near the US coast.

The Soviet navy also developed an important surface fleet, especially from the 1960s, including missile cruisers whose anti-ship missiles posed a major threat to Western warships. In 1967 and 1973, the Soviet navy was able to make substantial deployments in the eastern Mediterranean in order to advance Soviet views during Middle Eastern crises.[44] Soviet naval development led the USA, from 1969, to focus on planning for naval conflict with the Soviets, rather than amphibious operations: the emphasis now was on being able to destroy Soviet naval power in battle and in its home waters, and this led to a focus on big aircraft carriers and large submarines, both designed to attack the enemy fleet.

1980s

The early 1980s saw a marked heating up of the Cold War. The overthrow of the Shah in Iran in January 1979 had already led to greater US concern with the Persian Gulf. Manifested in the Carter Doctrine in January 1980, this led to the establishment, two months later, of the Rapid Deployment Task Force, which was to become the basis of Central Command, the Tampa-based Area Command responsible for the Gulf Wars which was co-equal with other regional commands. This Task Force was presented as a body able to provide a rapid response across the world. As it contained both army and marine units, this was also an important initiative in joint structures.

The Soviet invasion of Afghanistan in December 1979 was seen by Western governments, not as a frontier policing operation designed to ensure a pliant government, but as an act of aggression that needed to be countered, a view that drew on a tendency to exaggerate Soviet economic resources and military capability. Under Ronald Reagan, US President in 1981–9, and Margaret Thatcher, British Prime Minister in 1979–90, this determination was matched by action. Reagan's presidency witnessed a development of covert operations outside formal military structures, but, alongside US support for anti-Communist insurgents in Afghanistan, Nicaragua and Angola, the last thanks to a repeal of the Congressional ban on involvement, there was also a marked build-up in the US military. This focused on the deployment of tactical nuclear weapons, carried on Cruise and Patriot intermediate-range missiles, and on the development of new nuclear and space-mounted weaponry, but also included expansion in all the services. The 'Star Wars' programme, outlined by Reagan in a speech in 1983, was designed to enable the USA to dominate space, using space-mounted weapons to destroy Soviet satellites and missiles.[45]

Tensions rose to a peak in 1983; with the Soviets fearing attack during a NATO exercise; the shooting down, over Soviet airspace, of a Korean airliner suspected of espionage; and the deployment of Cruise and Pershing missiles in Western Europe. With the KGB providing inaccurate reports of US plans for a surprise nuclear first strike, the Soviets also deployed more weaponry, although they could not match the USA's use of information technology. Nevertheless, six Typhoons, the largest ballistic missile submarines built, entered Soviet service from 1980, as did their most impressive surface warships, including the *Kuznetsov*, their only big carrier.

Advanced technology contributed greatly to increased US effectiveness, and US planning benefited from major developments in the capability of airpower. This included the advances stemming from more powerful air-to-air radars; the enhancement of air combat resulting from heat-seeking short-range missiles, and their radar-guided, long-range counterparts; and the use of AWACS (Airborne Warning and Control System) aircraft. The USA planned to employ stealthy attack aircraft and 'smart' laser-guided weapons fired from stand-off platforms. Laser-guided projectiles and programmed cruise missiles would inflict heavy damage on Soviet armour, while advanced aircraft, such as the F-15 and F-16, would win air superiority and also attack Soviet ground forces. Stealth technology would permit the penetration of Soviet air defences, obliging the Soviets to retain more aircraft at home, and would also threaten their nuclear deterrent. Co-ordination would be made possible by computer networking, a new generation of spy satellites with six-inch resolution, AWACS aircraft, and the Global Positioning System.

THE END OF THE COLD WAR

The Soviet order sat increasingly uneasily on a society where individualism, consumerism and demands for change and freedom could not be accommodated by an inherently inefficient command economy nor by Communist ideology. The rise to power in the Soviet Union in 1985 of Mikhail Gorbachev, a leader committed to reform at home and good relations abroad, greatly defused tension, not least by leading to Soviet disengagement from Afghanistan and Angola. Gorbachev was also willing to challenge the confrontational world-view outlined in KGB reports. For example, he was convinced that US policy on arms control was not motivated by a hidden agenda of weakening the Soviet Union, and this encouraged him to negotiate. In 1987, the Soviet government accepted the Intermediate Nuclear Forces Treaty, which, in ending land-based missiles with ranges between 500 and 5,000 kilometres, forced heavier cuts on the Soviets, while also setting up a system of verification through on-site inspection. In 1990 NATO and the Warsaw Pact were able to agree a limitation of conventional forces in Europe, while, in July 1991, START I led to a major fall in the number of US and Soviet strategic nuclear warheads.

Aside from reducing international tension, Gorbachev also ended the Cold War, thanks to the unintended consequences of his reform policies. Although he sought to modernize Soviet Communism, his policies instead, unintentionally, unravelled its precarious domestic basis, and at the same time failed to provide sufficient food, let alone reasonable economic growth; while his pressure for reform on Soviet satellite states in Eastern Europe led to their fall, as Gorbachev was unwilling to use the Soviet military to maintain their governments

when they faced increasing popular pressure for change. These governments themselves had totally failed. East Germany, apparently the
most successful, but its economy wrecked by ideological mismanage-
ment, was on the edge of bankruptcy in the autumn of 1989: it had only
been able to continue that long thanks to large loans from the West.[46]

The end, when it came, in 1989–91, was rapid and relatively peaceful. Issues of classification are also raised, as the fall of the Soviet Union
was at once a stage of the Cold War and also an important stage in
decolonization for, however much the Soviet Union was in theory a
federation, it also rested on a powerful degree of Russian, as well as
ideological, imperialism. Counter-reform attempts by the Soviet military, keen to preserve the integrity of the Soviet Union, led to action
against nationalists in Georgia (1989), Azerbaijan (1990), Lithuania
(1991), Latvia (1991), and Moldova (1992), and there was an attempted
coup in Moscow by hardline Communists in August 1991, but they
were unable to prevail. Gorbachev also wanted to preserve the Soviet
Union, if necessary as a loose confederation, and, when the Baltic
republics (Estonia, Latvia and Lithuania) declared their independence,
he supported the attempt to maintain the authority of the Soviet
Union by sending troops into the republics in January 1991, leading to
clashes in Vilnius and Riga. However, the growing weakness of the
Soviet state, and the division and confusion of the government's
response, was accentuated by the strength of nationalist sentiment,
especially in the Baltic republics, the Caucasus and western Ukraine. As
with much of decolonization, it was the war that did not happen that is
worthy of consideration. Instead, in December 1991, nationalism in the
republics led to their independence, and thus to the collapse of the
Soviet Union, while Gorbachev resigned, to be replaced by Boris
Yeltsin. With Soviet Communism in ruins and Chinese Communism
increasingly market orientated, the Cold War was over.

Chapter 6

Wars Between Non-Western Powers, 1945–90

Conflict between non-Western powers was no mere postscript to the history of war in this period or, indeed, in any other. Nor is it helpful to treat such conflicts as in some way simply adjuncts of the Cold War. That element was indeed important, not least due to the provision of weapons, munitions, finance, training and advice by protagonists in the Cold War, but the conflicts also had an autonomy in cause, course and consequence. This is particularly so if the range of conflict is considered, as it included not only struggles between sovereign states, but also large-scale insurgencies and other instances of civil conflict. In many cases, conflicts owed their origins to the after effect of rapid decolonization, as groups that had succeeded in ousting imperial powers, or benefited from their departure, found it less easy to govern successfully or to manage relations with neighbours. These struggles drew, in part, on pre-existing tensions, for example between regions with different ethnicities, religions and/or economic interests, and these helped shape competing nationalisms; there was, however, also a powerful element of novelty stemming from the ideological struggles of the Cold War and their interaction with indigenous identities. In Indonesia, for example, the mid-1960s witnessed a very bloody civil war in which Communists were killed in large numbers by Islamic nationalists who were powerful in the army. Similarly, in Iraq the Communists were kept from power by Baath nationalists.

Wars in the Middle East tend to dominate attention under this heading. They were, indeed, important both in their own right and because their course, especially those of the Arab–Israeli wars of 1967 and 1973, was scrutinized carefully by analysts seeking insights into tactical and operational effectiveness. For example, Egyptian success with anti-tank weaponry in 1973 encouraged commentators to stress its importance. The use of advanced weaponry by the combatants, particularly of US aircraft and tanks by the Israelis, and Soviet counterparts by their opponents, made it possible to view these conflicts as testing grounds for a clash between the two powers. However, although Cold War factors were important in the Arab–Israeli struggle, there were a great many other inherent factors involved, and many conflicts between non-Western powers were not readily definable in terms of the Cold War.

BORDER WARS

Decolonization had led to a far greater number of independent states in Africa and Asia, and many of these became involved in conflict. Border disputes arising from the departure of colonial powers were responsible for numerous struggles, for example between India and Pakistan in 1947–8 and 1965, and, at a far smaller scale, Morocco and Algeria in 1962–3, and, despite the 1964 Cairo Declaration confirming Africa's frontiers, Mali and Burkina Faso in 1995; as well as for China's border war with India in 1962.

Border clashes were sometimes intertwined with insurrectionary movements. This was the case with the India–Pakistan war over Kashmir in 1947–8, when Pakistan tried to exploit Islamic opposition to Indian rule in Kashmir, leading the Indians to a military response.[1] The India–Pakistan wars indicated the value of the far larger Indian military, but other factors also played a role in Indian success. In 1965, the Indians chose to advance not in Kashmir, as the Pakistanis had anticipated, but, instead, in the Punjab, using tanks to drive on Lahore and Sialkot. The Pakistanis had been encouraged by India's defeat by China in 1962, but the Indians, with their Soviet T55 tanks, fought better than had been anticipated. In 1965, unlike in 1947–8, there was large-scale conventional conflict, including the use of large quantities of tanks and artillery. Other border conflicts were smaller in scale and obscure and tend to be ignored in military history, although, for the forces concerned, they were important, not least in tasking. For example, in 1969, the army and police in Guyana stopped a Venezuelan-backed secessionist rising in the Rupununi region.[2]

INTERVENTION WARS

In Africa, border clashes frequently interacted with rebellions. Libya intervened in Chad in the 1980s, both in order to pursue a territorial claim to a northern strip of the country and in order to support protégés seeking to control the entire country. Overt Libyan intervention in 1983 with about 6,000 troops led to a military response by France and Zaire (Congo), which enjoyed the benefit of intelligence provided by US aerial surveillance. The Libyan advance was reliant on Soviet doctrine and training, but this was not going to be a conflict decided by armoured vehicles and related tactics. Instead, the Chad forces opposed to Libya benefited from light vehicles and a raider's desire for mobility, and used mortars and anti-tank rockets in order to inflict heavy casualties on the Libyans.

These tactics were employed again in the 'Toyota War' of March 1987, with the Libyans losing over 3,000 troops and much of their armour as they were driven from most of the north of Chad. French aircraft were used against Libyan ground forces on a number of occasions, but the French did not act at the close of 1990 when a new faction invaded Chad from Sudan and overthrew the government. Attempted coups, rebellions and ethnic clashes continued there for years. Libyan claims were also seen as a challenge by other neighbours. In 1977, Egypt mounted a successful surprise attack on Libyan frontier positions in order to indicate its anger with Libyan pretensions and policies.

More generally, foreign military intervention could lead to the overthrow of governments, as with the Vietnamese conquest of Cambodia in 1978–9, and the Tanzanian overthrow of Idi Amin, the megalomaniac military dictator of Uganda, in 1979. Amin had seized power in a coup in

1971, ruled by terror, slaughtering opponents, greatly increased the size of the army, and attacked neighbouring Tanzania, alleging that its government supported military operations by Ugandan exiles. This served as an excuse for Ugandan attacks in 1971, 1972 and, more seriously, on three occasions in the winter of 1978–9. After the last, the Tanzanians, citing self-defence, invaded and overthrew Amin. The latter campaign was typical of many in Africa. The fighting quality of the Ugandan army varied greatly, with élite units mounting a resistance that most of the demoralized army was unwilling to offer. Tactical mobility was crucial in clashes, helping ensure that light anti-tank weapons were used to destroy armoured personnel carriers, which were largely road-bound. Libyan military intervention on behalf of Amin could not sway the struggle.

SOUTH ASIA

The removal of the constraints of Western control or hegemony led states to pursue regional territorial and political interests, often using force to that end. Thus, India sent troops into Kashmir in 1947; overran the princely state of Hyderabad in 1948; occupied the Portuguese possessions of Diu and Goa in 1961; conquered East Pakistan in 1971, helping to create the state of Bangladesh; annexed Sikkim in 1975; sent 100,000 troops to help Sri Lanka against Tamil insurgents in 1987 (withdrawing in 1990); and intimidated Nepal in 1995. Victory over Pakistan in 1965 led to a recovery of Indian confidence after defeat by China in 1962.

Indian operations revealed the growing capability of Third World military systems: in 1947, India sent troops by air to Kashmir, while, in 1961, it used 71,000 troops to overrun Goa, which had a garrison of only 4,000 men, in one day. Although allied to Portugal in NATO, the USA refused appeals for help. 160,000 Indian troops were sent into East Pakistan in 1971, while at the same time, other Indian units fought Pakistani forces in West Pakistan.[3]

The military also played a major role in maintaining the cohesion of India. In 1984, the Indian army stormed the Golden Temple of Amritsar, the leading Sikh shrine, which had become a major terrorist base, although this led to Sikh mutinies in the Indian military. From 1987, there was also the need to confront Muslim insurgency in Kashmir.[4] In 1998, India, which had exploded a nuclear device in 1974, demonstrated its ability to launch a rocket with a nuclear warhead. India's military build-up was directed not only against internal problems and Pakistan, but also against China, which was seen as a threat not only on their common border, but also because of Chinese support for India's neighbours, Pakistan and Burma. The geo-strategic tension between the two powers was an important aspect of the struggle for regional dominance in South Asia that was seen during the Cold War and became more important thereafter.[5]

China was successful in 1962 against India, whose forces were poorly prepared for high-altitude operations, but much less so in 1979 against Vietnam. In 1962, the Chinese heavily outnumbered the Indians, and benefited, as a result of road building, from superior logistics, at least in the zone of conflict. The Indians began the war on 10 October with an unsuccessful attempt to seize the Thag La Ridge, and the Chinese then responded with an offensive launched on 20 October, defeating and driving back the Indians. An Indian counter-offensive on 14 November was defeated, and the following day the Chinese outmanoeuvred the Indian defensive positions near Se La, inflicting heavy casualties. Having revealed that the Indians would be unable to defend Assam, the Chinese declared a unilateral ceasefire on 21 November and withdrew their troops. Theirs was a limited operation in which prospects for exploitation were gravely restricted by logistical factors. In total, the Indians had lost 6,100 men dead, wounded or prisoners.[6]

In 1979 the Chinese sent eventually about 120,000 troops to confront an equal number of Vietnamese, in response to Vietnam's attack on China's ally, Cambodia, the previous year. This attack had accentuated the long-term tension between China and Vietnam, a tension exacerbated by China's rapprochement with the USA. The Chinese captured three provincial capitals, but were knocked off balance by the Vietnamese decision to turn to guerrilla tactics. The Vietnamese benefited from their extensive recent experience of conflict, while the Chinese military lacked such experience and suffered from an outdated army and flawed doctrine. Affected by poor logistics, inadequate equipment and failures in command and control, the Chinese withdrew, with maybe 63,000 casualties, and without forcing Vietnamese forces to leave Cambodia. Nevertheless, they had shown that they would not be deterred by Soviet–Vietnamese links, and their invasion testified to growing Soviet weakness.[7] Vietnam did not withdraw its forces from Cambodia until 1990.

THE MIDDLE EAST

Other would-be regional powers also built up their forces, for example Iran with its oil wealth in the 1970s, and mounted attacks. Egypt sent troops to Yemen in an attempt to support the new revolutionary regime established in September 1962 by a military coup against the conservative rule of Iman Muhammad al-Badr. The Royalist opposition was backed by Saudi Arabia, which provided money, weapons and bases, while Jordan sent military advisors. The Egyptians had anticipated a commitment of only three months, but found themselves in an intractable situation that offered a parallel to other counter-insurgency operations of the period. Aside from the inherent difficulty of the task, which owed much to the bellicose and fissiparous character of Yemeni society, and to the harsh nature of the terrain, the Egyptian army was not prepared for operations in Yemen. It lacked adequate planning for operations there, was critically short of information about both Yemeni alignments and the terrain, was short of adequate communications equipment, and was not prepared, by training or doctrine, for counter-insurgency conflict. Instead, their experience was in conventional operations against Israel.

In the initial operations in October and November 1962, the Egyptians found their attempts to control the entire country thwarted by opposition that made more effective use of the terrain, not least by ambushing road-bound Egyptian columns. The Egyptians responded, at the close of November, by focusing on a defensive triangle of key cities where they intended to build up the Republican army; but their hopes were not realized, the nascent revolutionary force performing worse than the South Vietnamese military, and only becoming an important element from 1966. Royalist successes, instead, led the Egyptians to build up their own forces and to return to the offensive in February 1963, regaining, in Operation Ramadan, control over most major towns and much territory. To secure these gains from Royalist attacks, the number of Egyptian troops rose from 15,000 in the winter of 1962–3 to 36,000.

In many respects, there were parallels with the Vietnam War. The Royalists had bases in neighbouring Saudi Arabia and were supplied from there, and made good use of the terrain in Yemen, not least in mounting ambushes. The Egyptians, in contrast, had control of the air, which they used for bombing, ground attack and air mobility, as with the capture of Sadah in February 1962 after paratroopers had seized a runway on which troops could be landed. The Egyptian ability to take the initiative was, however, not matched by successful results. Unless occupied, territory could not be retained, but the occupation of territory did not itself produce benefits. Furthermore, the difficulty of achieving results, combined with the absence of an exit strategy hit the morale of the Egyptian forces. To them, Yemen appeared a hostile environment, both physically and culturally, and, as in the Vietnam War, difficulties in identifying the enemy contributed to this sense of alienation. Discipline was weakened, corruption developed in the officer corps, and military and domestic support for the war fell. The inflexibility of the Egyptian military made it difficult to adapt doctrine and tactics to engage the guerrillas, although there were some improvements in tactics, not least with the use of helicopter borne aerial re-supply.

In 1964, the Egyptian forces in Yemen were increased to 50,000 men, but they still faced problems in using the roads, and early in the year the capital, Sana, was besieged by the Royalists. The Egyptian attempt that summer to kill the iman led to the capture, successively, of two of his headquarters, but he was able to escape into Saudi Arabia, and the campaign did not lead to the end of the war. Once the Egyptians withdrew from the areas they had captured in the northwest, they were reoccupied by the Royalists. The following year, despite deploying 70,000 troops, the Egyptians again faced problems in responding to ambushes that cut supply routes and left their positions isolated and vulnerable. Much of the east of the country was overrun by the Royalists, and Egyptian frustration led to plans for an attack on Royalist bases in Saudi Arabia, which had already been repeatedly bombed.

At the same time, and the parallel with the Vietnam War is instructive, the Egyptians tried to negotiate. In August 1965 Nasser and King Faysal of Saudi Arabia signed the Jeddah Agreement, in which they undertook to stop helping their respective protégés, and, by the summer of 1966, there were only 20,000 Egyptian troops in Yemen. However, the hopeful signs of the previous autumn were wrecked by the failure of peace talks between the Republicans and the Royalists, and by Nasser's interest in using Yemen as a base for seizing control of Aden after the British withdrawl. As a result, the Egyptians reoccupied parts of Yemen they had abandoned, although it was the increasingly effective Republican troops that played the major role in operations against the Royalists in 1966–7. Israel's total victory over the Egyptian forces in Sinai in June 1967 led to pressure for an evacuation of Yemen, and the fig-leaf of an agreement with Saudi Arabia (which, despite its promises, continued to supply the Royalists) allowed them to do so, mostly in October 1967, although not finally until December 1967. Once the Egyptians had left, the Republicans proved more resilient than had been anticipated, successfully defending Sana against siege in the winter of 1967–8. Saudi support for peace finally led to the end of the war, and the formation of a coalition government in 1970.[8]

In contrast to Egypt's lengthy commitment to Yemen, Syria's unsuccessful invasion of Jordan in 1970, in support of a rebellion by Palestinian guerrilla forces, was a struggle between conventional forces: the Jordanians fought well and benefited from effective air support against Syrian ground forces which, in turn, lacked air assistance. The Jordanians succeeded in expelling the Palestinian guerrillas. In 1976, however, Syria successfully sent troops into Lebanon in response to an appeal from the President for support of the Maronite-dominated Lebanese Front against the Druze–PLO (Palestinian Liberation Organization) alliance. The Syrians then turned against the Maronites (Christians) and occupied much of the country.

Another regional power, Turkey, successfully invaded Cyprus in 1974, partitioning the island between the Greek and Turkish Cypriots.

Seeking to exploit the chaos following the overthrow of the Shah, and to gain both a favourable settlement of border disputes and regional hegemony, Iraq, which had used oil money greatly to build up its military, invaded Iran in September 1980, launching a struggle that lasted until 1988, and that involved more combatants (probably over 2.5 million by 1988) and casualties (reportedly up to one million killed) than other conflicts of the period. The Iraqis planned to use the same methods as those employed by Israel against Egypt in 1967: a surprise air attack to destroy the opponent's air force, followed by a tank offensive. However well conceived the operational plan, the Iraqis proved incapable of executing it. The surprise Iraqi attack on ten air bases on the night of 22 September failed because of a lack of adequate expertise and targeting equipment, a failure that ensured that the Iranian air force survived and was, in turn, able to attack Iraqi oil facilities successfully on 25 September, hitting the financial under-pinnings of the Iraqi war effort.

On the ground, the Iraqis lacked the mobility and tactical flexibility shown by the Israelis. Instead, their advance was slower and their tanks were frequently employed as artillery, downplaying their capacity for manoeuvre warfare. Iraqi forces also lacked adequate logistics and suffi-ciently flexible command systems. More seriously, their war aims were misconceived, and there was no clear exit strategy, in part because the nature of Iranian politics had been misread, for, far from collapsing, the Iranian forces fought back, helped by an upsurge in patriotism. To take Khorramshahr on 24 October–10 November, the Iraqis had to resort to hand-to-hand combat. The following May, the city was recaptured by Iranian forces making skilful use of night attacks. The Iranians also benefited from the use of helicopters, not least firing heat-seeking missiles against Iraqi tanks, and from the employment of SAM 7 surface-to-air missiles. The Iranians outnumbered the Iraqis, but international isolation made it difficult to keep their equipment maintained (always a major problem with foreign sources of supply), and the Iraqis bene-fited from assistance from most other Arab states, as well as from powers fearful of Iran and its espousal of Islamic fundamentalism, including the USA. This help was variously financial, particularly from Kuwait and Saudi Arabia, and the sale of weapons, especially by France and the Soviet Union.

The Iraqis used chemical weapons against Iranian attacks, and both sides employed missiles, targeting opposing capitals.[9] The war also saw the first modern 'martyrdom operation' by an Islamic group when an Iranian-backed Shia movement was responsible, in 1981, for the suicide bombing of the Iraqi embassy in Beirut. The war also spread to involve attacks on shipping in the Persian Gulf, which led to Western naval commitments there.[10]

LATIN AMERICA

Another would-be regional power, Argentina, engaged in an arms race and naval confrontations with Chile, with which it had a territorial dispute, and, in 1982, provoked war with Britain over the Falklands, an island group in the South Atlantic (see chapter Three). Argentina had come close to war with Chile in 1978 when it rejected a mediation settlement over three small islands in the Beagle Channel, but the fall of its military government after failure in the Falklands war finally led it to accept this verdict. Latin America, however, saw little intra-state conflict. The Football War of 1969, in which the army of El Salvador invaded Honduras after a visiting Honduran football team had been attacked in San Salvador and the football victory of El Salvador had been followed by anti-Salvadorean riots in Honduras, appeared ridiculous, and was certainly short, although the root causes were more complex. They owed much to longstanding difficulties exacerbated by large-scale Salvadorean migration into Honduras.

ARAB–ISRAELI WARS

In the Middle East, there was a series of wars between Israel and its Arab neighbours (1948–9, 1956, 1967, 1973 and 1982). The Arabs, who rejected the UN partition resolution of 29 November 1947, and sought to drive the Jews from Palestine as the British withdrew, proved unwilling to accept the culmination of the Zionist movement in the form of an independent Israel, and this ensured a high level of tension in the region from the outset of the period. Israel was able to establish its independence in the face of poorly coordinated and badly prepared attacks by neighbouring Arab states in 1948–9, although, in that conflict, the Arabs benefited from more weaponry and firepower as well as from taking the initiative. The Israelis had more troops by the last stage of the war, and also benefited from the determination borne of a conviction that their opponents intended genocide; they certainly at least intended what was later to be termed ethnic cleansing. More mundanely, the Israelis had interior lines of communication, while the supply of Czech small arms and, to a lesser extent, aircraft was crucial.[11]

The war ended with the partition of Palestine between Israel, which, determined to make the Palestinian home a Jewish homeland, gained far more than had been envisaged in the UN partition resolution in 1947, and Egypt and Jordan, each of which also gained part of the proposed Arab state. The latter was not established. Indeed, Jordan's army, the Arab Legion, was more concerned to seize the west bank of the Jordan than to destroy Israel. Although Jordan, which annexed the west bank in 1950, was able to reconcile itself to the existence of Israel, Egypt and Syria were far less willing to do so.

In 1956, as part of the Suez Crisis, Israel attacked Egypt on 29 October in concert with Britain and France, overrunning the Sinai Peninsula, but withdrew in the face of US and Soviet pressure. The weak resistance put up by the Egyptians reflected Israeli success in gaining the initiative, as well as the poorly trained nature of the Egyptian army, and its ineffective use of the weapons it had received. In particular, the Egyptians, who fought well in prepared positions, suffered from inadequate combined-arms training and from the rigid tactics of their armour, while Israeli success indicated that the reserve system, which provided the bulk of their army, worked. The Israelis also benefited from having numerical superiority in Sinai, in part because Gamal Abdel Nasser, Egypt's leader, correctly anticipated an Anglo-French invasion of the Suez Canal zone to the west. When Britain and France attacked, Nasser indeed ordered his already embattled troops in Sinai to retreat. The whole of the Sinai Peninsula was conquered in under 100 hours, at the cost of 172 Israeli fatalities. After the campaign, Israel, let down by the failure of Britain and France to sustain their invasion, agreed to withdraw in return for the deployment of UN troops along the frontier.

After the 1956 war, both Israel and, even more, her Arab neighbours increased their military expenditure, while Egypt's unification with Syria in 1958 created, in the United Arab Republic, the prospect of more united Arab action, especially in 1960. However, the union was overthrown by a group of Syrian officers in 1961, while the United Arab Command created in 1964 by a meeting of Arab leaders in order to prepare for war with Israel faced serious national divisions. Nevertheless, a serious Israeli–Syrian border clash in 1964 was followed by an upsurge of Palestinian guerrilla attacks on Israel in 1965–6, with Israeli reprisal attacks on Palestinian bases in Jordan. In November 1966, an Egyptian–Syrian defence treaty seemed to move Egypt closer to Syria's desire for war.

In 1967 rising regional tension, particularly Egyptian sabre rattling, led to a pre-emptive Israeli attack on Egypt. Nasser was encouraged in his blustering by his desire to retain the leadership of the Arab cause: the aggressive attitude of the new Syrian government towards Israel challenged his prestige. Nasser also felt under pressure from economic problems arising from his misguided attempt to force-start the economy through state planning. His expulsion of the UN peacekeeping force from the Sinai frontier and the closure of the Gulf of Aqaba to Israeli shipping provoked Israel and reflected a failure to appreciate the limitations of the Egyptian military, which, in turn, was overly concerned about Yemen, where several of its leading units were deployed. The Israeli assault began on 5 June with a surprise attack on the Egyptian air bases launched by planes coming in over the Mediterranean from the west. The Egyptians, who had failed to take the most basic precautions, lost 286 planes in just one morning, and, in addition, their runways were heavily bombed. As the war spread, it led to the Israeli conquest not only of the Gaza Strip and Sinai from Egypt, but also of the West Bank section of Jordan and the Golan Heights from Syria.

Gaining the initiative was crucial to the execution of Israeli's well-prepared plans, as were training and morale which were better than those of their disunited opponents. In Sinai, the Egyptians suffered from a failure to appreciate the calibre of the Israeli military and the nature of Israeli operations, and from an absence of adequate, effective reserves: the large number of poorly trained reservists in the Sinai were no substitute, and, more generally, Arab forces suffered from a lack of adequately trained troops. In 1967, Soviet T54 and T55 tanks used by the Egyptians were beaten by US Patton and British Centurion tanks used by the Israelis, who showed greater operational and tactical flexibility, not least in successfully searching for vulnerable flanks, and thus overcoming the strength of prepared Egyptian positions. The Egyptian command system, weakened by cronyism and complacency, proved totally inadequate to meet the challenge. Having broken into the Egyptian rear, the Israelis ably exploited the situation, and they also benefited from the destruction of the Egyptian air force at the outset of the war: Egyptian ground forces were badly affected by Israeli ground-support attacks, for which operations in Yemen had given them no preparation. When Field Marshal Amer instructed the army to retreat from Sinai to the Suez Canal on 6 June, the unplanned withdrawal was chaotic, the cohesion of the army collapsed, and resistance to the Israelis disintegrated. The Egyptians suffered about 10,000 fatalities and 5,000 men captured, as well as the loss of much of their equipment: about $2 billion worth was destroyed while Israel captured 320 tanks. The conflict in Sinai also underlined the key role of field maintenance and repair in mobile warfare; the Israelis proving more effective than the Egyptians in every case. As always, overnight repair of equipment and its return to the battle line proved a key element in the war-making ability of a modern army. Non-battle losses through mechanical failure are apt to be more costly than battle losses.

Jordan joined in on the Egyptian side on 5 June, only to have its air force destroyed and the West Bank overrun. The Israelis had not anticipated a ground war with Jordan, but Jordanian support for Egypt led the Israelis to attack once they were certain that the Egyptians had been defeated. Syria refused to provide assistance to Egypt, but it shelled Israeli positions, and, on 9 June, the Israelis, keen to take advantage of an opportunity to occupy the Golan Heights, attacked. As Egyptian and Jordanian forces had already been defeated, with the Jordanians accepting a ceasefire late on 7 June and Egypt early on 9 June, the Israelis were able to focus on the Syrians, reflecting the importance of sequential warfare, and their ability to respond rapidly to problems. Gaining the initiative, and using their aerial superiority for ground attack, the Israelis benefited from a collapse in Syrian morale. The failure of Syria's patron, the Soviet Union, to intervene was also important, not least because the Soviets had stirred up Syria against Israel and had made some preparations to intervene.[12] At the end of the war, Israeli forces were less than 60 kilometres from Damascus and less than 110 kilometres from Cairo.

Israel remained in occupation of the regions conquered in 1967, ensuring that it now controlled a large Arab population. In the long term, the presence of a large Arab population within Israel and, even more, in Israeli-occupied territories was to challenge the security of Israel, while the consequences of the occupation helped destabilize its politics. Furthermore, the failure of the Arab regular armies encouraged some of the Palestinians to resort to terrorism, not only in the Middle East but also further afield. Attacks on Israelis included one at the Munich Olympics in 1972. In addition, over 600,000 Arab refugees, many of whom had fled Palestine in 1948–9, were based in neighbouring Arab states, where they challenged the stability of Jordan, and helped overthrow that of an already divided Lebanon, which moved into full-scale civil war from 1975.

Meanwhile, Egypt and Syria, totally unwilling to accept Israel's gains in 1967 and to negotiate peace, had been rearmed by the Soviet Union[13] and, in 1968–70, Egypt launched major artillery bombardments of Israeli positions. Nasser was determined to show that the Six-Day War of June 1967 was only a stage in a longer conflict. In turn, the Israelis mounted their own bombardments and, from 1969, the conflict spread to the air until, in August 1970, the USA arranged a ceasefire.

In 1973, however, conflict resumed, in the Yom Kippur War, in which Egypt and Syria ultimately failed in their plan, to inflict defeats in a surprise attack and then to establish strong defensive positions that would lead to superpower mediation. Suffering from an over-confidence similar to that which had affected the Arabs in 1967, and from a failure to appreciate intelligence of Arab preparations, the Israelis were unprepared for the attack launched on 6 October. The Israelis' American-made M48 and M60 tanks had double the rate and range of fire of the Soviet T55 and T62 tanks, but the Arabs benefited from launching a surprise attack, Operation Badr, against the weakly defended Israeli Bar Lev line on the east bank of the Suez Canal, which rapidly fell, while the Syrians broke the Israeli line on the Golan Heights.

The fall of the Bar Lev line was a serious blow to Israeli prestige in the shape of a reputation for invincibility. Furthermore, in responding to the Egyptian attack, the Israelis found it difficult to penetrate the integrated air defence missile system that the Egyptians had received from the Soviets, while, east of the Suez Canal, the Egyptians repelled a series of Israeli counter-attacks, inflicting serious damage on Israeli armour which suffered from a doctrine that, based on the experience of 1967, exaggerated the effectiveness of tank attack and failed to provide adequate combined-arms capability, especially sufficient artillery support and mobile infantry. Israeli aircraft and tanks proved vulnerable to mobile ground-to-air and air-to-ground missiles, and to Sagger anti-tank guided missiles.

The Israelis, nevertheless, were able to drive the Syrians back, advancing into Syria, and repelling counter-attacks. In response to Syrian pressure for help, the Egyptians changed their strategy and moved their armoured reserve forward, attacking on 14 October. This was a mistake, because the Israelis were strong in defence, not least as the Egyptians advanced beyond their anti-aircraft cover. In an attack that highlighted the deficiencies of Egyptian tactics, the Egyptians lost heavily. In turn, benefiting from this destruction of the Egyptian reserve, the Israelis attacked, exploiting the Egyptian failure to cover their entire front, and, more generally, their limitation at manoeuvrist warfare, crossing the Suez Canal where the Egyptians were weakest from the night of 15–16 October, defeating Egyptian counter-attacks, and encircling Egyptian forces before a ceasefire ended the war on 24 October: a first ceasefire on the 22nd had been breached by Israeli advances on the 23rd and 24th.

As in 1967, the failure of Arab armies in 1973 demonstrated the vulnerability of forces with a lower rate of activity, the problems arising from losing the initiative, and the need for a flexible defence. Arab militaries lacked effective practice, especially information acquisition and management, unit cohesion, and command skills,[14] while Israeli forces were more effective in using the initiative. In the 1973 war, command skills were particularly tested by the need to adapt to large-scale use of tanks: attacks, such as the Syrian advance with 800 tanks through the Israeli lines, and one by Egypt on 14 October, in which the Egyptians lost about 260 tanks, were clashes for which there was planning but scant experience. Egypt and Syria lost about 2,250 tanks in the war, the Israelis 840.

The 1973 war was mostly waged on land and in the air, but, at sea, both sides deployed missile boats, the Israelis sinking at least nine Egyptian and Syrian ships and driving their navies back to harbour. As with aircraft carriers in World War II, the emphasis was on an accurate first strike, but, compared to then, all ships now depended in part on the use of electronic counter-measures to block missile attacks.[15]

The USA tried to ease regional pressures which threatened the world economy because of the concentration in the Middle East of oil production and reserves. The Carter administration helped arrange a peace settlement between Egypt and Israel, with the Camp David Accords of September 1978 followed by the Egypt–Israel treaty of March 1979 under which all Israeli settlers and troops were to have left the Sinai within three years. However, Israel's determination to act as a regional power and its concern about terrorism based in Lebanon which arose from instability there, led, in Operation Litani, to its invasion of southern Lebanon in 1978 and the destruction of the PLO's infrastructure before it withdrew its forces. Israel was now backing the militia of the Maronite Christians. The Israeli advance benefited from close air support. Israel's determination to take the initiative was further demonstrated in 1981, when Iraq's nuclear reactor was destroyed in an air raid.

In June 1982, still helped by the peaceful nature of relations with Egypt, the Israelis, in what they termed Operation Peace for Galilee, again invaded southern Lebanon, hitting the Syrian occupying force hard and, this time, advancing as far as Beirut, which they besieged in

July–August and occupied in September. The Israelis relied on helicopter support for their integrated advancing units of armour/infantry/ artillery/ engineers, and the Palestinian refugee forces in Lebanon were heavily outgunned. The Israeli Cabinet had not wanted an advance to Beirut or conflict with the Syrians, but were pushed into both by the Defence Minister, Ariel Sharon, who was a determined advocate of aggressive policies. The Syrians initially fought well, but once their missile batteries in Lebanon had been knocked out, and their air force badly pummelled by Israeli aircraft armed with Sidewinder missiles, and supported by electronic counter-measures, they proved vulnerable to Israeli attack, now bolstered by clear superiority in the air.

However, it proved impossible to 'stabilize' the local situation in Israel's interests. In August 1982 the Israeli candidate, Bashir Gemayel, was elected President of Lebanon, but he was assassinated the following month, destroying the basis for a settlement between Israel and Lebanon. Israel now found itself with an onerous commitment and with local allies that required support. The slaughter, in September 1982, by Israel's Lebanese allies, the Phalange militia, of Palestinians in the Sabra and Shatila refugee camps in Beirut, and the Israeli bombardment of the city, badly compromised Israel's reputation.[16]

More generally, conflict in Lebanon demonstrated the limitations of well-armed forces' weapons. In 1982 a multinational Western force was sent to Lebanon to try and bolster its stability, but the troops soon became targets. In September 1983, the US Sixth Fleet bombarded Druze militia positions on the hills near Beirut in support of the Lebanese army, firing shells the size of small cars; yet, the following month, neither the Americans nor the French could prevent the destruction of their headquarters in Beirut by lorries full of high explosive driven by suicidal guerrillas; the British, more attuned to terrorist moves, thanks to their experience in Northern Ireland, blocked a comparable move. As a result of their losses, and of a more general sense of political impotence, the US marines sent to Lebanon in 1982 were withdrawn in 1984.

Subsequently, the Israelis had to withdraw from the bulk of Lebanon (1985), and, eventually, to abandon the Security Zone established along the frontier with Israel: they faced a guerrilla force, the Hizbullah, willing to take casualties, enjoying foreign support, especially from Iran, and able to respond tactically (for example with surface-to-air missiles) to such Israeli advantages as airpower, while still maintaining pressure on Israel.[17] The collapse of Israeli influence in Lebanon was matched by Syrian success, and, in 1990, the Syrians played an important role in bringing the Lebanese civil war to an end.

In 1987, the *Intifada*, a rebellion against Israeli rule in occupied Arab territories, and specifically against the pace of Israeli settlement on the West Bank, began with stone-throwing crowds challenging Israeli authority. The *Intifada* was to underline the weakness of imposed political settlements in the Middle East where the bulk of any population felt alienated, and also to expose the limitations of regular troops in the face of popular resistance. The Israeli High Command found it difficult to deal with what was to them a novel form of warfare. There was no concentrated target, such as that which faced the Saudi Arabians in November 1979 when the Grand Mosque in Mecca was seized by Shia militants: it was stormed. The Oslo Agreement of 1993 and the subsequent creation of a Palestinian autonomous territory under Yasser Arafat failed to prevent an increased escalation of conflict between Israel and Palestinians from the late 1990s;[18] although Israel and Jordan signed a peace treaty in 1994.

REBELLIONS

Aside from anti-imperialist movements and wars between states, there was also conflict as governments faced rebellions. These overlapped with other categories of conflict. Thus, in Angola, the longstanding rebellion against the MPLA government by UNITA carried forward their rivalry in the war of independence against Portuguese control, a rivalry that included a tribal and regional dimension, with UNITA based in the Ovimbundu tribe of southern Angola. The Portuguese tried in early 1975 to transfer power to a coalition government willing to oversee free elections, but conflict began on 1 February when the MPLA and FLNA clashed in Luanda. Within six months, the MPLA had defeated its opponents and seized control of the government. This, however, did not prevent a lengthy civil war. The clash between UNITA and the MPLA was also closely intertwined with the Cold War, as the MPLA government looked to the Soviet Union and Cuba while UNITA received US backing, and also with the continuing struggle against 'white' rule in Southern Africa. South Africa provided money, weaponry and advisers to UNITA, as well as bases in neighbouring South West Africa, and more direct intervention, including air cover for UNITA in southern Angola. In 1975, South Africa sent a large force into Angola in order to weaken the MPLA. Further attacks followed in 1978 and 1979 as the South Africans attacked SWAPO bases in Angola, such as Lubango, from which their position in South-West Africa was under attack. Angolan forces were attacked anew by South Africa in 1981–2, and, after the failure of the Lusaka Accord of 1984, a ceasefire was not agreed until 1988.

The war had become too costly for the Soviet Union, Cuba and South Africa, and the failure of the UNITA/South African siege of the city of Cuito Cuanavale in the winter of 1987–8 encouraged negotiations. Ironically, US aid for UNITA was countered by the purchase of oil by American oil companies that helped enable the government to buy arms to fight UNITA. As a result of the ceasefire, the South Africans withdrew at once, while the Cubans finally left in 1991. However, the MPLA and UNITA ceasefire, only signed in 1989, speedily collapsed, leading to an upsurge in conflict, a fresh bout of diplomacy, and a peace in 1991 that lasted until UNITA rejected the results of the 1992 election. After the end of Portuguese power in Mozambique, South Africa had also supported the RENAMO rebels against the FRELIMO government.[19] The government was backed by troops from Zimbabwe and Tanzania and received Soviet arms.

Ethnic tensions played a role not only in Angola and Mozambique, but also in a host of conflicts in sub-Saharan Africa. Some of the most bloody occurred in the former Belgian colonies of Burundi and Rwanda where the Hutu and Tutsi were the major ethnic groups. In 1959 the Tutsi rulers of Rwanda were overthrown by the Hutu majority, with about 10,000 killed, and subsequent attempts by Tutsi émigrés to regain power by guerrilla action failed, and led to the killing of maybe another 30,000 Tutsi. This was to be the background to serious conflict in the early 1990s (see p. 170).

Across the world many rebellions were separatist in origin, and these occurred with increasing regularity after 1945. In 1946 the Shah led the Iranian army into Tabriz, producing a bloodbath that cowed Azerbaijani separatism, while, in 1959, the Chinese army defeated an uprising by Tibetans (guerrilla action had begun in 1955), and, in the 1960s, Congo suppressed Kataganese separatism. The Indonesian army suppressed Communist and Islamic opposition, including the Darul Islam (House of Islam) in west Java in the 1950s, as well as the Republic of the South Moluccas in 1952, and rebellion in Sumatra and Sulawesi in 1957–8. The latter was backed by CIA aircraft. The Indonesians also unsuccessfully sought to overthrow Brunei in 1962, by fomenting a rebellion, and to conquer northern Borneo from British-supported Malaysia in 1963–5. The Indonesians also annexed western New Guinea (as West Irian) in 1963, successfully invaded East Timor in 1975, and brutally resisted demands for independence by the FRETILIN (Frente Revolucionária de Timor-Leste Independente) movement in East Timor and the Free Papua Movement in Irian.

The reliance on force in East Timor proved seriously counter-product-ive, as it failed to assuage local separatism and also led to international condemnation, especially after the shooting of unarmed demonstrators at a cemetery in Dili on 12 November 1991 led to hundreds of deaths or injuries and was filmed by Western journalists. In 1999, the Indonesians responded to continued separatism, and to international pressure, by giving East Timor the choice of independence or regional autonomy. The people overwhelming chose independence, despite ser-ious pressure from militias supported by the army. After the election the coercion was stepped up, but international attention and anger mounted, and finally led the Indonesians to accept the popular verdict.

In the Middle East the Kurds had mounted separatist efforts against Iraq and Turkey since the inter-war period, leading to a response by both that was frequently intertwined with both international and global power politics. Thus, in Iraq, where conflict with Kurdish insurgents had been intense in 1961–6 and 1969–70, the Kurdish rising of 1974–5 was supported by Iran with artillery and anti-aircraft cover, as well as the provision of US and Israeli arms. However, in Syria, the Alawite-dominated regime and army brutally crushed a rising by Sunni Muslims at Hama in 1982. Religious uprisings were most common in the Islamic world, but they were generally unsuccessful; that in Sudan in 1970 being crushed by forces supported by tanks and aircraft. In 1959 the Moroccan army crushed a revolt by the Berbers in the Rif mountains.

In South Asia, attempts by the Pakistani army, which was dominated by troops from the Punjab in West Pakistan, to suppress the Bengali nationalism of East Pakistan, provoked a rebellion in 1970 which was supported by India, leading to the creation of the state of Bangladesh.[20] The Pakistani army was more successful in quelling a tribal uprising in Baluchistan in 1972–6 that arose from attempts to limit autonomy and tribal power. In 1983 Tamil separatism led to a protracted war in northern Sri Lanka; while India faced rebellion in Kashmir, and from Sikh radicals.

Rebellions led to a variety of military situations. Conflict in Congo in the 1960s was wide-ranging and bloody, but it did not involve such a large-scale use of troops and front lines as seen in the Nigerian Civil War of 1967–70. The slaughter of large numbers of Ibos – possibly 30,000 – in the massacres that followed the second coup of 1966 in Nigeria had led to a collapse of Ibo support for the notion of Nigeria. The new Nigerian federal government, composed of officers, and the product of the coup, was unsympathetic to the Ibo demand for a looser confederation, while the Ibo leadership challenged the legality of the government. After the Ibo republic of Biafra was proclaimed, the federal government launched a 'police operation' in July 1967 that became a civil war. The federal forces benefited from overwhelming numerical superiority, including an army of 120,000 troops, and from the availability of British and Soviet weaponry. The Nigerian navy was crucial, both in imposing a debilitating blockade of Biafra, and in enabling the Nigerians to seize ports and coastal positions. Although there were some able commanders and some brave troops on both sides, operations and fighting in the war showed the problems, for both sides, of rapidly expanding armies with untrained men.[21] The application of force proved difficult: air attacks were frequently ineffective,[22] and artillery was often poorly aimed. Infantry weaponry was a crucial factor in the fighting, while the Nigerian army also made good use of armoured personnel carriers. However, the role of ethnic and factional considerations weakened the federal army's fighting competence. Logistical support in the difficult terrain was not improved by chaotic command and organizational systems undermined by corruption.

The Biafrans, who fought a conventional war with front lines, had no answer to the airpower of their opponents, and little response to their armoured vehicles. After the initial stages of the conflict they were also heavily outnumbered. Unlike the Viet Minh and the Viet Cong, the Biafrans were swiftly cut off from foreign land links, and this exacerbated their lack of food and military supplies. The Nigerian government felt no hesitation in using starvation to help destroy the Ibos. The hard-pressed Biafrans finally collapsed after their airstrip at Uli was overrun in 1970, severing their only remaining supply link.[23]

This was the first major war in sub-Saharan Africa fought to a resolution with modern weapons in which all the commanders were African. The Nigerian army subsequently came, in the 1990s and 2000s, to play a regional role in peacekeeping in Sierra Leone and Liberia that reflected its own regional agenda. Poorly trained for the task, the Nigerians tended to use firepower as a substitute for policing; however, in both cases they faced very difficult situations: drug-taking, adolescent fighters operated on behalf of rebel factions and both countries had been reduced to a form of gangland chaos, making it difficult for regulars to clearly identify opponents who could be defeated. In Sierra Leone the civil war was declared over in January 2002 and an international peacekeeping force began to disarm combatants. However, in Liberia, a coup in 1980 was followed by a rebellion led by Charles Taylor that started in 1989, and after he became President in 1997, by a rebellion against him that started in 1999 and that led to his opponents advancing into the capital Monrovia in 2003. He resigned in the subsequent chaos, and Nigerian peacekeepers took over Monrovia.

Further east, Ethiopia eventually conceded independence to Eritrea in 1993 after a long secessionist movement in which the Ethiopian position had finally collapsed in April–May 1991, in part because of the fall of the Mengistu regime in Ethiopia in the face of successful opposition by the Ethiopian People's Revolutionary Democratic Front and the Tigré People's Liberation Front.[24]

Sudan, however, continued to be devastated by a civil war which had been waged from 1963 until 1972, and then again from 1983. Successive governments based in the Arabic-speaking Islamic north thwarted southern separatism, beginning with the suppression of a military revolt in 1956, soon after independence, but were unable to subjugate the south. The southern separatists of the Anya-Nya movement had initially lacked modern weapons, many relying on spears, but its use of guerrilla tactics gravely weakened the army's position in the south. The size of Sudan also told against the army. It was more successful in its policy of turning for support to the Nuer tribe, rivals of the Dinka tribe which was prominent in the resistance. The latter, however, benefited from support from, or at least bases in, the neighbouring states of Ethiopia, Uganda and Zaire (Congo), as well as from Israeli military equipment. The internationalization of the conflict appears less intense than those in Indo-China, because of the absence of US intervention, but it was important in fuelling the war. The Sudanese government received Soviet weapons and advisors, and also support from Egypt. The importance of international backing was shown in 1971 when agreements between Sudan and both Ethiopia and Uganda (which led to the end of Israeli aid via Uganda) cut support for the rebels and encouraged them to negotiate. The 1972 Addis Ababa agreement included southern autonomy as well as the incorporation of southern troops into the army, but in 1983 government pressure, including an attempt to introduce Islamic *sharia* law, led to a revival of guerrilla warfare, soon under the leadership of the Sudan People's Liberation Army (SPLA). Civilians became a target for both sides, with food aid and famine used as weapons. The ground-to-air missiles of the SPLA made the aerial re-supply of government garrisons, such as Juba, hazardous. Although a truce was agreed in the autumn of 2002, peace seems unlikely, not least because of the strength of uncompromising militant Islam on the government side.[25]

Many other rebellions were small-scale, for example the unsuccessful attempts in 1966 by the former kingdom of Buganda to secede from Uganda; the Shifta war of 1963-7, when Somalis in northeast Kenya unsuccessfully sought to break away to join Somalia; and the separatist movement in the Senegalese province of Casamance, that began in the early 1980s and still continues. Such struggles are important to the history of individual states, and, in aggregate terms, make up much of the military history of the world. They also ensured that insurgency and counter-insurgency capability, operations and doctrine played a major role in this history. In such struggles effectiveness was often intertwined with political will. For example, in Cuba in 1958, when Batista's divided, demoralized and incompetent army attacked Castro's guerrillas, the offensive was poorly coordinated and lacked both adequate airpower and foreign support. Once the campaign had failed, the government suffered a crucial loss of nerve and lost the initiative, with fatal consequences.

The political context was also crucial in other insurrections. Governments that were flexible and able to devise effective and interrelated political and military strategies enjoyed more success. Thus, in the defeat of the Hukbalahap Rebellion, the peasant-backed Communist guerrilla movement on Luzon in the Philippines, in 1946–54, the government benefited from US arms, but counter-insurgency operations were supplemented by land reform to win over the peasantry. Oman suppressed rebellious tribesmen in the extensive Dhofar region in 1965–75, in part thanks to foreign, particularly British and Iranian, assistance, but also because Sultan Qaboos, who deposed his father in 1970, was a more adept politician. The problems faced by insurgency warfare spurred recourse, from the 1970s, for example in Northern Ireland, to terrorism, with its more limited requirements and its lesser risk to its participants.[26]

COUPS

Conversely, governments faced with insurgency challenges also had to confront the risk that elements in the military might themselves seize power, and this helped determine the relationship between military capability and organization.[27] Thus in the mid-1950s, the field forces of the Iraqi army, with the exception of the Royal Guards Brigade, were, for security reasons, not usually provided with ammunition. Coups were an important part of the military history of the period. In July

1958 the Iraqi monarchy was overthrown in a coup that seized the usual targets of such uprisings, including the broadcasting headquarters and the airport.

In Africa and elsewhere, coups followed decolonization, although any listing has to note the very different levels of violence seen in coups, which, in large part, reflected their contrasting causes. Many coups arose from the rejection of the civilian governments established at independence and their attempt to control the military, for example the coup in Sudan in 1958, and that in Cambodia which deposed Prince Sihanouk in 1970; but the politicization of the military by civilian governments, keen to use its strength to help achieve political goals, also encouraged the military to overcome inhibitions about the use of force. Other coups were the product of inter-military divisions. Coups in Africa included Egypt (1952 and 1954), Sudan (1958, 1985, 1989), Togo (1963), Zanzibar (1964), Zaire (1965), Nigeria (1966, 1985), Ghana (1966, 1972, 1978, 1979), Sierra Leone (1967 and 1997), Mali (1968), Libya (1969), Uganda (1971, 1980, 1985, 1986), Madagascar (1972), Rwanda (1973), Ethiopia (1974), the Central African Republic (1979, 1981, 2003), Equatorial Guinea (1979), Liberia (1980), Upper Volta (1982), Mauritania (1984, 2003), Lesotho (1986) and Ivory Coast (1999). In Pakistan, military regimes were created in 1958, 1969, 1977 and 1999.[28]

The frequency of coups in Latin America indicated, however, that coups were not only linked to decolonization. Coups there included those in Peru (1948, 1962 and 1967), Venezuela (1948 and 1958), Bolivia (1951), Colombia (1953 and 1957), Guatemala (1954, 1978, 1982 and 1983), Argentina (1955, 1962, 1966, 1970 and 1976), the Dominican Republic (1963), Brazil (1964), Chile (1973), Paraguay (1989), Grenada (1983), and Ecuador (2000). Coups usually led to the creation of military governments, reflecting the widespread conviction among Latin American militaries that their function included the suppression of internal enemies; for example, left-wing tendencies. The use of force also sometimes played a role in changes in civilian government, such as those in Peru and Colombia in the 1980s and '90s .[29]

Although some military regimes were short-term, others were long-lasting, for example in Brazil from 1964 until 1985, and in Chile from

1973 until 1990. In the short term, authoritarian regimes reliant on force were less powerful or rigid in practice than they appeared, and they operated by accepting the circumvention of their nostrums and structures by their own members, as well as by vested interests and by the public itself. In the long term these regimes found it difficult to contain political problems and to satisfy popular demands. Thus in Thailand, the military lost power in 1992, while, in Indonesia, General Suharto, the Chief of Army Staff, who had benefited from the coup of 1965 to take over power in 1967, and become President in 1968, was forced to surrender power in 1998.[30] However, in Myanmar (Burma), where the military ruled as the State Peace and Development Council, the elections held in 1990 were annulled when a pro-democracy movement won, and the military has held on to power since. Unsuccessful coups, such as those in Gabon in 1964, Sudan in 1971, Iran in 1980, Spain and Gambia in 1981, and Nigeria in 1990, and plans for coups, as in Egypt in August 1967, were also an important feature of military history, and ensured that many governments had to see coup-avoidance as one of the most important goals of their military policy.

FORCE AND THE STATE

Another important feature of military history, more generally, was the use of force as the arm of the state, whether military or civilian. This could involve peaceful operations, but was often brutal. Thus, in 1977, 1979 and 1991 the Iraqi army suppressed Shia agitation, in the latter two cases with heavy casualties. The militarized nature of many regimes was readily apparent. Under General Qassem, who ruled Iraq from 1958–63, the heavily fortified Ministry of Defence compound was the centre of government, protected by about 2,000 troops. When Qassem was overthrown, the compound was attacked from the air before being besieged. Having surrendered, Qassem was killed.[31]

The continuum between coups and civil wars was not easily segmented for the purposes of definition. Nor was that between ethnic tension and civil war, as was shown in 1987–90 in Natal, then part of white-ruled South Africa, when the Zulu Inkatha movement fought the

United Democratic Front, which was linked to the then-banned African National Congress. This struggle for dominance involved control over land and employment, and the ability to negotiate with the apartheid government. Police involvement further complicated the struggle, which was at once a conflict between groups within a state where the government could still deploy considerable force, and a disorganized upsurge of ethnic violence and lawlessness.[32]

Civilian governments also used force to intimidate the population. Having, in the Great Proletarian Cultural Revolution, used Red Guards to terrorize alleged reactionaries, Mao Zedong, from late 1968, accepted the use of the army to restore order. In 1989, under his less authoritarian successor, Deng Xiaoping, the army was still used to suppress brutally the Democracy Movement in Beijing. In 1992, the Peruvian President, Alberto Fujimori, used the army to shut down the Congress and the courts, while, in Zimbabwe in the early 2000s, Robert Mugabe used troops to try to break a national strike and to crush demonstrations. Troops were also used for policing, as in Jamaica in 1999 when there were joint patrols with the police. The military was also employed as the arm of the state in First World countries. In Britain, 19,000 servicemen were deployed in the winter of 2002–3 in Operation Fresco in order to provide emergency cover for striking firefighters.

CONCLUSIONS

The internal use of force is central to the military history of much of the world, although it both militarized society and compromised military professionalism. This aspect of military history has been underrated in part because it plays no important role as far as the USA, the world's leading military power, is concerned.[33] The US military played a role in the racial integration of the American South and was the last resort in the event of apparent challenges to internal stability, but the constraints on the use of force were far greater than in most Third World states, while the availability of the National Guard kept the regular military at a remove from the issue. However, militarized states, such as those in Latin America, owed their character not so much to conflict with each other as to the domestic use of force,[34] and this was accentuated by radical challenges, such as those of the Tupamaros guerrillas in Uruguay and the Shining Path in Peru. This situation continued after the end of the Cold War, and helps define much of modern military history.

Chapter 7

Searching for a New World Order since 1990

The end of the Cold War with the collapse, as a result of domestic pressures, of the Soviet Union (dissolved in 1991) did not lead to the 'end of history', or the 'peace dividend', foretold by some of the more superficial commentators, who believed all too readily that it represented a triumph for US-led democratic capitalism, and that there would be no future clash of ideologies to destabilize the world. However, in what was a revolution in strategic affairs,[1] the Western powers, led by the USA, which saw itself as victor in the Cold War, were now able to intervene more frequently against states that earlier would have looked for Soviet support, not least because UN resolutions were not vetoed in the Security Council. In addition, the established parameters within which peacekeeping was generally expected to take place (first, that conflict had already ended, second, that the government of the state in question accepted the deployment of peacekeepers), were interpreted increasingly loosely, as seen in various examples of so-called 'peace' support, making, enforcement . . .[2]

RUSSIA

American force-projection was not challenged by a revived Russia because the collapse of the Soviet Union was not followed by a stronger Russia. Instead, it faced serious economic difficulties as the dismantling of the old command economy exposed the uncompetitive nature of much Soviet-era industry, while it proved difficult to establish effective monetary and fiscal mechanisms. Western loans were necessary in order to prevent a total collapse of Russia in the 1990s and, even so, debt payments caused a severe crisis in 1998, leading to default and devaluation.

Geo-strategically, Russia was in a very different position as a result of the 1991 independence of the fourteen non-Russian republics of the Soviet Union. Her frontiers did not change in the Far East but, elsewhere, there was a major retreat, with the return of territory not only that had been gained as a consequence of World War II, but also of Russian gains stretching back to the seventeenth century. In terms of overland force-projection, there were no longer frontiers with Afghanistan, Iran, Turkey, Romania, Hungary and Czechoslovakia, while the openings to the Caspian, Black and Baltic Seas were much reduced. Indeed, control over the Black Sea Fleet was a major issue of tension with Ukraine in 1992–4. On the Baltic, Russia retains St Petersburg, which freezes in winter, and Kaliningrad, which, however, was separated from the rest of the country when Lithuania became independent. The extension of Western economic and strategic interests into the former Soviet republics was a particular issue of sensitivity for the Russians, with NATO guarantees to the Baltic republics (Estonia, Latvia and Lithuania) being a matter of contention; although the subsequent establishment of US bases in Central Asia, in order to facilitate intervention in Afghanistan in 2001–2, caused less contention. However, whereas decolonization was eased for Britain by America's role as a guarantor of Western interests (albeit on its own terms), US power projection and strength proved less welcome to many politicians in the Russian Federation.

With Russian weakness, the arithmetic of deterrence, underlined as it was by the risk of mutually assured destruction, no longer discouraged overt Western intervention in the Third World. Indeed, in January 1994, the US and Russian leaders agreed not to target each other's states with their strategic nuclear weapons. The end of the Cold War also increased the number of potential allies for the West, and thus deepened its logistical capability and strengthened its capacity for force-projection. At the same time, this capacity was put at the service of a mixture of regional goals, and a universalist aspiration to secure a more benign world order, that posed serious challenges not only to Western military capability but also to related political goals. In particular, there were acute issues of prioritization between alternative commitments, and also of how best to devise sensible political missions that matched military capability, and how best to organize and enhance the latter in order to secure missions. A variety of military devices and doctrines, such as US preparation for confronting two major regional crises, and US (from 1992) and British reconceptualization of naval warfare toward littoral power projection, were important, but did not address the issues of sensible tasking and the political management of conflict.

THE GULF WAR, 1990–91

The 1990s opened with a second Iraqi invasion, this time of Kuwait. A far smaller and weaker target than Iran, oil-rich Kuwait rapidly fell on 2 August 1990, and, six days later, Saddam Hussein declared Kuwait Iraq's nineteenth province. The response defined high-spectrum warfare for the following decade. Concerned about the impact of Iraqi expansion in the centre of the world's oil production, George H. Bush, the US President, rapidly began diplomatic and military preparations for conflict, and Iraq's failure to press on ensured that the initiative thereafter rested with its opponents. On 3 August two US carrier groups were ordered towards the region and, on 8 August, in response to a Saudi request for ground troops two days earlier, the first US troops arrived. The build-up of coalition forces in neighbouring Saudi Arabia, forces benefiting from the availability of Saudi oil and bases, was matched by a blockade intended to hit Iraqi trade, especially oil exports.

Iraq's refusal to meet a UN deadline for withdrawal, led, on 17 January 1991, to the start of a major air offensive. Although aircraft from twelve countries were involved, the US was central to the offensive, which worked because of the rapid success in overcoming the sophisticated Iraqi anti-aircraft system; Saddam had used French and Soviet technology to produce an integrated system in which computers linked radars and missiles. Iraq's heavily outnumbered air force did not intervene in force; instead the MIG-29s flew to Iran where they were added to the air force. The air offensive benefited from state-of-the-art US weaponry: B-2 Stealth bombers able to minimize radar detection bombed Baghdad – one of the most heavily defended cities in the world – and did so with impunity, while the US made effective use of guided bombs. Thermal-imaging laser-designation systems were employed to guide the bombs to their target, and pilots launched bombs into the 'cone' of the laser beam in order to score a direct hit. The use of stealth and precision meant that it was possible to employ a direct air assault aimed at over-coming the entire Iraqi air-system, rather than an incremental roll-back campaign. The destruction of the air-defence system, with only one aircraft lost (to an Iraqi MIG-29) on the first night, was a triumph, not only for weaponry but also for planning, that made full use of the oppor-tunities presented by the weapons, while also out-thinking the Iraqis, for example by getting them to bring their radars to full power, and thus exposing them to attack. As a result of the subsequent air assault, Iraqi ground forces were short of supplies, their command and control system was heavily disrupted, so that they could not 'understand' the battle, and their morale was low.[3]

In February 1991, Iraq was driven from Kuwait in a swift campaign in which the Iraqis were out-generalled and out-fought by coalition forces that benefited not only from superior technology, but also from their ability to maintain a high-tempo offensive while executing a well-conceived plan that combined air and land forces. Allied (Coalition) fighting quality, unit cohesion, leadership and planning, and Iraqi defi-ciencies in each,[4] all played a major role in ensuring victory. The Iraqis had surrendered mobility by entrenching themselves to protect their conquest of Kuwait. The US employed satellite surveillance, Patriot anti-missile missiles against Iraqi attacks, and Cruise missiles and guided bombs to provide precise bombardment. In the ground war, which began at 4 am on 24 February, the Iraqis were defeated with heavy casu-alties, while their opponents lost few men, the US suffering 143 battle fatalities, 33 from 'friendly fire'. Predictions that Iraqi entrenchments would be difficult to take, and that the Iraqis would force attritional warfare on the coalition, causing heavy casualties,[5] proved mistaken. While the Iraqis were attacked on the direct route to Kuwait City, their right flank was outmanoeuvred by a rapid US advance to the west which put tremendous pressure on the Iraqis as the outflanking US forces turned, on 27 February, to attack them and destroyed much of the Iraqi army. The following morning, President Bush ordered a ceasefire, with the Iraqis, in 100 hours of non-stop combat, having lost over 50,000 dead, as well as 81,000 prisoners and nearly 4,000 tanks.

Despite the rapid victory, the US doctrine of AirLand Battle proved more difficult to execute in practice than to advance in theory, and to train for, not least due to the problems of synchronizing air and land forces under fast-moving combat conditions.[6] However, compared to earlier conflicts, such as the Linebacker II air offensive on North Vietnam in December 1972, there was unified control over air operations – a single air manager (the Joint Force Air Component Commander), target acquisition and accuracy were effective, and the pace of the air attack was maintained;[7] even if some of the high-tech weaponry, such as the Patriot missile and British runway-cratering bombs, did less well than was claimed at the time. In addition, important parts of the Allied military did not use weaponry that was available. For example, the US used 9,300 precision-guided munitions, but most of their aircraft were not equipped or their pilots trained for their use and, instead, employed unguided munitions, which made up 90 per cent of the aerial munitions used. This was despite the extensive and effective use of precision-guided munitions in the Linebacker I and II campaigns in Vietnam in 1972. Similarly, although the US had developed stealth aircraft, most of their aircraft lacked this capability.

The conflict also saw Iraqi Scud missile attacks on Israel, and, although they did not achieve their desired aim of bringing Israel into the war, and thus jeopardizing Arab support for the USA, especially from Saudi Arabia and Syria, they underlined Israeli vulnerability. Concerned that, as a result of its inaction, their deterrence had been lessened, the Israeli government wished to take reprisals, but, aside from discouraging weather conditions, the Israelis were affected by US opposition to such action. The USA did, however, provide Israel with satellite information and Patriot batteries. The need to counter the military and, even more, the political threat from Scud missiles dramatized the implications of the spread of weaponry. American anti-missile doctrine had long focused on Soviet inter-continental ballistic missiles, but the Scuds indicated that short-range anti-missile defences and doctrine were also necessary, and drew attention to the problems of relying on the Patriot missiles for that purpose.

For the US and British navies, the war marked the major change that followed the end of the Cold War. In place of a doctrine focused on defeating Soviet naval forces in a struggle for maritime routes, came littoral force-projection and amphibious capability at the expense of a state, Iraq, with no real naval power.

The failure to keep military objectives and political goals in harmony, however, helped ensure that the Gulf War did not lead to the hoped-for overthrow of Saddam Hussein. The US decision to end the offensive was taken in haste, in a war that was very high-tempo, without an adequate consideration of how to translate the outcome of the campaign into a durable post-war settlement. This was linked to military factors, specifically the persistence of 'friction' and 'fog': 'At the operational level, it is clear that Schwarzkopf lost track of the position of his forces and Iraqi troops at a critical point in the battle'. A failure to distinguish victory from operational success helped ensure that the wrong decisions were taken when 'battlefield commanders were allowed to improvise decisions that should have been made at the highest political levels'.[8] The civilian leadership permitted the decision to end the war to be governed by military considerations, specifically the expulsion of Iraqi forces from Kuwait, but the major goal, in fact, was political: the need to create a stable post-war situation in the Gulf, and the military pre-conditions for such stability were ultimately a political judgement. Secretary of State James Baker, however, offered little guidance during meetings held to discuss whether it was time to end the war.

Instead, after the coalition ceased its advance, Hussein was able to use his forces, particularly the Revolutionary Guard and its artillery and tanks, to smash a rebellion by the country's Shia majority, causing heavy casualties and destroying Shia shrines in Karbala and Najaf. In contrast, in Operation Provide Comfort, a multi-service, multinational task force protected the Kurds in northern Iraq from action by Hussein's forces.

The war was followed by the long-term use of Allied airpower to try to prevent Iraq from rebuilding its military, an expensive commitment that had only limited success; not least because policing Iraqi 'no-fly zones' was easier than influencing developments on the ground.

The understandable focus on the US contribution to the war, which included over half a million military personnel, has led to an underestimation of its impact on other states. For all those militaries that took part, the war raised issues of force-projection, logistics, and interoperability, although the last was eased by the experience of many in cooperation through NATO.[9] The contribution of those that did not send forces into the combat zone, but did provide financial support and/or indirect military help by freeing coalition units for operations, principally Germany and Japan, was important, although it also raised questions about their future military role.

US OPERATIONS

Although it was far smaller in scale and was to be overshadowed by the Gulf War, the US had already shown on 20–24 December 1989, in Operation Just Cause, that airborne forces could play a major role, in overthrowing the government of General Noriega in Panama, which had played a prominent role in drug-smuggling into the USA. Overwhelming force brought the US rapid success with few casualties, although, in part, that reflected the limited nature of the resistance.[10]

The operation was far more successful than the attempt to rescue the American hostages in Iran in 1980, or Operation Urgent Fury against Grenada in 1983. Urgent Fury had been motivated by concern about Grenada's leftward move, and the possibility that this would lead to a Soviet military presence. The Caribbean island was seized by US forces, but the operation saw inadequate inter-service coordination, which led to delay and to most US losses being to 'friendly' fire. These problems had been remedied by 1989, so that, in Panama, joint operations worked, as they had not done on Grenada, and objectives had been more clearly defined, while new weapons, including the AC-130 Gunship, performed successfully.

The improvement in joint operations was an important aspect of a more profound period of change in the US military following the end of both conscription and the Vietnam War. Morale, cohesion and effectiveness in the army had been particularly poor in the early 1970s, and it proved necessary to rebuild military capability. This was done. Operationally effective, the move away from mass conscript forces potentially lessened the domestic political sensitivity of military commitments, but failure in Beirut in 1982–4, a poorly conceived and managed intervention, and the more lasting impact of the Vietnam War, encouraged the formulation of what became known as the Weinberger doctrine (after Casper Weinberger, Secretary of Defense), which pressed for commitments only in the event of predictable success and a clear exit strategy, and called for the use of overwhelming force. This helped ensure that the protection of the military took precedence over diplomatic goals and, instead, became the strategic objective.[11]

SOMALIA AND HAITI

Due to American intervention, Somalia in the 1990s generally rates a mention in global military history, but this intervention was in fact tangential to a bitter and lengthy period of conflict in that country. Following Somalia's failure in the Ogaden war with Ethiopia in 1977–8, a weaker President Barré had faced growing opposition from clans which, increasingly, obtained heavier arms. The Somali National Movement mounted a serious challenge from 1978, although, in 1988, the government was able to drive them from the northern towns they had seized, albeit causing heavy civilian casualties in the process. In 1989–90, other resistance movements further eroded Barré's position, and he fled into exile in January 1991, mounting unsuccessful attempts to return that April, as well as in April and September 1992. Somalia was split into areas controlled by clan factions, each of which deployed artillery and armoured vehicles, as well as the light lorries carrying heavy machine-guns which were a distinctive feature of Somali warfare, and several of which made use of child fighters.

The UN intervened in 1992, in order to bring humanitarian relief, although also, if necessary, to disarm the factions. The UN forces, however, were inadequate to the latter task, and the ambiguity of the mission helped to lead to chaos. The US, who, in Operation Restore Hope, initially provided 28,000 men of the 37,000-strong UN force, were determined to remove Mohamed Farah Aidid, whose faction dominated the capital Mogadishu. Aidid opposed the UN intervention, and on 5 June 1993 his men ambushed a Pakistani unit, killing 25. This led the UN, supported by the US, to move against Aidid. On 3 October 1993, US Task Force Ranger captured several Aidid supporters (but not Aidid) in a raid, but then met opposition, with two helicopters shot down. In the clash that continued until the force was relieved by US, Pakistani and Malaysian troops early next day, the Rangers lost 16 dead and 83 wounded, while about 300 Somalis were killed. In reaction to their losses, the US abandoned aggressive operations in Somalia. The UN forces withdrew in March 1994. Faction fighting continued and the number of factions increased, as did civilian casualties.[12] Thereafter, no US troops were sent on peacekeeping missions to Africa, and, in 2003, when pressure built up for UN intervention in the mounting crisis in Congo, the US administration made it clear that it would not send troops, while in Liberia the US essentially only provided logistical support for Nigerian peacekeepers.

Nine years earlier, in Operation Uphold Democracy in 1994, the USA had sent 20,000 troops to Haiti in pursuit of a UN mandate to restore Jean-Bertrand Aristide, the president deposed by a military coup in 1990, and as a way to stop the flight of Haitian refugees to the USA. This restoration was achieved by negotiation rather than force, although it proved difficult to make Haitian society conform to the goals of the subsequent US-dominated UN peacekeeping mission, and the subsequent history of Haiti was far from benign.[13] The peacekeeping and humanitarian support goals of the interventions in Haiti and Somalia were correctly described as low-intensity conflict, as any comparison to the wars with Iraq would demonstrate, but they were difficult and dangerous for the troops involved, and the mission culture that stemmed from the nature of peacekeeping added to the difficulty. It proved hard to secure adequate and timely intelligence, both military and political, and to bring the two into line, while the unpreparedness of the US military for operating in urban environments was revealed. The relative ease of Operation Just Cause in Panama was no real preparation for the problems, both military and political, of Mogadishu. The fate of the latter intervention ensured that Operation Uphold Democracy was supported by adequate force, and it was no accident that US defence expenditure rose markedly in the mid-1990s. Yet the adequacy of force depends largely on the political context and the skill with which the mission is crafted. The US preference for being prepared for war-fighting led to a practice of overwhelming force that worked in Panama and Haiti, but that differed from the British preference for minimum necessary force,[14] as well as from the necessity for long-term commitment focused on nation-building.

CHECHNYA

Meanwhile, the Russians, who were even worse prepared for such tasks, had encountered serious problems in the Caucasus, where Islamic independence movements were able to rely on considerable popular support built on a tradition of ethnic strife, as well as on the mountainous terrain. The Russians responded by invading the rebellious region of Chechnya in December 1994, capturing the capital, Grozny, in January 1995, after a lengthy siege in which they employed devastating firepower, particularly intensive artillery barrages and bombing. Russian brutality and intransigence, however, encouraged resistance which the Russians were unable to crush. In 1996, they withdrew under a peace agreement.

The 1994–6 campaigns revealed the deficiencies of the badly led, equipped, trained, motivated and under-strength Russian forces. Not least among these deficiencies was the lack of appropriate training and doctrine for counter-insurgency warfare, although it is also necessary to emphasize large Chechen numbers and the extent to which the Chechens were both well-armed and determined; many had also been trained through conscription in the Soviet army. The Russian preference for firepower reflected the dominance in their doctrine and practice of preparations for war with the West,[15] while, more seriously, the Russians appeared to have no response other than force; and could not use that effectively, nor really afford it. The Russians added to the usual problems affecting a counter-insurgency policy that of the difficulty of transforming it into peacekeeping; they failed at both.

The renewed Russian attack on Chechnya in 1999–2000 led to the fall of Grozny in January 2000, but indicated similar military deficiencies. As with other forces battling insurgency, the Russians suffered from the problem of inadequate intelligence which reflected the limitations of surveillance in such contexts. In such a situation, there was an over-reliance on firepower responses, often poorly directed. Guerrilla opposition in Chechnya, including suicide bombings, continued, and, in response, the Russians mounted raids on guerrilla areas and seized suspected Chechens. Opposition was firmest in the mountainous south.[16]

THE FORMER SOVIET UNION

Russian intervention, in turn, created problems for the newly independent republics in the Caucasus. Thus, the Georgian army used force from 1992 to resist separatism by the Muslim province of Abkhazia, but the latter received Russian military assistance. In addition, following the collapse of the Soviet Union, the newly independent republics of Armenia and Azerbaijan fought, until 1993, over control of the region of Nagorno-Karabakh, a struggle won by Armenia,[17] while, in Central Asia, there was a bitter clan-based civil war in Tajikistan, and, on a smaller scale, Uzbeks and Meskhetian Turks fought in the Fergana region of Uzbekistan. Further west, the 'Trans-Dniester Republic', supported by former Soviet forces in the 14th Army, sought to break away from the newly independent republic of Moldova.

The Russian government, under Boris Yeltsin, had sought to create a single army for the Commonwealth of Independent States (CIS) that was established by some of the former Soviet republics, and Russia, Armenia, Belarus, Kazakhstan, Kyrgyzstan, Tajikistan and Uzbekistan agreed to pool their forces under CIS control. This arrangement was not sustained, however, as the other states, angered by Russian dominance of the CIS command system, created their own independent forces. Security pacts, nevertheless, were signed in 1992 by some of the states, and Russia, Armenia, Kazakhstan, Tajikistan and Uzbekistan agreed to allocate troops for peacekeeping.[18] The CIS produced a 25,000 strong Russian-dominated peacekeeping force for Tajikistan which helped ensure the defeat of the southern groups, including Islamic fundamentalists that had contested the dominance of northerners, although the resolution was not peace but rather a guerrilla struggle. However, differences about financing joint forces led to the ending of the unified command structure.

The USA and other Western powers benefited from the collapse of the Soviet Union to establish a degree of military cooperation with some of the successor states. For example, from 1994, Ukraine's military was given US money under military cooperation programmes to fund joint events, as well as Ukraine's participation in the NATO Partnership for Peace Programme and the support of Ukrainian Peacekeepers in Kosovo, where they operated with US forces. The US also funded the training of Ukrainians in the USA under the International Military Education and Training Program, while the USA helped support the training of NCOs in Ukraine.[19] This policy did more than lessen tension, as US–Soviet military cooperation sought to do; it also had a strategic impact in terms of creating a culture of military cooperation, however much the autocratic character of the Ukrainian government compromised this politically.

NORTHERN IRELAND

The British meanwhile had failed to suppress IRA (Irish Republican Army) terrorism in Northern Ireland, although they had contained the situation sufficiently to allow negotiations that produced a peace settlement in 1998. British troops had been deployed on local streets from 1969 in order to maintain control in the face of serious rioting, but, despite the confidence of the Unionists and of some of the army that a military solution was possible, IRA terrorism proved impossible to suppress. Given the difficulties of their task, the British army maintained a high level of professionalism, but that did not protect them from criticism from many who seemed less willing to condemn the deliberate terrorist policy of civilian and military murder employed by the IRA. In 1972 alone there were 1,853 bomb incidents, although, that year, the army also successfully regained control of 'no-go areas' in Londonderry and Belfast hitherto controlled by the IRA. This led the IRA to follow the course of terrorism, rather than that of waging guerrilla warfare. The British made heavy use of helicopters to supply fortified posts, as roads were vulnerable to mines, and used intelligence-gathering in order to strike at terrorists,[20] but there was a limit to what could be achieved. At the same time, the terrorists were unable to drive the army out of Northern Ireland. Of all modern forms of warfare, that of terrorism seems most likely to lead to an impasse.

YUGOSLAVIA

While the fall of the Soviet Union led to conflict in the Caucasus, the disintegration of Yugoslavia in 1991 had the same effect in the Balkans. In 1991 about 70,000 men out of a population of only two million Slovenes mobilized in order to resist Yugoslav attempts to prevent Slovene independence. The Serb-dominated Yugoslav army did not push the issue to widespread conflict, but it made a far greater effort in Croatia, which, unlike Slovenia, had a border with Serbia and also contained a large Serb minority. Franjo Tudjman, the authoritarian President of Croatia from 1991–9, used nationalism to provide both identity and rationale for his power, and the same was true of Serbia under Slobodan Milošević. This war spilled over into Bosnia, a part of Yugoslavia that was ethnically mixed, with large Croat, Serb and Muslim populations, and which suffered from both Croat and Serbian expansion. Each of the communities in Bosnia formed an army, and the Bosnian Serbian and Bosnian Croat forces cooperated with the armies of Serbia and Croatia, pursuing both their own and joint objectives.

The conflicts in Yugoslavia were brutal, but also limited. War involved demonstration and negotiation, a politics by military means that was intensely political, and a mixture of sudden and brief brutality, truces, and convoluted strategies of diplomacy. This conception of war is rooted in the Balkan tradition of limited operations, while full-scale war was in the domain of an Emperor or Sultan, who cannot be resisted if provoked too far; but also reflected the politics of the area and the forces available.

Western intervention to end the conflict was undermined by a combination of US reluctance, not least from the military leadership, and European weakness, but settlements were eventually imposed in Bosnia in 1995, and in Kosovo in 1999, at the expense of the expansionism and ethnic aggression of a Serbian regime that unsuccessfully looked for Russian sponsorship. Although the West played a major role, with 3,515 sorties flown in Operation Deliberate Force in 1995 (the first NATO combat mission), the ability of Serbia's opponents, especially the Croats, to organize military forces capable of mounting credible opposition in the field was important in preventing Serb victory. This ability was seen in the autumn of 1995 when the Croats and the Bosnian Muslims, who had been brought together in large part by US pressure, were able to mount successful offensives against the Bosnian Serbs. Combined with NATO air attack and diplomatic pressure, this pushed the Serbs into accepting the Dayton peace agreement.

The brutal slaughter of civilians by the Serbs (and, to a lesser extent, by their opponents) was an all too familiar feature of conflict in much of the modern world, and reflected the extent to which ethnic groups were seen as the units of political strength, and thus as targets. In 1995, the Bosnian Serbs murdered about 7,000 unarmed Muslim males in Srebrenica. What was termed ethnic cleansing – the expulsion of members of an ethnic group – was more common. It was generally associated with the Serbs, but was also used by the Croats, for example in the Krajina,[21] and, although that does not excuse Serb actions, it helps explain the paranoia that characterized their policymakers. In turn, such action against civilians helped create pressures on outside powers to adapt existing views on peacekeeping in order to adopt a proactive policy of peace enforcement focused on humanitarian goals.[22]

In order to suppress separatist demands and to destroy support for the Kosovo Liberation Army, the Serbs also used the tactics of ethnic cleansing in Kosovo, part of Serbia with a majority ethnic Albanian and Muslim population. The Western response over Kosovo and Serbia was coercive diplomacy which became a forceful humanitarian mission, Operation Allied Force. The resulting 78-day bombing and cruise missile assault by US, British and French forces in 1999 was less effective than Operation Deliberate Force had been in 1995, and caused far less damage to the Serb military than was claimed, although it did help lead in 1999 to the Serb withdrawal and the Serb acceptance of a ceasefire. Thereafter, the continuing isolation of Serbia, in a form of economic and financial warfare, helped cause an erosion of support for Milosĕvić, and his fall in the face of Serbian popular action in 2000.

In 1999, George Robertson, the British Secretary of State for Defence, publicly scorned commentators who warned about the difficulty of winning the Kosovo conflict by airpower alone, and also about the contrast between output (bomb and missile damage) and outcome. The air attack itself suffered the loss of only two aircraft, but the subsequent Serbian withdrawal from Kosovo revealed that NATO estimates of the damage inflicted by air attack, for example to Serb tanks, had been considerably exaggerated. Benefiting from the limitations of Allied intelligence information and its serious consequences for Allied targeting, and from the serious impact of the weather on air operations (a large number cancelled or affected), the Serbs, employing simple and inexpensive camouflage techniques that took advantage of terrain and wooded cover, preserved most of their equipment despite 10,000 NATO strike sorties. Furthermore, the air offensive had not prevented the large-scale expulsion of Kosovans from their homes, and this badly compromised the success of the operation. Indeed Operation Horseshoe, the ethnic cleansing campaign, increased as the air attack mounted.

The Serb withdrawal may have owed more to a conviction, based in part on Russian information, that a NATO land attack was imminent, as well as to the withdrawal of Russian support, than to the air offensive, although French, German and, eventually, US rejection of British pressure for such an invasion indicated their doubts of its feasibility, and indeed a land attack faced a serious logistical challenge, and was dependent on the willingness of neighbouring countries to provide access and bases. This contributed to the mistake of not preparing adequate options in the event of the air offensive failing. The crisis suggested that airpower would be most effective as part of a joint strategy, for ground and air threats to the Serbs were not separate. The eventual threat to the Serbs on the ground from a NATO invasion made their forces vulnerable to air attack, as it made dispersal, rather than concentration, a less viable proposition.[23]

Although the damage to the Serbian army from air attack was limited, the devastation of Serbia's infrastructure, in the shape of bridges, factories and electrical power plants, was important, not least because it affected the financial interests of the élite as well as their morale, and the functioning of the economy. Thus, there was a marked contrast between the tactical and strategic impact of airpower.

The Kosovo conflict revealed serious (although not unbridgeable) strains in NATO, as well as various limitations in advanced militaries, not least US concerns about the effectiveness of their Apache helicopters. The report produced by the National Audit Office in 2000 on British operations the previous year depicted major operational problems with the air force: on cloudy days the planes were unable to identify targets and were grounded, which, ironically, prevented an excessive depletion of bombs. In addition, many bombs mounted on aircraft were unable to survive the shock of take-off, while heat and vibration damage affected missiles, and Tornado jets were reportedly unable to drop precision-guided bombs effectively. A lack of lift capacity led to a British reliance on Russian built Antonovs hired from private contractors, but whose use was dependent on Russian certification. The SA80 rifle, the main British infantry weapon, was found to be faulty, while Serbian forces were readily able to monitor British radio communications.

Differences within the Western alliance, not least among US policymakers, were more serious in hindering a clear articulation of mission and the stages of its achievement, and helped ensure an incremental plan of air attack that failed to overcome Serbian resolve and that contributed to a somewhat negative impression of airpower capability. There were also more profound strategic problems, not least those posed by the goal of stopping Milosěvić from pursuing a particular policy in Kosovo while not seeking his overthrow. Milosěvić's determination to thwart this by stepping up ethnic cleansing enabled, or rather forced, NATO to overcome many of its differences over political and military strategy; although this determination also exposed the shortcomings of NATO planning: only a very short air offensive with relatively few aircraft had been anticipated; there was inadequate preparation for Serbian persistence, not least a failure in operational plans and in targeting systems; and a more general inability to work with the unpredictabilities of the situation, ranging from poor weather to the difficulties of assessing Serbian responses.[24] Furthermore, the length of the campaign created greater political pressure and more reasons for disagreement, and all within a context in which commanders and targeters were constrained by the strict parameters set by a determination to minimize civilian losses and to ensure no Allied losses; a goal that ruled out ground operations.

Thus, strategically, operationally and tactically, the military had to plan in ways that compromised doctrinal 'purity'; although these constraints were made acceptable by the inability of the Serbs to inflict serious damage on NATO forces, which ensured that the costs of President Clinton's aversion to risk, and of NATO differences, were contained. The determination to detach Russia from Serbia, and not to defeat the latter to the point that the Kosovan separatists were able to win independence, complicated the situation, and helped ensure that the hesitation that stemmed from NATO consensus-building had a political rationale.

The precarious nature of the Balkan settlement led to long-term military commitments by peacekeeping forces in Bosnia and Kosovo, and this ensured that most refugees returned home, including about 750,000 of the 800,000 displaced Kosovan Albanians by the close of July 1999. The disadvantage, however, was an expensive long-term commitment to Kosovo. The disturbed situation in the Balkans also led to a commitment in Macedonia in order to end an insurrection by Albanians there, with the provision, in 2001–2, of the force necessary to monitor an amnesty that was the background to elections held in September 2002.

Problems in the Balkans distracted attention from the more promising situation elsewhere in Eastern Europe, where the transition to non-Communist governments willing to contest power at the ballot box was managed without military intervention, as was the division of Czechoslovakia into the Czech Republic and Slovakia. Eastern European militaries were transformed into bodies under the control of democratic governments, and with their structures, tasking, doctrine and weaponry no longer determined by membership of the Warsaw Pact. In terms of capability, this was not an easy transition, although it was eased by the absence of challenges from Russia; but in political terms, it was successful, far more so than the transition to democracy in many parts of the world.[25]

THE WAR ON TERRORISM

The attacks launched by Osama bin Laden's al-Qaeda (The Base) terrorist movement on New York and Washington on 11 September 2001 helped ensure that the US administration took a more determined position in warfare in the early 2000s than had been the case in the Balkans. The replacement of Bill Clinton by George W. Bush as President in January 2001 was also significant, while, at least initially after September 11, the Americans benefited from widespread international support in their self-proclaimed 'War on Terrorism'. The US administration felt it necessary in resisting terrorism, to strike back against it, and this led to attacks, overt and covert, on what were identified as terrorist bases, and supporters which represented another stage in the movement towards action that had followed the end of the Cold War.

In 2001, Russia lent diplomatic support to the US air offensive against the Taliban regime in Afghanistan, which had provided sanctuary for al-Qaeda , despite the fact that this campaign entailed the establishment of US bases in Central Asian republics that had been part of the Soviet Union. The Taliban had emerged from the chaos that was Afghanistan in the early 1990s. The Afghan regime of President Najibullah, who had been put in power by the Soviets in 1986, finally fell in April 1992, when the guerrillas entered Kabul: the government had been greatly weakened by the defection of its strongman, Abdul Rashid Dostum. Victory was followed by an upsurge in already strong ethnic and regional tensions, and, in particular, the northerners who had seized the capital in 1992 were opposed by Gulbuddin Hekmatyar, a Pushtun and the leader of the Afghanistan Islamic Party, who attacked Kabul. As the country was divided by warlords and the economy collapsed, looting became the best way to supply warring forces.

This situation was challenged by the Kandahar-based and Pakistan-backed Taliban movement, which sought stability and religious orthodoxy. Benefiting from Pushtun support, and the profits of opium dealing, the Taliban overran much of the country in 1996, seizing Kabul that year. Bribes helped dissolve much of the opposition. However, in the non-Pushtun areas, particularly in the north, the Taliban encountered serious resistance, and this helped provide the USA with allies when they attacked the Taliban regime in 2001.

The fall of the Taliban regime, which had refused to hand over Osama bin Laden and other al-Qaeda members, was seen as a success for US airpower, which included long-range B-52 and B-2 'stealth' bombers, extensive aerial refuelling, aircraft and Tomahawk cruise missiles from carrier groups and warships in the Arabian Sea, AC-130 gunships, unpiloted drones, and CBU-130 'Combined-Effects Munitions' which spread cluster bombs. The availability of dual mode, laser and GPS guidance for bombs increased the range of precision available, while the air assault benefited from the effective and, crucially, rapid management of information from a number of sources, including forward air controllers and ground-based GPS devices; and the absence of hostile airpower and of effective ground-fire was also important.

However, the Taliban ultimately had to be overcome on the ground by rival Afghan forces, particularly the United Front, the so-called Northern Alliance, while the lack of coherence of the Taliban regime and the porosity of alignments in Afghanistan were also both important to the war's outcome. Warlords switched allegiance, and the Taliban position collapsed on 9–13 November 2001, with the fall of the cities of Mazar-e Sharif, Herat and Kabul. The Taliban was unable to regroup after the fall of Mazar-e Sharif: defections that stemmed from its divisions accentuated a failure of command and control. American airpower and Afghan ground attack combined to ensure the fall of more firmly defeated Kunduz on 26 November. Taliban forces tried to regroup at Kandahar, but abandoned it on 7 December.[26]

The Taliban position had been broken by the combination of US air attack and Afghan ground assault, the latter an instance of the proxy-warfare seen throughout the Cold War, while the willingness of President Musharraf of Pakistan to cut links with the Taliban and provide assistance, including permitting US overflying and moving troops into border areas, was important. The air attack helped switch the local political balance within Afghanistan, but the victorious campaign did not lead to the clear-cut pro-USA triumph that had been hoped for. Instead, it became readily apparent that the war had provoked a regrouping and realignment of factions, uneasily presided over by the weak new pro-Western President, Hamid Ka'rzai. Far better than nothing, but not forcing opponents to accept the will of the victor. Furthermore, analysis of the impact of the air attack revealed that, while it had been considerable in the initial attacks in northern Afghanistan, it subsequently became less so in the ground operations launched by US and allied forces against Taliban and al-Qaeda survivors near Tora Bora (December 2001) and, in Operation Anaconda, east of Gardez (March 2002). This was attributed to the Taliban ability to respond by taking advantage of terrain features, for camouflage and cover.[27]

Operations by the International Security Assistance Force against al-Qaeda supporters in Afghanistan were the most prominent aspect of the US and US-allied 'War on Terrorism' that followed September 11, 2001, but they were far from the only moves. Instead, US special operations units were deployed against Islamic terrorist movements linked to al-Qaeda, particularly on and near the Philippine island of Mindanao where, from 2003, the US provided military support to the army against the Abu Sayyaf Group. The same year, the republic of Georgia was provided with help against an al-Qaeda force in the region of the Pankisi Gorge, which was also a base for Chechnyan rebels.

Counter-terrorist operations posed serious difficulties for military responses, not least the identification of opponents and the brevity of the period in which it was possible to engage. There are also conceptual problems in such conflict: the terminology used towards opponents delegitimizes them – instead of 'troops' and 'war', we have 'terrorists' and 'terrorism' – but this can make it more difficult to conceive of a strategy that matches political with military methods and goals, and may make it more difficult to probe the possibilities for an exit strategy.

THE REVOLUTION IN MILITARY AFFAIRS

Striking against terrorist bases, as in Afghanistan, became part of a US doctrine of pre-emptive attack against hostile states. As a result, conflict returned to the Persian Gulf in early 2003 when Iraq was attacked by a preponderantly American force, with a large British military participation and smaller Australian, Polish, Czech and Slovak contingents. The campaign, and the preparations for it, were conducted in the glare of media attention and pundit discussion, and there was considerable speculation as to how far it corresponded with current notions about a Revolution in Military Affairs (RMA), as well as related debates about the character of modern military capability and development.

The RMA linked developments in weapon systems with a doctrine that meshed with theories of modernization that rest on the adoption of technological systems. Furthermore, the RMA met the need to believe in the possibility of High Intensity Conflict and of total victory, and appeared to counter the threats posed by the spread among rivals of earlier technologies and their development of new ones. Integral to the RMA are a number of concepts each rich in acronyms and jargon; the common focus is on smart doctrine: operational planning and practice in order to take advantage of a new generation of weapons and the possibilities posed by advances in information technology. The emphasis on precise information as a means, as well as a tool, of conflict, relates to its use in order to locate forces accurately, as well as to destroy enemy units with semi-automated weapons. Accurate targeting is required if precision weaponry is to be effective. This, in turn, entails 'information dominance', in order to deny such a capability to opponents. The RMA also calls for 'network-centric warfare': a focus on the new capability of information systems, rather than on traditional practices and structures of command and control.[28]

In one respect, information dominance is a continuation and application of the intelligence warfare that had characterized the Cold War, particularly the development of satellite surveillance capable of providing 'real time' information. By the end of the twentieth century the USA, Britain, Australia, Canada and New Zealand were allied participants in Echelon, an electronic eavesdropping service; Britain significantly not being linked to its European Union (EU) partners; while France and Germany also cooperated in such covert monitoring. Access to satellite information became a major issue in military planning. The USA, which dominates the field, is unhappy about EU attempts to acquire capability, seeing this as unnecessary duplication, a view not shared by the EU, not least because of a determination to give bite to its security and defence policy. Irrespective of EU policy, leading member states sought to establish their own satellite reconnaissance, France developing the Helios I satellite system. American satellite surveillance played a major role in the 2003 Iraq crisis, not least in target monitoring.

More generally, at the same time, intelligence was increasingly devolved to, and developed at, 'micro'-levels: individual units, weapons such as pieces of artillery and, eventually, soldiers; for each, there was more information, and it was both up-to-date and, therefore, constantly changing. This underlined the need to integrate information and activity systems effectively, and thus the extent to which command and control were under great strain at every level.

In the language of the RMA, weaponry is designed to ensure what are termed dominant manoeuvre, precision engagements, full-dimensional protection, focused logistics and information warfare. All of these are seen as the goals and methods of future military structures, and particular organizational forms, and weapons are presented as intended to serve these ends, rather than simply moulding structures or methods. Joint operations are seen as crucial to the manoeuvrist warfare that is advocated, and as stemming from the interest of all services in 'deep battle'. To foster joint operations, there has been a proliferation of joint organizations, not least because, alongside AirLand concepts, have come greater US and British interest in sea-based strategies.[29] In the USA, these organizations include the creation, in 1992, of an Expeditionary Warfare Division in the office of the Chief of Naval Operations and, more generally, the Goldwater-Nichols Department of Defense Reorganization Act of 1986, which strengthened the position of the Chairman of the Joint Chiefs of Staff and established a joint acquisition system. In Britain the plethora of joints included the Joint Rapid Deployment Force, the Joint Headquarters, and the Joint Services Command and Staff College; while France has joint war college training. Joint institutions provide powerful advocates for new doctrines and plans, such as the US *Joint Vision 2010* and *Joint Vision 2020* plans. Similarly, the US defence industry is heavily committed to new weaponry designed to provide the desired RMA.[30]

Whether or not they were willing or could afford to invest in the wider ranges of the RMA, a problem that was of particular importance for Russian ambitions,[31] emphasis on advanced weaponry and relevant training encouraged a number of states to follow the UK and USA in moving toward a force structure that put a greater emphasis on mobility and training. This encouraged states that still used conscription, such as France and Russia, to begin phasing it out, a process that continues today. Under President Chirac French military planning became less concerned with nuclear defence and retaliation and more interested in large-scale power projection, a process aided by the slimming down and professionalization of the army that followed the end of conscription.[32] In June 2000, the Italian Parliament passed a Bill phasing out conscription by 2005. It was designed to replace the army of 270,000 with a professional service of 190,000. The Turkish army has also begun to talk about abolishing conscription as part of a programme of modernization.

THE GULF WAR OF 2003

In 2003, the USA focused on Iraq – a definite and defiant target with regular armed forces – rather than on the more intangible struggle with terrorism, which challenged Western conventions of war-making. The attack was presented in terms of 'drying up the swamp' – eliminating a state allegedly supporting terrorism, as well, more specifically, as destroying Iraq's supposed capability in weapons of mass destruction, specifically chemical and bacteriological warheads.

Operation Iraqi Freedom, the US campaign in Iraq in 2003, with its rapid and successful advance up the Euphrates valley on Baghdad, was widely praised for its manoeuvrist character and for its ability to gain and seize the initiative, disorientating the Iraqi military and government and hitting their capacity to respond. 125,000 US combat troops on the ground were the key element, although Britain supplied 45,000 troops and Australia 2,000. Predictions that the Iraqis would use chemical weapons and blow up bridges and dams, or that it would be hard to subjugate the Iraqi cities, and that they would pose problems like those faced by the Germans in Stalingrad in 1942, with the US military being chewed up in the course of their capture, were totally disproved. These predictions had rested on the assumption that the Iraqis had responded to their defeat in 1991 by deciding not to take on the US in manoeuvrist warfare, where technology would give the Americans an advantage, and, instead, to abandon the desert and focus on the cities, hoping to repeat the success of Mohamed Aidid in Mogadishu in 1993. Indeed, both in 1991 and in 2003, Saddam Hussein counted on the US suffering if they could be forced to abandon the distant use of firepower for close combat.

However, the coherence of the Hussein regime, its ability to intimidate the population, and the possibility of exploiting US vulnerability along their long lines of advance, were undermined by the tempo of American attacks. The Iraqi attacks on supply lines, for example at the Euphrates bridge-town of Nasiriya, attracted considerable media attention, but the forces available for such attacks were a local irritant rather than operationally significant, and, despite short-term problems, which were understandable given the tempo of the advance, US logistics proved able to support the offensive. The use of Fedayeen irregulars, some of whom fought vigorously, did, however, lead to somewhat naïve complaints about such tactics by the Fedayeen as disguise and fake surrender.

Much of the Revolutionary Guard ran away in the face of US firepower. Units that redeployed or stood and fought were pulverized, with particular effort being devoted to destroying Iraqi armour. This represented the tactical value of airpower, which accomplished more than the 'Shock and Awe' attacks on Baghdad from the night of 19 March at the outset of the struggle, although the latter's impact on Iraqi command and control was significant; the possible killing or wounding of Saddam Hussein in an air-strike, had it occurred, would have reflected the strategic value of airpower in disrupting opposing leadership. The US made particular use of JDAMS (Joint Direct Attack Munitions) which used GPS to make conventional bombs act as satellite-guided weapons, and were an important addition to the improvement in US airpower capability that characterized post-Vietnam developments.[33] Although there were differences of opinion between Britain and the USA over targeting, the air assault did not face the constraints that had affected the attack on the Serbs in Operation Allied Force in 1999. Instead, with a clear target, it was possible to use airpower effectively, and, in turn, to contribute to its reputation for effectiveness. About 70 per cent of the aerial munitions used were 'smart' or guided, rather than 'dumb' or unguided, in contrast to 10 per cent against Iraq in 1991.

The US also benefited from the use of helicopter gunships and unmanned aerial vehicles, and from improvements in the accuracy of artillery fire. The Iraqi T-55s and T-72s that were not destroyed by air attack could not prevail against the US M1A1 Abrams tanks, while the US use of night vision goggles enabled them to maintain the pace of the assault, and thus to prevent the Iraqis from resupplying and regrouping. The Iraqis made effective use of rocket-propelled grenades, but, although there had been improvements in quality as a honed-down force was sought, their military was far weaker than in 1991, in large part because the impact of international sanctions since then had limited the build-up of modern weaponry.

Once they had closed on Baghdad, the US initially, from 5 April, launched 'thunder runs', armoured thrusts into the city, demonstrating that their opponents could not prevent these advances, and therefore undermining their position. Manoeuvre warfare was thus shown to work in an urban context. Having captured Baghdad, where organized resistance collapsed on 9 April, the US forces pressed on to overrun the rest of Iraq, without encountering the large-scale opposition that was feared, particularly in Hussein's home town of Tikrit, which fell on 14 April. The British meanwhile had taken Basra, Iraq's second most populous city.

A prime element of debate before the campaign, which was revived during it, when US supply lines came under serious attack, had related to the number of troops required for a successful invasion. The Secretary of Defense, Donald Rumsfeld, and other non-military commentators had been encouraged by the overthrow of the Taliban regime in Afghanistan to argue that airpower and special forces were the prime requirements, and that the large number of troops pressed for by the military was excessive. In the event, military pressure led to the allocation of sizeable numbers, but the campaign did not see the full committal of forces originally envisaged, because the Turkish refusal to allow an invasion across their frontier with Iraq ensured that troops from the US Fourth Infantry Division prepared for that invasion could not be used at the outset of the war. However, US special forces, landed by air from the night of 22–3 March, helped direct Kurdish pressure (and US bombing) on Hussein's forces in northern Iraq. Kurdish and US forces captured Kirkuk on 10 April, and on 11 April Mosul surrendered. The consequences of the rapid fall of Iraq did, however, expose one of the problems with having insufficient troops in that it proved imposs-ible to restore order and the workings of government as rapidly as was anticipated. Terrorism proved a particular challenge.

The collapse of the Hussein regime led to talk of pressing on to attack other states that harboured terrorism, particularly Iran and Syria. However, it is more likely that US success in overthrowing Hussein will encourage a degree of compliance with its demands, as seen with Libya in late 2003, and thus lessen the apparent need for such conflicts, while the US failure to restore order in Iraq and the costs of their continuing commitment will foster a measure of caution.

At the same time, the war led the Americans to devote renewed effort to their already vigorous debate about force structure and tasking. At the risk of considerable simplification, this located discussion about weaponry within consideration of the continued validity of a military centred on separate services. Rumsfeld was particularly keen on break-ing with what he saw as a conservative inheritance out of keeping with the need for rapidly delivered force. Interest in new weaponry focused on AirLand combinations, but included research into low-yield nuclear weaponry that was seen as an important way to upgrade the USA's nuclear capability.

Although no other power could match such developments, the impact of US weaponry in Iraq in 2003 encouraged interest elsewhere in procuring similar weapons. This was true of Britain, where the development of drones was stepped up, and also of Japan, which felt increasingly threatened by North Korea's development of rockets, leading, in response, to Japanese interest in anti-missile defences and in satellite surveillance. Article Nine of the Japanese Constitution states that 'land, sea, and air forces, as well as other war potential, will never be maintained'; as a result, Japan has 'Self-Defence Forces', which were 258,000 strong in 2003.

THIRD WORLD CONFLICT

As with the situation prior to 1990, it would be misleading to ignore the number of conflicts between Third World forces,[34] some of which, as in Afghanistan[35] and Somalia, provided the background for Western intervention. Indeed, the process by which the Taliban seized power in Afghanistan is more typical of the character of post-1990 conflict than the American intervention in that country in 2001. Conflict between Third World forces took a number of forms, ranging from regular warfare across front lines, to insurrections, ethnic conflict, terrorism, and coups. Most of this conflict occurred in Africa, but there were also important instances in Latin America, Asia and Oceania. The numbers involved could be considerable: in 1999, it was estimated that Indian security forces in Kashmir, which included not only the army, but also the Central Reserve Police Force and the Border Security Force, numbered 400,000. As an instance of regular conflict between Third World forces, in 2000, Ethiopia invaded Eritrea in a frontier struggle that was also a conflict over hegemony. As with many 'Third World' wars, it is difficult to be precise about events, but the Ethiopians benefited from superior airpower, better armour (Russian T-72 tanks), and greater numbers, only to find that the Eritreans fought well, taking advantage of the terrain.

In contrast, in Liberia from 1989 and Sierra Leone from 1991, the chaos that accompanied what was referred to as 'failed states' saw conflict that lacked much central direction. In both, drugged teenagers, many of them orphans, and outright looters, had little, if any, idea of the cause they were fighting for, except for their own personal gains. Political objectives beyond the capture of power were hazy, and 'wars' benefited from the large-scale availability of small arms and were financed primarily by criminal operations and extortion. There were no chains of command or (often) even uniforms that distinguished 'troops' from each other or from other fighters,[36] and, politically, this was an instance of a more widespread process in which warlords moved from being rebels to presidents or vice versa, while ethnicity helped exacerbate conflict.[37]

In Rwanda, civil war was neither so disorganized nor so sustained, but was extremely bloody when it occurred. In 1990 the Tutsi *émigrés* of the Rwanda Patriot Front invaded Rwanda from Uganda, beginning a civil war that lasted until peace agreements, in 1993, that were monitored by a small, largely Belgian UN peacekeeping force. However, that year, a Tutsi coup in Burundi against the Hutu government led to the killing of over 100,000 Hutus, increasing tension, and, in April 1994, an extremist group of Hutus seized power in Rwanda, touching off the slaughter of about 800,000 Tutsi. The failure of the international community to end genocide raised a question-mark against both the UN's ability to enforce norms and the willingness of the world's leading power, the USA, to act.[38]

In Afghanistan, after the fall of the Taliban and the establishment as President of the US-backed Hamid Ka'rzai, there was not comparable chaos to that in Liberia, but that was because the weakness of the central government was counter-pointed by the strength of provincial governors, such as Abdul Rashid Dostum and Ismail Khan, autonomous figures with a tradition of independence and their own armies. Government indeed involved a process of negotiation with these warlords that accepted their regional power. Peace, in turn, depended on their restraint, but it was threatened by challenges to the regional position of warlords, as well as to that of the central government. A Taliban resurgence in the summer of 2003 led, however, to the collapse of the government position in much of the south and east of the country, with the President wielding scant authority outside the capital.

Angola is not a failed state, but, until the killing of the UNITA leader, Jonas Savimbi, in 2002, it faced a debilitating insurrectionary war that rested on ethnic tension, especially Ovimbundu support for UNITA, and was financed by exploitation of the country's diamond wealth. Diamonds were also important in financing conflict in West Africa, especially Sierra Leone. In turn, the Angolan government benefited from control of the country's oil. Having rejected the results of the 1992 election, UNITA had resumed its conflict with the government, which was now weakened by the withdrawal of the Cuban and Soviet assistance that had greatly helped it in the 1970s and '80s. Defeated by the scale of the country, neither side was able to win. The operational effectiveness of the government's conventional forces declined in the wet season, which favoured UNITA guerrilla tactics. Both sides mounted attacks on the supply-systems of the others, but without lasting effect, other than to cause large numbers of civilian casualties, and even larger numbers of refugees. However, international pressure and a failure to win led Savimbi to negotiate anew in 1994, producing a *de facto* partition of the country that lasted until 1997 when the government attacked UNITA. UNITA now suffered from both the loss of its supply route through Congo and from divisions, with Savimbi's leadership under challenge. In 1999, Jamba, where Savimbi had established his capital in 1984, and which the government had failed to take in the 1980s, finally fell. UNITA forces were in a poor position by 2001 and the government used its oil wealth to enhance its military capability. The death of Savimbi on 22 February 2002 was rapidly followed, on 4 April, by the signature of a peace agreement.[39]

As an in-between stage, Congo became both a failed state and one in which regular forces from other African countries intervened in order to influence the direction of conflict there, to dominate neighbouring areas, and to obtain control over raw materials. Mobutu Sese Soko, the dictator since 1965, fell in 1997 as a result of foreign invasion, while another invasion was launched in 1998 in an unsuccessful attempt to overthrow his replacement, Laurent Kabila. Uganda and Rwanda supported competing rebel factions; Rwanda in part in order to defeat the Hutu militias that had staged the genocide of 1994 and that had taken refuge in Congo; while Zimbabwe, Angola, Chad and Namibia backed Kabila, in part in response to the dynamics of their own internal security situation: Angola wished to stop Congolese support for UNITA, which had been important under Mobutu. Probably between 3.1 and 4.7 million people died in Congo in 1998–2003, most of disease and starvation, but many of them in ethnic conflict between tribal militias, as murderous attacks on villages proved a particularly common means of waging war. Far from being at the cutting edge of 'new-generation' warfare, this conflict saw much of the killing with machetes, and bows and arrows and shotguns were employed alongside the frequent use of mortars and submachine guns. The conflict also led to cannibalism, and to the use of child warriors also seen in West Africa. The outside powers armed their own Congolese allies, particularly, for Rwanda, the Rally for Congolese Democracy and the Union of Congolese Patriots. These overlapped with tribal militia groups, such as those of the Ugandan-backed Lendus, which competed with the Rwandan-allied Hemas in the north-eastern province of Ituri, a major centre of conflict. Other aspects of African conflict that were distant from Western warfare included the use of traditional charms and spirit mediums.[40]

More generally, rivalries between states interacted with insurrections and other civil conflicts elsewhere. Thus, warfare between Eritrea and Ethiopia, which involved large-scale fighting of a conventional type,[41] spilled over into internal conflicts in Somalia. Foreign assistance was sought, and, if necessary, hired, to help resist insurrection. Thus, between 1993 and 2003, Ange-Félix Patassé, the President of the Central African Republic, survived seven coup attempts, including one in 2002 by General François Bozizé, one-time head of the army, that involved serious street fighting in the capital, Bangui. Patassé turned for support to Libya, which provided backing until 2002, and then the Congolese MLC (*Mouvement de Libération du Congo*) rebel group, but, in March 2003, Bozizé at the head of 1,000 men overran Bangui. The unpaid army was unwilling to resist, and the MLC did not fight. Instability in the Central

African Republic reflected the knock-on effects of war elsewhere, for conflict in Congo hit its trade links down the River Congo.

In West Africa, in 2002–3, the Liberian government under Charles Taylor, whose seizure of power had originally owed much to backing from Ivory Coast, supported rebels in the three neighbouring states, Sierra Leone, Guinea and Ivory Coast, before being forced to step down in 2003. Guinea itself was linked to rebels against Taylor – Liberians United for Reconciliation and Democracy – a misnamed group of thugs, as was the army of Ivory Coast. France intervened to support the government of Ivory Coast against the MPCI (Mouvement Patriotique de Côte-d'Ivoire): the rebel group that failed to seize power in 2002, but that remained strong in the largely Muslim north. Britain had earlier intervened in Sierra Leone, in 2000, supporting UN stabilization, retraining the army, and, in Operation Barras, rescuing hostages from the West Side Boys, one of the gangs that intimidated much of the country.

In the Congo, Kabila was assassinated in 2001. This was an aspect of the continuing role of force in the seizure of power across parts of the Third World, a role that puts a focus on the attitude of the armed forces and of paramilitary units. Military establishments have a disproportionate independence and impact in post-colonial systems where nothing else seems to work very well and too many countervailing institutions have lost credibility and authority. Thus, in 1999, the Pakistani army staged a successful coup, although the military lost power in other states, for example Thailand in 1992. In 2000 US and Brazilian pressure on Paraguayan military leaders led them to thwart an attempted coup. In turn, in some countries, groups outside the military sought to use force to seize, or at least contest, power. Thus, in 2003, organized crime linked to nationalists was responsible for the assassination of the Serbian Prime Minister, Zoran Djindjic.

Alongside its use to gain and hold power at the centre, force was also widely used against regional separatism. Thus, southern secessionism in Yemen was crushed in 1994, the Chinese suppressed Muslim separatism in Xinjiang in 1990 and 1997, while, in 1998, the Tajik army suppressed a rebellion in the Khojand region of Tajikistan where many Uzbek speakers lived. In Nigeria the army was used against tribal separatists in the oil-producing Niger delta, while, in 1997, a separatist revolt on Anjouan, one of the islands in the Comoros, was suppressed. The breakdown in May 2003 of a five-month ceasefire in the Aceh region of Sumatra, led the Indonesian army to announce that it would destroy the Gam separatist movement, in part by moving the population into tented camps so as to deny them cover. This conflict, which had begun in 1976, opposed a military using the means of conventional warfare, including ground-attack aircraft, amphibious landings, parachutists and tanks, against a smaller guerrilla force lacking international support but strong in determination. In some cases separatism was not the issue. Thus, from 2002, Nepal faced a serious Maoist insurgency which posed major problems for its military.

Sales of arms continue to provide fresh munitions for Third World forces, and their governments, encouraged by international competition as well as by concern over domestic stability, have been only too willing to spend money on the military. In 2002 Africa alone spent about $14 billion on defence. Expenditure on arms by terrorist movements was restricted by measures, including attempts to limit money laundering, but, despite the efforts of aid donors, no such restraint affected states. Instead, developments in their military capability were affected by attempts to control the trade in weaponry and its components, in particular restricting the sale of components for weapons of massive destruction. Despite the terrible poverty of much of their population, India pushed up defence spending by 14 per cent in 1999 alone, and Pakistan by 8.5 per cent, to total allocations of $9.9 billion and $3.3 billion respectively, though Pakistan's nuclear weaponry programme may have been funded by Saudi Arabia.

Rivalry over Kashmir between the two powers led to the Kargil conflict in 1999, in which the attackers killed by the Indian army included Pakistani regulars as well as guerrillas, and took them close to war in 2002, with the Indians moving over 600,000 troops to the frontier. Religious hatred exacerbated a national rivalry that was made more serious by increased nuclear capability, which led, first, India and, then, Pakistan to test nuclear weapons in 1998; while, that year, Pakistan test-fired its new Ghauri intermediate-range missile, India firing its new long-range Agni 2 missile the following year; its range, 2,000–3,000 kilometres, extending to Tehran and covering most of China and

South-East Asia. In March 2003 both states test-fired short-range surface-to-surface missiles that could have been used to carry nuclear warheads.

CONCLUSIONS

In the 1990s and 2000s casualties were far greater in conflicts that did not directly involve Western powers than in those that did, and this was particularly true of civil wars in Angola, Congo, Rwanda and Burundi. In Burundi conflict between Hutu and Tutsi has led to maybe 300,000 deaths since 1993, a further phase in a sequence of violence that included large-scale clashes in 1965, 1969, 1972 and 1988. The savagery of the killing was accentuated by the use of cruelty, torture, dismemberment, sexual mutilation and cannibalism to increase pain and express hatred. Aside from deaths due to slaughter, conflicts also led to the destruction of economies, as military units focused on plundering villages, while infrastructures collapsed, with resulting deaths from privation as well as from disease. In part, the latter reflected disruption, for example to water supplies, but the spread of disease, by both troops and refugees fleeing conflict, was also important. In Africa, rape by troops helped transmit HIV, while refugees spread malaria. This is an appropriate point on which to close the chapter, for the impact on civilians of war is far more intense than is suggested by the use of the concept of limited warfare, let alone the commonplace emphasis on the 'spectator' character of warfare for Western audiences. Instead, the large number of refugees in the world is a reminder not only of the use of force in waging war on peoples, but also of the consequences of conflict across the globe.[42]

Chapter 8

Conclusions

The widespread fascination with meta-narratives (overarching interpretations) that apparently explain military affairs, whether technologically, organizationally or culturally derived, seriously risks undermining our awareness of the variety of conflict and the complexities of assessing and explaining relative capability, as well as of reasons for success, and the nature of military change. Instead, the central role of political purpose and the consequent 'tasking' of the military needs to be underlined. This clearly emerged when the attacks on 11 September 2001 led the USA to shift from a focus on possible conflict with China to a concern with the Islamic world, terrorism and related challenges; although it would be unwise to neglect the long-term nature of the likely challenge from China, not least because Chinese demographic growth and economic expansion are linked to a hostile ideology. In the case of Europe, political tasking is also at issue, and the military history of, say, the 2020s is likely to be different depending on the future character of NATO and the EU, with consequent influences on doctrine, strategy and force configuration. As a result, the political contingencies that might determine these and other choices become central to military history. Over the last century wartime cooperation across the North Atlantic was crucial both to the defeat of autocratic hegemonic tendencies in Europe and to the security of the USA. Such a scenario, which underlay NATO, depends, however, on continued effort and on circumstances, and is no way inevitable, a point that Franco–American tensions in 2002–3 made abundantly clear.

The history of recent decades indicates the limitations of military power as a tool of policy, and also of advanced technology as the war-winning element. This might appear a surprising view given the USA's existence as the sole superpower, indeed, what was termed by French commentators in 2002–3, the hyper-power. It is often argued in the USA that the so-called Revolution in Military Affairs, based, in particular, on information warfare capability, enables the most technologically advanced power, now the USA, to overcome both distance and resistance in order to secure victory with minimal casualties, and without worrying about the issues of inter-operability in cooperating with allies who lack the ability to match its doctrinal suppositions.

This is, in fact, another version of the mechanization of the military imagination that has been so potent since the advent of the airplane and the tank, and probably had earlier anticipations with the chariot and gunpowder. It is obviously important to seize and develop every advantage that new weaponry can bring, but it is mistaken to imagine that a technological edge guarantees victory at low cost, or, indeed, victory; while some of the claims for information-led warfare mistakenly 'equate bombardment with war'.[1] To be sure, advantages in weaponry are valuable in symmetrical warfare – between opposing forces that operate in a similar fashion – but, even then, a host of other factors intrude, including strategy, tactics, leadership, unit cohesion and morale, as well as contextual issues, such as the respective determination of the powers engaged.

Technological and other force advantages are seen to lie not only in the inherent strength of weapons and military units, but also in the means for their use. As the application of force in order to use and/or gain advantage attracted attention, so there was an interest in the West in understanding opposing systems in order to achieve a superior 'OODA' (Observe, Orient, Decide and Act) loop, not least one that 'got inside' opposing decision-making processes. This was seen in both the Gulf Wars.

In asymmetrical warfare, which, crucially, is a range of very varied situations requiring different responses, rather than a single condition, the advantages conferred by superior weaponry and battle-winning systems are severely curtailed. Compare, for instance, the frustration of US forces in the asymmetrical Vietnam War, with contemporaneous Israeli success in the symmetrical and short Six Day War of 1967, and then look to the intractable difficulties facing the highly professional Israeli military as it struggled to resist the impact of suicide bombers and fighters in the early 2000s. The financial burden on Israel of the struggle was considerable, pushing up defence spending by up to two billion dollars annually from the start of the *Intifada*, which exacerbated the problems in public finance that put a heavy strain on Israeli society. The vulnerability of advanced militaries to terrorist attack was shown not only by the destruction of Israeli heavy tanks by mines but also, in October 2000, by the ramming at Aden of the destroyer USS *Cole* by a small boat loaded with explosives, which led to 17 American deaths and extensive damage to the ship.

Finally, technological advantage, in both types of conflict, inevitably inspires the development of counter-measures involving weapons, tactics, and strategy. Thus, the impact of airpower has been greatly lessened by the development of anti-aircraft weapons whose cost-benefit payoff is immense compared to that of a state-of-the-art aircraft. Indeed, it has been suggested by Jeffrey Clarke that the development of precision-guided munitions owed much to the increasing effectiveness of air defences, rather than to the 'vision of network-centric, effects-based warfare' of RMA proponents.[2] There is no reason to imagine that this process of advances in counter-measures will cease.

The diffusion of new technology provides opportunities for those involved in asymmetrical warfare against major powers, for example with the prospect of using biological and chemical weapons. Irrespective of this, for major powers, there will remain military limits to effective force projection; and skilful policy-making will continue to require a shrewd understanding of capability and limits. This process is not new. Former great powers also struggled to learn and adjust to their capabilities and limits – in the process evolving particular strategic cultures[3] – and, in light of historical parallels, it is logical to suppose that, while US power will dominate the twenty-first century, it will also encounter its limits. This apparent contradiction will provide an important element of the military history of the century, and an understanding of it is important if the US public and policymakers are to be brought to appreciate what the USA can and cannot reasonably do in the world.

The technological sweep of current US power is awesome, and will become even more so in the future. Directed by secure and extensive communication systems, aircraft that can fly from the USA to bomb targets half-way round the world, refuelling in mid-air, are different to what Britain (most recently in 1919) and, even, far more recently, the Soviet Union (in 1980–88) could throw at Afghanistan in the past, as is the degree of aerial surveillance; indeed the weaponry would have been the stuff of fantasy for earlier generations. For example, the Afghan war of 2001–2 showed that unmanned aircraft, hitherto used for surveillance, could be employed to fire missiles, and accurately. This was not so much a robotic weapon as a sophisticated firing platform controlled from a distance, but it offered a marked enhancement of capability at the intersection of artillery and airpower. It is no surprise that, of all the US services, the Air Force has the clearest vision of how it wants to fight, in part because it is the service that most heavily depends on the promise of new technology.[4]

The spread of technology, however, has not lessened the need for considered planning and the appropriate use of force, not least because of the range of possible challenges facing the USA and the variety of tasks its military will be called upon to discharge. Industrial technology enables far greater mobility (speed and distance), and thus expands the potential area for conflict, so that, while the role of 'contact points', where societies with very different technologies interact, remains an important aspect of relative military capability, now the 'points' cover the entire surface of the world. This is particularly apparent with the spread of US bases and airborne force-projection, which, in turn, create demand for applied technology, such as rapidly erected aircraft hangars.

Although the range of industrial technology, especially with airpower, means that two combatants can be fighting each other in a far more contrasting fashion than ever before, this does not ensure that technological superiority is decisive: the quickening of mobility through technology does not necessarily mean that wars are quicker, briefer or more successful than pre-industrial conflicts. The USA fired 79 sea-launched cruise missiles at terrorist targets in Afghanistan and Sudan in 1998, an impressive display of force, but not one that stopped the terrorists. Similarly, the ability to force a way along particular routes and to gain control of individual sites did not mean the subjugation of a society, a point that became readily apparent in Afghanistan from 2002 and Iraq from 2003.

CULTURAL LANDSCAPES

The problems of subjugating a society should encourage attention to the social, political, economic and cultural factors that make it more or less likely that military strength and success will have consequences. As with warfare itself, this approach leads us to focus on the varied cultural 'landscapes' of the world, and their interaction. Historically, it is clear that the willingness to accommodate, and indeed acculturate to, the more powerful, especially conquerors, has been far from constant. In general, the availability of syncretic options, for example the assimilation of local religious cults by the conqueror's religion, and the cooption of local élites, have been the most important means of success. They ceased to be so with the decline of imperialism, although, in certain dictatorships, such as North Korea, leadership cults provided such a pseudo religion. In the modern world accommodation is generally expressed in terms of 'hearts and minds', and the emphasis is on the need to win them over, in particular in order to stage successful counter-insurgency operations. In some societies, however, the display of coercion and force is seen as the best way to win over people, a process demonstrated by the Ethiopians in Eritrea, the Russians in Chechnya,[5] and the Indonesians in Aceh.

It is unclear how far capitalism will lead to an accommodation with US power, both through a desire to benefit in economic terms, by means of trade and investment, and because of the prestige of the USA as the leading economic power and the source of the themes, modes and goods of the global culture of Hollywood and consumerism. Aside, however, from the rejection of this culture by particular groups, most prominently the range of opinions somewhat misleadingly simplified as radical Islam, there is also the prospect that force will be employed against Western hegemony in order to alter the availability and terms of transactions within this world, as states and social groups seek to gain more resources, or to retain control of their own. More generally, pressure for water, oil and other resources lends specific intensity to what may also be a more generalized competition for living standards and jobs. While these factors may seem the product of economic change, population growth and environmental degradation in the modern world, they in fact, look back across the ages to competition over watering holes, grazing lands and the most fertile soil. The modes of conflict change greatly, as do their political, social, economic and cultural contexts, but the root causes appear inherent to human society, and they are readily apparent in conflict in parts of the world at present, although other factors also play a role.

Today the capability of a high-tech military to deliver a hard punch is formidable, particularly in symmetrical conflict, but the problems of dealing with intractable local opposition remain, whether the conflict is defined as a war, as peace-keeping or as a police action. Both political and religious ideologies serve to prepare some groups or societies for long conflicts. Major-General John 'Boney' Fuller, a leading British thinker on military affairs, wrote to an American correspondent in July 1965:

> Today your government and its military advisors appear to have accepted the concept that the way to defeat Communism in Vietnam is by bombing when clearly the precepts garnered from World War Two should have told them that ideas cannot be dislodged by bombs.[6]

The course of the Vietnam War amply demonstrated Fuller's argument, although there is a marked unwillingness on the part of some commentators to accept that that conflict threw doubt on the efficacy of firepower.[7] Air attack in the Vietnam War brought important tactical and operational benefits, but it proved to have only limited value as a strategic tool, and was certainly not war-winning. Fuller's reference to World War II might appear misleading, as the use of atomic bombs led to the surrender of Japan, but, by 1965, there were powerful constraints on such use, most particularly possession of atomic bombs by the USA's leading Communist rivals, both the Soviet Union and China.

Furthermore, cultural constraints and considerations of effectiveness each played a role in discussion of 'anti-societal' strategies. Mao Zedong claimed that the loss of many million Chinese in a nuclear attack would not prevent the others from fighting on. To wipe out much of society by the use of such weapons appeared to some hostile commentators to be the equivalent of the race warfare known later as 'ethnic cleansing' or indeed of genocide: a means that was unacceptable, however potentially effective it might be as a way to destroy the ideas referred to by Fuller. The unacceptability of such slaughter did not prevent planning for atomic confrontation and war, but it was generally done as a means to deter or repel threats and aggression, and not as a means to launch wars of aggression.

It is possible that this may change, and that the deterrence provided by fears of mutual destruction will ebb. It has also been suggested that the cultural restraints that characterized governmental responses to the availability of nuclear weaponry during the Cold War, may not be seen among new Asian nuclear powers.[8] Furthermore, interest, in the USA and elsewhere, in low-yield nuclear weapons may lead to their development and to a lessening of the restraints on the use of atomic weaponry, with consequent dangers of its escalation. The development of other weapons of mass destruction may also contribute to a lessening of restraints. If so, these changes may usher in a new age in human impact on the environment, and in the character of conflict.

The nature of a very different type of cultural landscape can be seen with the increased prominence of the relationship between warfare and the media. In the television age events are immediately relayed on screen, and this is a new aspect of warfare in this period, one that reflects other changes in society. This culminated during the 2003 Gulf War in cameramen going into combat with the troops, ensuring that the messiness, or at least unpredictability, of conflict was extensively shown, as were interviews with ordinary soldiers. This new aspect of conflict creates pressures on both political and military leaders, for it is necessary to be seen to be successful in the very short term, and there is massive public exposure to casualties and chaos. Whereas the simultaneity of news was limited in the 1940s and '50s, it has become more immediate with developments in satellite transmission, as well as with the manufacture of lighter-weight cameras. Furthermore, the panoptic view of the camera has become normative, and this has made it difficult for Western powers to sustain limits on reporting. An awareness that opponents will try to manipulate news, as Saddam Hussein vigorously did, encouraged in 2003 an accessibility to the media as an important part of news management.

US MILITARY POWER

The nature of the US force structure has been important to the character of US military power in recent decades, and will continue to be so in the future. An emphasis on preparation for great-power symmetrical warfare, first with the Soviet Union and then with China, affected the ability of the USA to engage in other conflicts successfully, and led to a stress on airpower and long-range missiles, both of which were important for helping the USA to dominate at the high end of the power spectrum. In the 1950s jet aircraft carrying nuclear bombs appeared to be the best response to overwhelming Soviet conventional superiority. This doctrine and force structure, in turn, led to an emphasis, first, on submarine and land-based inter-continental ballistic missiles and, later, on space-based weapons.

This approach downplayed the multiple-tasking of forces and preparation demanded by the range of commitments the USA might face, and led to a relative shift of resources away from conventional forces, especially the army. The result became clear in the Vietnam War, where the commitment of large numbers, courage and can-do spirit could not compensate for the lack of adequate training and doctrine in counter-insurgency warfare on the ground, and in close-support air operations. In particular, the effective coordination of air and ground forces in the Vietnam War was affected by the independence of the air force and by the type of air war it had prepared for. The doctrine and structure of airpower misleadingly emphasized its capacity to deliver decisive victory independently, rather than through support of land and sea operations.

The risk remains that war will not conform to the high-tech model that is both sought and anticipated. This helps fuel the debate over the RMA, both with scepticism on the part of the USA's allies,[9] and with opposition within the US military to some of the doctrinal and force-profile prescriptions of RMA enthusiasts, in particular the emphasis on airpower and special operations and the reduction of the army, or at least a decrease in its influence, and the transformation of its structures. Robert Scales has argued that, in place of the division, the focus for force projection should be the brigade,[10] a force similar to Marine Expeditionary Units. The risk of a technologically driven process of change is that it will lead to heavy investments in capabilities that do not match geo-strategic requirements.[11] Instead, these requirements subordinate capability to goals that, in turn, may lead to a force structure that reflects political needs. Thus, for example, for the USA it is important to maintain land power, primarily as that is the only effective way to occupy territory, but also, in part, as an expression of shared responsibility with regional partners.[12]

In turn, RMA enthusiasts attack what they discern as conservatism in doctrine and practice, not least service parochialism,[13] but, in practice, the aggregate military capability discussed by these enthusiasts is not the same as capability or success in any particular scenario, while there is the problem of securing the 'exit-result': that those who are beaten accept that they have lost and are willing to heed US wishes, which is the necessary prelude to a successful exit-strategy. This is a particular problem with global interventionism, whether practised by the USA or by other powers, as the ability to project strength and win the battle does not mean that the war, more specifically the war to force changes in policy and attitude, has been won. To be sure, it is better to be prepared for the wrong war than not to be prepared at all, but that will not suffice. The dominant note on which to conclude when surveying the character of modern war is that of variety, and this sets the tasking for the USA. Major powers have to be ready for a range of military possibilities, and force structures and doctrines have to be developed accordingly.

Aside from this socio-political constraint on the effectiveness of the RMA, the theory also underrates continuities in warfare. The US military, like that of other powers, is affected by the extent to which small-unit deployment for battle has not changed greatly since 1918. High-quality manpower, training, motivation, discipline and leadership are still essential at the small-unit level, not least for low-intensity operations, and closing with the enemy remains difficult and costly on the battlefield. Weaponry is rarely the key.

At the start of the new millennium planning for total war between the major powers became less pertinent than at any time for over a century. This reflected the situation after the Cold War, especially the dominant role of the USA within the West; the degree to which other Western states could not wage war without US consent and co-operation (as the British discovered, negatively, over Suez in 1956 and, positively, in the Falklands War in 1982); and the decline of Soviet, and then Russian, power. According to the International Institute for Strategic Studies, in 2000 the USA spent $295 billion on its military budget, Russia $59 billion, China $41 billion, and the 17 European NATO powers $162.5 billion. By 2001, US military spending had risen to $310 billion, more than the next nine largest national military budgets combined, and a contrast that challenged inter-operability between the USA and its allies. For 2002, the sum was about 40 per cent of the world's total military spending; although costs for items such as pay and social benefits varied greatly across the world, as did expectations about food and accommodation. President Bush declared that year, 'Our men and women deserve the best weapons, the best equipment and the best training. And therefore I've asked Congress for a one-year increase of more than $48 billion for national defence – the largest increase in a generation'. Indeed, having had a budget of $276 billion in 1998, the US Defense Department's proposed budget for 2004 is over $400 billion.

The consequences of the end of the Cold War were not restricted to relations between the USA and the Soviet Union. The collapse of the Russian economy, of the ability and willingness to sustain the Soviet

Union's levels of delivery of advanced weaponry, and of the value of Soviet diplomatic and military support also affected former clients such as Iraq, Syria and Ethiopia; although the availability, legally or otherwise, of surplus Cold War equipment introduced a powerful degree of instability in weapons movements, while Russia sought to use its armaments industry to gain foreign capital. Russian weaknesses, nevertheless, gave the USA a major advantage around the world, and ensured that both the USA, and its ally Israel, had a stronger military position in the Middle East, encouraging their opponents to rely increasingly on asymmetrical responses including terrorism.

The contrast in expenditure between the USA and other powers owed much to US wealth, to the economic growth of the 1990s, and to the willingness to increase greatly the federal deficit, particularly in 2003; but the contrast also reflected the impact of the 11 September 2001 suicide attacks on New York and Washington by Islamic terrorists, in a jet-fuelled *jihad*, and the consequent political consensus in the USA enabling an enormous arms build-up. In contrast, other priorities for government expenditure, such as social welfare, played a far larger role in many, although not all, of the poorer and economically weaker states that were second- or lower-rank military powers, particularly the European NATO powers and Canada.

In addition, many of these states found their military not up to the tasks they might envisage. Thus, in 1993, the Spanish government decided that it could not contribute a brigade to the UN forces in Bosnia, as conscripts could not be expected to serve and there were insufficient regulars; while, in 2003, aside from the political reasons for its reluctance to assist the USA against Iraq, France was affected by the problems of rebuilding its military after the end of conscription, and was also committed to helping suppress an intractable insurrection in Ivory Coast.

At the same time, it is necessary to appreciate the continued role of mid-range military powers (from regional stability and limited power projection to niche technology, economic capability and political interests). Similarly, it is important to note the role of Third World forces: from regional and internal stability to peacekeeping and police operations.

The contrast in military capability between the USA and other powers is likely to continue, and to be accentuated by the large military and military-industrial investment on research and development in the USA. The results are readily apparent in the use of satellites and related high-speed technology, not least in the development of a national missile defence system against incoming missiles.[14] Furthermore, the US satellite-based global positioning system, employed for surveillance and targeting, is unmatched elsewhere, and is being strengthened as the USA invests in a new network of spy satellites, contributing to the militarization of space.[15] Heavy US investment in military research and development ensures that the USA will not only continue to dominate the production and export of advanced weaponry, but also that the capacity of other powers to match this will decline. This is particularly important to Russia, whose arms exports rose rapidly in 1997–2001, passing the USA in 2001 itself, but which, despite a commitment to new-technology weaponry, lacks comparable expenditure on military research and development.

American military capability does not, however, meet all the country's defence needs, which reflects not only the worldwide political and economic strategic concerns of the USA, but also the extent to which opposition does not present itself only in conventional terms. The former concern ensures the need to respond to more than one crisis at a time, which is not a new problem, and indeed characterized much of the post-war period. Thus, at the time of the Vietnam War, the USA was threatened by the danger that North Korean guerrilla attacks on South Korea would escalate and, alongside the response from the South, provoke a full-scale conflict. Furthermore, in April 1969, Nixon considered bombing North Korea after a US electronic reconnaissance aircraft was shot down. In the event, heavily committed in Vietnam, he resorted to a show of strength with a carrier task force.[16] The multiple character of challenges became more pronounced after the end of the Cold War as US interests were no longer defined by that conflict.

Alongside the asymmetrical resistance posed by guerrilla forces, has come a different challenge in the shape of high-tech or at least new-tech opposition, by rogue states and terrorist organizations willing to invest in new forms of weaponry, especially biological, chemical and low-grade nuclear devices. International attempts to prevent the development of such weaponry, such as the prohibition by the 1972 Biological and Toxic Weapons Convention, have failed to do so. Thus, the Soviet Union, despite signing the Convention, built up a major capability in this field, while Iraq also sought to become a regional power in part by linking such weaponry to its missile programme, although in 1991 it did not use these weapons and apparently by 2003 no longer possessed them. The capability was not restricted to states. In 1995, Aum Shinrikyo, a large-scale Japanese terrorist movement, carried out a biological attack on the Tokyo underground railway system.

The contrast in military capability with Europe encouraged the US administration to press ahead with a unilateral approach in the 2003 Iraq crisis, and led some US commentators to argue that Europe could not prove an effective support or a strategic competitor.[17] As another sign of unilateralism, in 2003, Congress required the Energy Department to be ready to resume underground nuclear tests within eighteen months, a step that would breach the 1996 Nuclear Test Ban Treaty.

Like other hegemonies in history, that of the USA partly rests on force, as was dramatically displayed against Iraq in 2003; and America's international political presence is increasingly militarized.[18] The USA benefits from the absence of insurrectionary movements and political breakdown in North America, but the global pretensions of its power, the far-flung nature of its economic, political and strategic interests, and the nature of American public assumptions, makes it vulnerable to feeling that it has to act in areas where, in practice, it will be difficult to enforce its will and to avoid long-term entanglements. This is particularly true in Latin America and the Middle East.

CHINA

Aside from the USA, only China, with its rapid economic growth, is able to act as a threatening great power, but its military is far weaker, its essential military and security concerns are internal, and its Communist leadership seeks peace with its neighbours and the West. Furthermore, China's potential challenge is restricted by the circumspection of its military projection: there are US forces in East Asia, not Chinese forces in the West Indies. Since 1950 China has clashed with the USA in the Korean War, and with India, Vietnam and the Soviet Union; but all, bar the Korean War, were short-term conflicts, and despite developing as a naval and nuclear power,[19] the Chinese were, and are, wary of military, and indeed diplomatic, commitments further afield. China is also concerned about what it sees as a rise in Japanese military assertiveness, as well as by Indian plans.

Despite this, China and the USA have rival interests in East Asia, especially over Taiwan, and there is also a powerful distrust between the two states that reflects their very different political cultures. In 1996, the Chinese threat to Taiwan led to the dispatch of two US aircraft battle groups, and it is likely that any attack on the island would lead to a response. However, Chinese anti-ship missiles pose a growing threat to any US naval deployment,[20] while, in 2002, China bought eight additional kilo-class submarines from Russia. In response, Taiwan purchased American submarines and destroyers. Since the 1996 Sino–Russian Summit, Chinese purchases of Russian military technology and arms have increased, enhancing Chinese capability and assisting its military modernization, as well as supporting the Russian arms industry. For example, the Russians proved willing to sell the up-to-date aircraft they had hitherto been unwilling to provide, giving China enhanced capability.

Concern about growing Chinese military strength, especially at sea, in turn, led Australia, Japan, Malaysia, Singapore and South Korea to develop their naval strength, Japan deciding in 2003 to build two carriers capable of carrying helicopters or V/STOL aircraft; although it is unclear whether China has an appropriate navalist strategic doctrine to match its growing strength.[21] Whatever the level of threat, the economic weight of East Asia has not been matched by an ability to produce political structures or, at least, practices capable of coping with worrying developments, and this has provided opportunities for maverick and destabilizing policymaking in the case of North Korea. As a consequence, the US military role remains very important.

While at present the September 11 effect has focused US attention on the Middle East, concern about North Korea's development of nuclear weapons, which had already taken them close to war with the US in 1994, has also directed attention to East Asia. In 2003, the US administration expanded the scope of its missile defence programme to include an emphasis on distant areas; this being clearly understood as a reference to those threatened by North Korea. The different US responses in 2003 to the apparent development of weapons of mass destruction by Iraq and North Korea suggested to commentators that possession of such weapons by North Korea did act as a deterrent, vindicating suggestions that the spread of nuclear weaponry was likely to create a series of deterrence relationships around the world;[22] although it is less clear that, as has been claimed, this spread 'has all but brought large-scale interstate warfare to an end'.[23] Furthermore, the crisis underlined US caution about becoming involved in more than one conflict at a time, an important constraint, and one that served as a reminder of the need to match military capability to attainable political goals.

Such a restraint is not the only necessary aspect of political intelligence. During the Cold War, the US 'tendency to regard violent nationalism in the Third World as the product of a centrally directed international Communist conspiracy was a strategic error of the first magnitude'.[24] American attempts in 2003 to settle the Palestine problem indicate that there are grounds to hope that a similar mistake is not being made with modern Islam, although the extent to which the religious dimension of conflict has become stronger in the Middle East is a major problem. This strengthening also extends to the USA, certainly as seen in the attitudes of President George W. Bush.

The recent cult for the 'face of battle' approach to military history suggests that it is particularly advantageous to write about recent conflicts because those can be recalled most vividly and the accounts of participants can be readily compared. The emphasis on images, in an increasingly visual society, contributes to the same end. The net effect was seen with the Gulf War of 2003, when instant punditry became round-the-clock as embedded correspondents were called upon to comment not only on their own experiences, and those of the units to which they were attached, but also on the course of the war. This, however, is a misleading approach, because the assessment of effectiveness requires careful study, while most of the information available to high-spectrum participants, for example satellite material, is not in the public domain. The embedding of correspondants also raised expectations about the rapidity of developments.

Instant punditry has readily gravitated to the new-age approach to warfare; indeed, the precision of the cruise missiles and their attacks on Baghdad appeared almost designed for television cameras. However, it is already apparent that assertions made at the time about a new age of warfare have been overstated. Analysis of the Afghan campaign of 2001–2 has undermined the popular claims about novelty, and has underlined the extent in that campaign of positional warfare, the role of close-combat capability, and the continuing need for a system of integrating fire and manoeuvre,[25] which, indeed, remains the case at every level of war.

CONFLICT AROUND THE WORLD

The general focus in military history is on the leading power, the USA throughout our period, which reflects the paradigm-diffusion model: the notion that there is a paradigm military method and power, and that its influence is spread by a process of diffusion.[26] While this, indeed, plays a role, it is also necessary to take note of the eccentricity of the leading military power, and to appreciate that to conclude by considering the USA and its campaigns would be misleading. By its very nature, the foremost power is atypical, and it is necessary to look at the nature of warfare for other states. Most states and groups of states could not afford the over $3 billion that Operation Allied Force, the US-dominated Kosovo operation, cost in 1999, and there is also, in most states, a lack of relevant command and control systems for joint theatre-wide operations.

At the close of the book it is appropriate to look not at US operations in Iraq, but at the most bloody conflict in the world, that in Congo; and the most persistent large-scale conflict, that in Sudan. The latter has been made more intractable by the rise of militant Islam on the government side and by international involvement, including from Eritrea, Ethiopia and Uganda on the rebel side and from Iran on the government side.

The war in Congo has cost more lives and involved more states than that in Iraq;[27] and yet, partly because it appears to threaten no crucial security interests, Congo receives little attention and is held to be of scant importance other than for debates over international peacekeeping and failed states in Africa. Aside from the war's consequences for a large part of Africa – both Congo and its neighbours – it is also significant as a more general indicator of the fragility of state structures and the extent to which other aspects of cohesion, particularly ethnic links, can lead to large-scale violence. The theses that underlay US and Israeli action in 2003 – that defeated societies could be reconstituted (Iraq) or could be made to act in an acceptable fashion (Palestine) – appear less pertinent in the case of Africa, and may, indeed, be over-optimistic, as well as self-serving, in the Middle East; as was seen previously in South Vietnam, when it proved impossible for the dominant military power to force a society to operate as it wished it to do. In Congo, in 2003, war appears both the means by which group action is conducted, not least in order to obtain resources, and, in the absence of (voluntary) disarmament, the sole way in which order is likely to be created.

The militarization of society that is caused by the spread of tribal and other militias is matched in other areas described in terms of failed states. This is not necessarily an irreversible process. Lebanon, for example, is less divided than it was in the late 1970s and early 1980s. Nevertheless, there is need in any discussion of war in the modern world to consider these societies alongside those where war, indeed large-scale violence, is monopolized by the state. The economics, organization and timetable of conflict in the former are such that it is less technological, less clear-cut and lower in tempo than war involving regular forces, but it is not therefore less worthy of attention.

These two military paradigms overlap when local or distant regular forces are brought into contact with these societies, as in Afghanistan in 2001–4, more particularly in the overthrow of the Taliban and in operations after their fall. These conflicts bring into play two different forms of warfare, and, given their respective social contexts, it is not clear that the system of regular forces with advanced weaponry is necessarily more effective. This system may win battles, but it is difficult to use these victories to enable the creation of new political systems that bring stability, peace, and what are judged, by the USA, to be acceptable international postures. The current 'War on Terrorism' is just an aspect of this wider problem, which is likely to become worse, not least because of social volatility and economic strains. For these reasons, and because most of the world's population growth is in the Third World, it is there that conflict will be focused. If 'First World' readerships continue to define war largely in terms of the actions and doctrines of their own militaries, they will be wrong to do so.

References

Chapter 1: Introduction

1 D. R. Snyder, 'Arming the *Bundesmarine*: The United States and the Build-up of the German Federal Navy, 1950–1960', *Journal of Military History*, 66 (2002), p. 481.
2 D. J. Dean, *The Air Force Role in Low-Intensity Conflict* (Maxwell Air Force Base, AL, 1986); C. H. Builder, *The Icarus Syndrome: The Role of Air Power Theory in the Evolution and Fate of the US Air Force* (New Brunswick, NJ, 1994).

Chapter 2: Aftermath Conflicts

1 *Selected Military Writings of Mao Tse-tung* (Beijing, 1963).
2 L. M. Chassin, *The Communist Conquest of China: A History of the Civil War 1945–1949* (London, 1966).
3 O. A. Westad, *Decisive Encounters: The Chinese Civil War, 1946–1950* (Stanford, CA, 2003).
4 H. M. Tanner, 'Guerilla, Mobile, and Base Warfare in Communist Military Operations in Manchuria, 1945–1947', *Journal of Military History*, 67 (2003), p. 1222.
5 S. I. Levine, *Anvil of Victory: The Communist Revolution in Manchuria, 1945–1948* (New York, 1987).
6 T. Tsou, *America's Failure in China, 1941–1950* (Chicago, IL, 1963); O.Y.K. Wou, *Mobilizing the Masses: Building Revolution in Henan* (Stanford, CA, 1994); J.K.S. Yick, *Making Urban Revolution in China: The CCP-GHD Struggle for Beiping-Tianjin, 1945–1949* (Armonk, NY, 1995).
7 G. Lockhart, 'In Lieu of the *Levée-en-mass*. Mass Mobilization in Modern Vietnam', in D. Moran and A. Waldron, eds, *The People in Arms: Military Myth and National Mobilization since the French Revolution* (Cambridge, 2003), pp. 227–31.
8 C. M. Woodhouse, *The Struggle for Greece, 1941–1949* (St Albans, 1976); H. Jones,

'A New Kind of War': America's Global Strategy and the Truman Doctrine in Greece (Oxford, 1989); T. Jones, 'The British Army, and Counter-Guerrilla Warfare in Greece, 1944–1949', Small Wars and Insurgencies, 8 (1997), pp. 80–106; C.R. Shrader, The Withered Vine: Logistics and the Communist Insurgency in Greece, 1945–1949 (Westport, CT, 1999).

9 P. Grose, Operation Rollback: America's Secret War Behind the Iron Curtain (New York, 2000).

10 V. Mastny, The Cold War and Soviet Insecurity (Oxford, 1996); S. J. Corke, 'History, Historians and the Naming of Foreign Policy: A Post-modern Reflection on American Strategic Thinking during the Truman Administration', Intelligence and National Security, 16 (2001).

11 T. Lai et al., A Tragic Beginning: The Taiwan Uprising of February 28, 1947 (Stanford, CA, 1991).

12 I have benefited from discussing this with Tim Rees.

13 M. W. Cagle and F. A. Manson, The Sea War in Korea (Annapolis, MD, 2000).

14 D. C. James, 'Command Crisis: MacArthur and the Korean War', in H. R. Borowski, ed., The Harmon Memorial Lectures in Military History, 1959–1987 (Washington, DC, 1988), pp. 218–19.

15 X. Zhang, Red Wings Over the Yalu: China, the Soviet Union, and the Air War in Korea (College Station, TX, 2002).

16 The extensive literature includes C. Blair, The Forgotten War: America in Korea, 1950–1953 (New York, 1987); B.I. Kaufman, The Korean War: Challenges in Crisis, Credibility and Command (Philadelphia, 1986); M.P. Hickey, The Korean War: The West Confronts Communism (Woodstock, NY, 2000); and W. Stueck, Rethinking the Korean War: A New Diplomatic and Strategic History (Princeton, NJ, 2002).

17 C. C. Crane, American Airpower Strategy in Korea, 1950–1953 (Lawrence, KS, 2000).

18 S. H. Lee, Outposts of Empire. Korea, Vietnam and the Origins of the Cold War in Asia, 1949–1958 (Liverpool, 1995), p. 85; A. Roland, The Military-Industrial Complex (Washington, 2001).

19 A. R. Millett, 'Introduction to the Korean War', Journal of Military History, 65 (2001), p. 935.

Chapter 3: Wars of Decolonization

1 P.M.H. Groen, 'Dutch Armed Forces and the Decolonisation of Indonesia: The Second Police Action, 1948–1949, A Pandora's Box', War and Society, 4 (1986), pp. 79–104.

2 N. Stewart, The Royal Navy and the Palestine Patrol (London, 2002).

3 A. Short, The Communist Insurrection in Malaya, 1948–1960 (London, 1975); R. Stubbs, Hearts and Minds in Guerrilla Warfare: The Malayan Emergency, 1948–1960 (Oxford, 1989); J. Coates, Suppressing Insurgency: An Analysis of the Malayan Emergency, 1948–1954 (Boulder, CO, 1992); T. Jones, Postwar Counterinsurgency and the SAS, 1945–1952 (London, 2001).

4 R. G. Thompson, Defeating Communist Insurgency: The Lessons of Malaya and Vietnam (New York, 1966); R. L. Clutterbuck, The Long, Long War:

Counterinsurgency in Malaya and Vietnam (New York, 1966).

5   B. Fall, *Hell in a Very Small Place* (New York, 1966).

6   I. M. Wall, *France, the United States and the Algerian War* (Berkeley, CA, 2001).

7   A. Horne, *A Savage War of Peace: Algeria, 1954–62* (London, 1977); A. A. Heggoy, *Insurgency and Counter Insurgency in Algeria* (Bloomington, IN, 1972); A. Clayton, *The Wars of French Decolonisation* (Harlow, 1994); C. R. Shrader, *The First Helicopter War: Logistics and Mobility in Algeria, 1954–1962* (Westport, CT, 1999); M. Connelly, 'Rethinking the Cold War and Decolonization: The Grand Strategy of the Algerian War for Independence', *International Journal of the Middle East*, 33 (2001), pp. 221–45; M. S. Alexander and J. F.V. Keiger, eds, *France and the Algerian War, 1954–62: Strategy, Operations and Diplomacy* (London, 2002); D. Porch, 'The Algerian War, 1954–1962: The Inversion of the "Levée en Masse"', in D. Moran and A. Waldron, eds, *The People in Arms* (Cambridge, 2002), pp. 234–55.

8   J. Paget, *Counter-Insurgency Operations: Techniques of Guerrilla Warfare* (London, 1967); R. W. Heather, 'Intelligence and Counter-Insurgency in Kenya, 1952–56', *Intelligence and National Security*, 5 (1990), pp. 57–83; I.F.W. Beckett, *Modern Insurgencies and Counter-Insurgencies* (2001), pp. 121–30.

9   I. Speller, *The Role of Amphibious Warfare in British Defence Policy, 1945–1956* (London, 2001).

10   R. Fullick and G. Powell, *Suez: The Double War* (London, 1979); D. Kunz, *The Economic Diplomacy of the Suez Crisis* (Chapel Hill, NC, 1991); M. Vaisse, ed., *La France et l'opération de Suez de 1956* (Paris, 1997).

11   T. R. Mockaitis, *British Counterinsurgency, 1919–1960* (London, 1990); R. Holland, *Britain and the Revolt in Cyprus, 1954–1959* (Oxford, 1998).

12   Southampton University Library, MBI/J79.

13   H. James and D. Sheil-Small, *The Undeclared War: The Story of the Indonesian Confrontation, 1962–1966* (London, 1971).

14   S. Harper, *Last Sunset: What Happened in Aden* (London, 1978).

15   T. H. Henriksen, *Revolution and Counter Revolution: Mozambique's War of Independence, 1964–1974* (Westport, CT, 1974); J. P. Cann, *Counter Insurgency in Africa: The Portuguese Way of War, 1961–1974* (Westport, CT, 1997); L. Heywood, *Contested Power in Angola: 1840s to the Present* (Rochester, NY, 2000), p. 175.

16   R. M. Fields, *The Portuguese Revolution and the Armed Forces Movement* (New York, 1976).

17   M. Dhada, 'The Liberation War in Guinea-Bissau Reconsidered', *Journal of Military History*, 62 (1998), p. 592.

18   A. Clayton, *France, Soldiers and Africa* (London, 1988); J. Chipman, *French Power in Africa* (Oxford, 1989).

19   L. H. Gann and T. H. Henriksen, *The Struggle for Zimbabwe: Battle in the Bush* (New York, 1981); J. Cilliers, *Counter-Insurgency in Rhodesia* (London, 1985).

20   L. Freedman and V. Gamba-Stonehouse, *Signals of War: The Falklands Conflict of 1982* (London, 1990).

21   D. Anderson, *The Falklands War 1982* (London, 2002) is the best short introduction. Important other works include R. A. Burden, *Falklands: The Air War* (London, 1986); D. K. Brown, *The Royal Navy and the Falklands War* (London,

1987); M. Middlebrook, *The Fight for the 'Malvinas': The Argentine Forces in the Falklands War* (New York, 1989); M. Clapp and E. Southby-Tailyour, *Amphibious Assault Falklands: The Battle of San Carlos Water* (London, 1996).

Chapter 4: Cold War Conflicts

1   H. M. Friedman, *Creating an American Lake: United States Imperialism and Strategic Security in the Pacific Basin, 1945–1947* (Westport, CT, 2001).
2   R. H. Whitlow, *US Marines in Vietnam: The Advisory and Combat Assistance Era, 1954–1964* (Washington, DC, 1977); R. H. Spector, *Advice and Support: The Early Years, 1941–1960, United States Army in Vietnam* (Washington, DC, 1983); D. Toczek, *The Battle of Ap Bac, Vietnam: They Did Everything but Learn from It* (Westport, CT, 2001).
3   D. Kaiser, *American Tragedy: Kennedy, Johnson, and the Origins of The Vietnam War* (Cambridge, MA, 2000).
4   N. E. Sarantakes, 'In the Service of Pharaoh? The United States and the Deployment of Korean Troops in Vietnam, 1965–1968', *Pacific Historical Review*, 68 (1999), pp. 425–49.
5   W. J. Duiker, *Sacred War: Nationalism and Revolution in a Divided Vietnam* (New York, 1995); R. E. Ford, *Tet 1968: Understanding the Surprise* (London, 1995); R. Brown, 'Limited War', in C. McInnes and G. D. Sheffield, eds, *Warfare in the Twentieth Century: Theory and Practice* (London, 1988), pp. 177–84.
6   D. T. Zabecki, 'Artillery Fire Doctrine', in S. C. Tucker, ed., *Encyclopedia of the Vietnam War* (3 vols, Santa Barbara, CA, 1998), vol. I, 49.
7   M. L. Pribbenow, 'The 'Ology War: Technology and Ideology in the Vietnamese Defense of Hanoi, 1967', *Journal of Military History*, 67 (2003), pp. 175–200.
8   D. J. Mrozek, *Air Power and the Ground War in Vietnam: Ideas and Actions* (Maxwell Air Force Base, AL, 1988).
9   C. D. Walton, *The Myth of Inevitable US Defeat in Vietnam* (Portland, OR, 2002).
10 T. C. Shelling, *Arms and Influence* (New Haven, CT, 1966).
11 S. W. Wilson, 'Taking Clodfetter One Step Further: Mass, Surprise, Concentration and the Failure of Operation Rolling Thunder', *Air Power History*, 48 (2001), pp. 40–47.
12 J. A. Nagl, *Counterinsurgency Lessons from Malaya and Vietnam: Learning to Eat Soup with a Knife* (Westport, CT, 2002).
13 L. Baritz, *Backfire: A History of How American Culture Led Us into Vietnam and Made Us Fight the Way We Did* (New York, 1985); J. J. Clarke, *Advice and Support: The Final Years, 1965–1973, United States Army in Vietnam* (Washington, DC, 1988).
14 S. P. Mackenzie, *Revolutionary Armies in the Modern Era: A Revisionist Approach* (London, 1997), pp. 172–3.
15 R. A. Hunt, *Pacification. The American Struggle for Vietnam's Hearts and Minds* (Boulder, CO, 1995); E. M. Bergerud, *The Dynamics of Defeat: The Vietnam War in Hau Nghia Province* (Boulder, CO, 1990).
16 G. Herring, 'Peoples Quite Apart: Americans, South Vietnamese and the War in Vietnam', *Diplomatic History*, 14 (1990), pp. 1–23.

17   R. H. Collins, 'The Economic Crisis of 1968 and the Waning of the "American
     Century"', *American Historical Review*, 101 (1996), pp. 413, 417.

18   M. Charlton and A. Moncrieff, *Many Reasons Why: The American Involvement in
     Vietnam* (London, 1978), p. 115.

19   G. Q. Flynn, *The Draft, 1940–1973* (Lawrence, KS, 1993).

20   It was captured in March 1968, T. N. Castle, *One Day Too Long: Top Secret Site 85
     and the Bombing of North Vietnam* (New York, 1999).

21   P. Wood, *Call Sign Rustic: The Secret Air War over Cambodia, 1970–1973*
     (Washington, DC, 2002).

22   W. Thompson, *To Hanoi and Back: The US Air Force and North Vietnam, 1966–1973*
     (Washington, DC, 2000).

23   D. Andrade, *America's Last Vietnam Battle: Halting Hanoi's 1972 Easter Offensive*
     (Lawrence, KS, 2001).

24   M. L. Michel, *The 11 Days of Christmas: America's Last Battle* (San Francisco, CA,
     2002).

25   N. V. Long, 'Post-Paris Agreement Struggles and the Fall of Saigon', in J. S.
     Werner and D. H. Luu, eds, *The Vietnam War: Vietnamese and American Perspectives*
     (Armonk, NY, 1992), pp. 203–15; G. J. Veith and M. L. Pribbenow, '"Fighting Is An
     Art": The Army of the Republic of Vietnam's Defense of Xuan Loc, 9–21 April
     1975', *Journal of Military History*, 68 (2004), pp. 163–214.

26   Amidst the extensive literature, H. G. Summers, *On Strategy: A Critical Analysis of
     the Vietnam War* (Novato, CA, 1982); L.J. Matthews and D. E. Brown, eds, *Assessing
     the Vietnam War* (Washington, DC, 1987); M. J. Gilbert, ed., *Why the North Won the
     Vietnam War* (New York, 2002).

27   A. Saikal and W. Maley, eds, *The Soviet Withdrawal from Afghanistan* (Cambridge,
     1989); S. R. McMichael, *Stumbling Bear: Soviet Military Performance in Afghanistan*
     (London, 1993); M. Galeotti, *Afghanistan: The Soviet Union's Last War* (London,
     1995); H. Bradsher, *Afghan Communism and Soviet Intervention* (Oxford, 1999);
     L. W. Grau and M. A. Gress, eds, *The Russian General Staff: The Soviet Afghan War:
     How a Superpower Fought and Lost* (Lawrence, KA, 2002), pp. 305–6.

28   S. Green, *Living by the Sword: America and Israel in the Middle East, 1968–1987*
     (London, 1988).

29   P. Gleijeses, *Conflicting Missions: Havana, Washington, and South Africa, 1959–1976*
     (Chapel Hill, NC, 2002).

30   J. T. Stanik, *El Dorado Canyon: Reagan's Undeclared War with Quaddafi* (Annapolis,
     MD, 2003).

31   C. G. Cogan, 'Desert One and Its Disorders', *Journal of Military History*, 67 (2003),
     pp. 201–16.

32   J. Prados, *Presidents' Secret Wars: CIA and Pentagon Covert Operations from World War
     II through Iranscam* (New York, 1985).

33   P. C. Schmitter, ed., *Military Rule in Latin America: Function, Consequences and
     Perspectives* (London, 1973).

34   M. D. Gambone, *Capturing the Revolution: The United States, Central America and
     Nicaragua, 1961–1972* (Westport, CT, 2001).

35   N. Cullather, *Secret History: The CIA's Classified Account of Its Operations in*

Guatemala, 1952–1954 (Stanford, CA, 1999).

Chapter 5: Cold War Confrontations

1 A valuable introduction is provided by J. L. Gaddis, *What We Now Know: Rethinking the Cold War* (Oxford, 1997).
2 J. J. Carafano, *Waltzing into the Cold War: The Struggle for Occupied Austria* (College Station, TX, 2002).
3 S. W. Duke and W. Krieger, eds, *US Military Forces in Europe: The Early Years, 1945–1970* (Boulder, CO, 1993).
4 J. A. Huston, *Outposts and Allies: US Army Logistics in the Cold War, 1945–1953* (Selinsgrove, PA, 1988).
5 Among the vast literature on this subject, J. Prados, *Presidents' Secret Wars: CIA and Pentagon Covert Operations from World War II through Iranscam* (New York, 1985); C. Andrew and V. Mitrokhin, *The Mitrokhin Archive: The KGB in Europe and the West* (London, 1999); S. Dorril, *MI6: Fifty Years of Special Operations* (London, 2000); R. Aldrich, *The Hidden Hand: Britain, America and Cold War Secret Intelligence* (London, 2001); K. Conboy and J. Morrison, *The CIA's Secret War in Tibet* (Lawrence, 2002). For criticism of the CIA, M. Goodman, 'Espionage and Covert Action', in C. Eisendrath, ed., *National Insecurity: US Intelligence after the Cold War* (Washington, DC, 1999), pp. 23–43, and R. Jeffrey-Jones, *Cloak and Dollar: A History of American Secret Intelligence* (New Haven, CT, 2002).
6 J. M. Diefendorf, A. Frohn and H. J. Rupieper, eds, *American Policy and the Reconstruction of West Germany, 1945–1955* (Cambridge, 1993); N. Wiggerhaus and R. G. Foerster, eds, *The Western Security Community: Common Problems and Conflicting National Interests during the Foundation Phase of the North Atlantic Alliance* (Oxford, 1993); S. Mawby, *Containing Germany: Britain and the Arming of the Federal Republic* (London, 1999).
7 M. J. Hogan, *A Cross of Iron: Harry S. Truman and the Origins of the National Security State, 1945–1954* (Cambridge, 1998).
8 H. Zimmermann, *Money and Security: Troops, Monetary Policy, and West Germany's Relations with the United States and Britain, 1950–1971* (Washington, DC, 2002).
9 D. G. Muller, *China as a Maritime Power* (Boulder, CO, 1983), pp. 18–19, 29, 38.
10 D. Holloway, *Stalin and the Bomb* (Oxford, 1994).
11 G. Herken, *The Winning Weapon: The Atomic Bomb in the Cold War, 1945–1950* (New York, 1990); H. R. Borowski, *A Hollow Threat: Strategic Air Power and Containment Before Korea* (Westport, CT, 1982); G. H. Quester, *Nuclear Monopoly* (New Brunswick, NJ, 2000).
12 M. Trachtenberg, 'The Making of a Political System: The German Question in International Politics, 1945–1963', in P. Kennedy and W. I. Hitchcock, eds, *From War to Peace: Altered Strategic Landscapes in the Twentieth Century* (New Haven, CT, 2000), pp. 118–19.
13 R. Rhodes, *Dark Sun: The Making of the Hydrogen Bomb* (New York, 1995).
14 S. T. Ross, *American War Plans, 1945–1950* (New York, 1988).
15 R. E. McClendon, *Autonomy for the Air Arm* (Washington, DC, 1996); H. S. Wolk,

Towards Independence: The Emergence of the US Air Force, 1945–1947 (Washington, DC, 1996); W. S. Borgiasz, The Strategic Air Command: Evolution and Consolidation of Nuclear Forces, 1945–55 (New York, 1996); C. H. Builder, The Icarus Syndrome: The Role of Air Power Theory in the Evolution and Fate of the US Air Force (New Brunswick, NJ, 1998).

16 S. J. Ball, The Bomber in British Strategy: Doctrine, Strategy and Britain's World Role 1945–60 (Boulder, CO, 1995).

17 T. A. Hughes, Over Lord: General Pete Quesada and the Triumph of Tactical Air Power in World War II (New York, 1995).

18 H. York, Race to Oblivion: A Participant's View of the Arms Race (New York, 1970).

19 C. C. Crane, 'To Avert Impending Disaster: American Military Plans to use Atomic Weapons during the Korean War', Journal of Strategic Studies, 23 (2000), pp. 2–88.

20 A. J. Bacevich, The Pentomic Era: The US Army between Korea and Vietnam (Washington, DC, 1986).

21 A. J. Bacevich, 'The Paradox of Professionalism: Eisenhower, Ridgway, and the Challenge to Civilian Control, 1953–1955', Journal of Military History, 61 (1997), pp. 303–33.

22 Southampton, University Library, MBI/I149.

23 D. L. Snead, The Gaither Committee, Eisenhower, and the Cold War (Columbus, OH, 1999).

24 C. Craig, Destroying the Village: Eisenhower and Thermonuclear War (New York, 1998).

25 M. J. White, The Cuban Missile Crisis (Basingstoke, 1995); A. Fursenko and T. Naftali, 'One Hell of a Gamble': Khrushchev, Castro, Kennedy – The Cuban Missile Crisis, 1958–1964 (1997); L. V. Scott, Macmillan, Kennedy and the Cuban Missile Crisis: Political, Military and Intelligence Aspects (Basingstoke, 1999).

26 T. Greenwood, Making the MIRV: A Study in Defence Decision Making (Cambridge, MA, 1975).

27 D. K. Stumpf, Titan II: A History of a Cold War Missile Program (Fayetteville, NC, 2000).

28 T. Terriff, The Nixon Administration and the Making of US Nuclear Strategy (Ithaca, NY, 1995); B. Heuser, NATO, Britain, France and the FRG: Nuclear Strategies and Forces for Europe, 1949–2000 (Basingstoke, 1997).

29 G. Smith, Doubletalk: The Story of the First Strategic Arms Limitation Talks (New York, 1980); M. Mandelbaum, The Nuclear Question: The United States and Nuclear Weapons, 1946–1976 (Cambridge, 1979); F. Kaplan, The Wizards of Armageddon (New York, 1983).

30 J. Györkei and M. Harváth, eds, Soviet Military Intervention in Hungary, 1956 (Budapest, 1999).

31 H. G. Skilling, Czechoslovakia's Interrupted Revolution (Princeton, NJ, 1976).

32 A. Norberg and J. O'Neill, Transforming Computer Technology: Information Processing for the Pentagon, 1962–1986 (Baltimore, MD, 1996); A. Roland and P. Shiman, Strategic Computing: DARPA and the Quest for Machine Intelligence, 1983–1993 (Cambridge, MA, 2000).

33 A. Horne, *The French Army and Politics 1870–1970* (London, 1984), p. 89.

34 J. Pay, 'The Battlefield since 1945', in C. McInnes and G. D. Sheffield, eds, *Warfare in the Twentieth Century* (London, 1988); G. Hartcup, *The Silent Revolution: Development of Conventional Weapons, 1945–85* (Oxford, 1993); W. B. Haworth, *The Bradley and How It Got That Way: Technology, Institutions, and the Problem of Mechanized Infantry in the United States Army* (Westport, CT, 1999).

35 J. W. Kipp et al., *Historical Analysis of the Use of Mobile Forces by Russia and the USSR* (College Station, TX, 1985); D. Glantz, *Soviet Operational Art: In Pursuit of Deep Battle* (Totowa, NJ, 1991); W. C. Frank and P. S. Gillette, eds, *Soviet Military Doctrine from Lenin to Gorbachev, 1915–1991* (Westport, CT, 1992).

36 D. J. Stein, *The Development of NATO Tactical Air Doctrine, 1970–1985* (Santa Monica, CA, 1987); D. J. Mrozek, *The US Air Force After Vietnam: Postwar Challenges and Potential for Responses* (Maxwell Air Force Base, AL, 1988).

37 J. L. Romjue, *From Active Defense to AirLand Battle: The Development of Army Doctrine, 1973–1982* (Fort Monroe, VA, 1984) and 'The Evolution of American Army Doctrine', in J. Gooch, ed., *The Origins of Contemporary Doctrine* (Camberley, 1997), pp. 70–73; R. Lock-Pullan, '"An Inward Looking Time": The United States Army, 1973–1976', *Journal of Military History*, 67 (2003), pp. 483–512, esp. 485–6, 505–9.

38 E. Grove and G. Till, 'Anglo-American Maritime Strategy in the Era of Massive Retaliation, 1945–60', in J. B. Hattendorf and R. S. Jordan, eds, *Maritime Strategy and Balance of Power: Britain and America in the Twentieth Century* (New York, 1989), pp. 286–99; M. A. Palmer, *Origins of the Maritime Strategy: The Development of American Naval Strategy, 1945–1955* (Annapolis, MD, 1990); S. M. Maloney, *Securing Command of the Sea: NATO Naval Planning, 1948–1954* (Annapolis, MD, 1995).

39 M. Milner, *Canada's Navy: The First Century* (Toronto, 1999).

40 P. Vial, 'National Rearmament and American Assistance: The Case of the French Navy during the 1950s', in W. M. McBride, ed., *New Interpretations in Naval History* (Annapolis, MD, 1998), pp. 260–88.

41 G. Calhoun, 'Freedom Fighter', *The Daybook*, VII/4 (n.d.), pp. 6–9, 14–16.

42 J. Miller, *Nuclear Weapons and Aircraft Carriers: How the Bomb Saved Naval Aviation* (Washington, DC, 2001).

43 E. J. Marolda and O. P. Fitzgerald, *The United States Navy and the Vietnam Conflict, II: From Military Assistance to Combat, 1959–1965* (Washington, DC, 1986); R. J. Francillon, *Tonkin Gulf Yacht Club: US Carrier Operations off Vietnam* (Annapolis, MD, 1988).

44 G. E. Hudson, 'Soviet Naval Doctrine and Soviet Politics, 1953–1975', *World Politics*, 29 (1976), pp. 90–113.

45 D. R. Baucom, *The Origins of SDI, 1944–1983* (Lawrence, KS, 1992); F. Fitzgerald, *Way Out There in the Blue* (New York, 2000).

46 G. A. Ritter, *Continuity and Change: Political and Social Developments in Germany after 1945 and 1989/90* (London, 2000), p. 24.

Chapter 6: Wars Between Non-Western Powers, 1945–90

1 L. P. Sen, *Slender was the Threat: Kashmir Confrontation, 1947–1948* (Bombay, 1969); S. N. Prasad and D. Pal, *Operations in Jammu and Kashmir* (New Delhi, 1987). Re 1965, D. R. Mankekar, *Twenty-two Fateful Days: Pakistan Cut to Size* (Bombay, 1966); A. Khan, *The First Round, Indo-Pakistan War, 1965* (New Delhi, 1979).

2 A. H. Young and D. E. Phillips, eds, *Militarization in the Non-Hispanic Caribbean* (Boulder, CO, 1986), p. 129.

3 B. Cloughley, 'The 1971 War in West Pakistan', *Army Quarterly and Defence Journal*, 129 (1999), pp. 174–81.

4 K. C. Praval, *Indian Army After Independence* (New Delhi, 1987).

5 J. W. Garver, *Protracted Contest: Sino-Indian Rivalry in the Twentieth Century* (Seattle, WA, 2001).

6 N. Maxwell, *India's China War* (London, 1970).

7 K. C. Chen, *China's War against Vietnam: a Military Analysis* (Baltimore, MD, 1983) and *China's War with Vietnam, 1979: Issues, Decisions, and Implications* (Stanford, CA, 1987); S. J. Hood, *Dragons Entangled: Indochina and the China–Vietnam War* (Armond, NY, 1992).

8 E. O'Ballance, *The War in Yemen* (Hamden, CT, 1971); A. A. Rahmy, *The Egyptian Policy in the Arab World: Intervention in Yemen, 1962–1967, a Case Study* (Washington, DC, 1983); S. M. Badeeb, *The Saudi–Egyptian Conflict over North Yemen, 1962–1970* (Boulder, CO, 1986); D. M. Witty, 'A Regular Army in Counterinsurgency Operations: Egypt in North Yemen, 1962–1967', *Journal of Military History*, 65 (2001), pp. 401–40.

9 D. Hiro, *The Longest War: The Iran–Iraq Military Conflict* (London, 1989).

10 M. S. Navias and E. R. Hooton, *Tanker Wars: The Assault on Merchant Shipping During the Iran–Iraq Conflict, 1980–1988* (London, 1996); M.A. Palmer, *On Course to Desert Storm: The United States Navy and the Persian Gulf* (Washington, DC, 1992), pp. 109–33.

11 A. Ilan, *The Origin of the Arab–Israeli Arms Race* (Basingstoke, 1996), pp. 153–74.

12 M. B. Oren, *Six Days of War: June 1967 and the Making of the Modern Middle East* (Oxford, 2002).

13 A. Vitan, 'The Soviet Military Presence in Egypt, 1967–1972: A New Perspective', *Journal of Slavic Military Studies*, 8 (1995), pp. 547–65.

14 K. M. Pollack, *Arabs at War: Military Effectiveness, 1948–1991* (Lincoln, NE, 2002).

15 C. Herzog, *The War of Atonement* (London, 1975).

16 Y. Evron, *War and Intervention in Lebanon: The Israeli–Syrian Deterrence Dialogue* (Baltimore, MD, 1987).

17 Z. Schiff and E. Ya'ari, *Israel's Lebanon War* (London, 1984).

18 A. Bregman, *Israel's Wars, 1947–93* (London, 2000).

19 W. Steenkamp, *South Africa's Border War, 1966–1989* (Gibraltar, 1989).

20 H. Feldman, *The End and the Beginning: Pakistan, 1969–1971* (London, 1975); H. Zaheer, *The Separation of East Pakistan: The Rise and Realization of Bengali Muslim Nationalism* (New York, 1994); J.F.R. Jacob, *Surrender at Dacca: Birth of a Nation* (New Delhi, 1997).

21   O. Obasanjo, *My Command: An Account of the Nigerian Civil War, 1967–1970* (London, 1981).
22   M. I. Draper, *Shadows, Airlift and Air War in Biafra and Nigeria, 1967–70* (Aldershot, 1999).
23   J. de St. Jorre, *The Nigerian Civil War* (London, 1972); A. Clayton, *Frontiersmen: Warfare in Africa Since 1950* (London, 1998), pp. 92–8.
24   R. Iyob, *The Eritrean Struggle for Independence: Domination, Resistance, Nationalism, 1941–1993* (Cambridge, 1995).
25   D. Wai, *The African–Arab Conflict in the Sudan* (London, 1981); H. Assefa, *Mediation of Civil Wars: The Sudan Conflict* (Boulder, CO, 1987); M. W. Daly and A. A. Sikainga, eds, *Civil War in the Sudan* (London, 1993).
26   B. Hoffman, *Inside Terrorism* (New York, 1998).
27   S. Biddle and R. Zirkle, 'Technology, Civil–Military Relations, and Warfare in the Developing World', *Journal of Strategic Studies*, 19 (1996), pp. 171–212.
28   C. Welch, ed., *Soldier and State in Africa* (Evanston, IL, 1970); S. Decalo, *Coups and Army Rule in Africa* (New Haven, CT, 1976).
29   P. Silva, ed., *The Soldier and the State in South America: Essays in Civil–Military Relations* (New York, 2001).
30   R. Challis, *Shadow of a Revolution: Indonesia and the Generals* (Stroud, 2001).
31   U. Dann, *Iraq under Qassem: A Political History, 1958–1963* (Jerusalem, 1969), esp. pp. 366–70.
32   M. Kentridge, *An Unofficial War: Inside the Conflict in Pietermaritzburg* (Cape Town, 1990).
33   R. F. Weigley, 'The American Military and the Principle of Civilian Control from McClellan to Powell', *Journal of Military History*, 57 (1993).
34   S. E. Finer, *The Man on Horseback: The Role of the Military in Politics* (London, 1962); S. P. Cohen, *The Pakistan Army* (Berkeley, CA, 1984); H. Crouch, *The Army and Politics in Indonesia* (2nd edn., Ithaca, NY, 1988); J. S. Ikpuk, *Militarisation of Politics and Neo-Colonialism: The Nigerian Experience* (London, 1995); J. Peters, *The Nigerian Military and the State* (London, 1997).

Chapter 7: Searching for a New World Order since 1990

1   L. Freedman, *The Revolution in Strategic Affairs* (Oxford, 1998).
2   R. Durwood, *Arms Control, Disarmament, and the New World Order* (Camberley, 1995), p. 4.
3   J. A. Olsen, *Strategic Air Power in Desert Storm* (London, 2003).
4   R. H. Scales, *Certain Victory: The US Army in the Gulf War* (Fort Leavenworth, KS, 1993); R. M. Swain, *'Lucky War': Third Army in Desert Storm* (Fort Leavenworth, KS, 1994); A. H. Cordesman and A. R. Wagner, *The Lessons of Modern War, IV: The Gulf War* (Boulder, CO, 1996).
5   R. Utley, *The Case for Coalition – Motivation and Prospects: French Military Intervention in the 1990s* (Camberley, 2001), p. 46, n. 26.
6   R. R. Leonhard, *The Art of Maneuver: Maneuver Warfare Theory and AirLand Battle* (Novato, CA, 1991), pp. 261–99; A. Bin, R. Hill and A. Jones, *Desert Storm:*

  A *Forgotten War* (Westport, CT, 1998).
7 M. Mandeles, T. G. Hone and S. S. Terry, *Managing 'Command and Control' in the Persian Gulf War* (London, 1996).
8 T. G. Mahnken, 'A Squandered Opportunity? The Decision to End the Gulf War', in A. J. Bacevich and E. Imbar, eds, *The Gulf War of 1991 Reconsidered* (London, 2003), pp. 144–5.
9 R. M. Connaughton, *Peacekeeping and Military Intervention* (Camberley, 1992), p. 21.
10 E. A. Huelfer, 'The Battle for Coco Solo, Panama 1989', *Infantry*, 90 (2000), pp. 23–32.
11 C. Dauber, 'Implications of the Weinberger Doctrine for American Military Intervention in a Post-Desert Storm Age', *Contemporary Security Policy*, 22/3 (2001), pp. 76–8.
12 C. Adibe, *Managing Arms in Peace Processes: Somalia* (New York, 1995); K. Allard, *Somalia Operations: Lessons Learned* (Washington, DC, 1995); T. Farrell, 'Sliding into War: The Somalia Imbroglio and US Army Peace Operations Doctrine', *International Peacekeeping*, 2 (1995), pp. 195–213; M. Bowden, *Black Hawk Down: A Story of Modern War* (New York, 1999).
13 B. Shacochis, *The Immaculate Invasion* (New York, 1999).
14 C. Lord, *Intermediate Deployments: The Strategy and Doctrine of Peacekeeping-Type Operations* (Camberley, 1996), pp. 17–18.
15 A. Raevsky, 'Russian Military Performance in Chechnya: An Initial Evaluation', *Journal of Slavic Military Studies*, 8 (1995), pp. 681–90.
16 A. Lieven, *Flaying the Bear: Chechnya and the Collapse of Russian Power* (New Haven, CT, 1998); S. Knezys and R. Sedlickas, *The War in Chechnya* (College Station, TX, 1999); S. Smith, *Allah's Mountains: The Battle for Chechnya* (2nd edn, London, 2001); R. Seely, *Russo-Chechen Conflict, 1800–2000: A Deadly Embrace* (London, 2001).
17 E. O'Ballance, *Wars in the Caucasus, 1990–1995* (Basingstoke, 1996).
18 D. Gates, *The UN and Europe's Security Institutions: Dashed Expectations?* (Camberley, 1995).
19 L. I. Polyakov, 'American Defense Transformation: A View from Ukraine', in C. C. Crane, ed., *Transforming Defense* (Carlisle, PA, 2001), p. 181.
20 M. Urban, *Big Boys' Rules: The SAS and the Secret Struggle against the IRA* (London, 1992); P. Taylor, *Brits: The War Against the IRA* (London, 2001).
21 J. Gow, 'After the Flood: Literature on the Context, Cause and Course of the Yugoslav War – Reflections and Refractions', *Slavonic and East European Review*, 85 (1997), pp. 446–84; S. L. Burg and P. S. Shoup, *The War in Bosnia-Herzegovina: Ethnic Conflict and International Intervention* (Armonk, NY, 1999); T. Ripley, *Operation Deliberate Force: The Campaign in Bosnia 1995* (Lancaster, 1999).
22 M. Melvin and S. Peach, 'Reaching For the End of the Rainbow: Command and the RMA', in G. Sheffield and G. Till, eds, *Challenges of High Command in the Twentieth Century* (Camberley, 1999), pp. 120–21.
23 I. H. Daalder and M. E. O'Hanlon, *Winning Ugly: NATO's War to Save Kosovo* (Washington, DC, 2000); T. Judah, *Kosovo: War and Revenge* (New Haven, CT,

2000); B. S. Lambeth, NATO's Air War for Kosovo: A Strategic and Operational Assessment (Santa Monica, CA, 2001); S. T. Hosmer, The Conflict over Kosovo: Why Milosevic Decided to Settle when He Did (Santa Monica, CA, 2001); A. J. Bacevich and E. A. Cohen, eds, War Over Kosovo: Politics and Strategy in a Global Age (New York, 2002).

24 W. K. Clark, Waging Modern War: Bosnia, Kosovo, and the Future of Combat (New York, 2001).

25 R. Joó, The Democratic Control of Armed Forces (Paris, 1996).

26 C. Connetta, Strange Victory: A Critical Appraisal of Operation Enduring Freedom and the Afghanistan War (London, 2002); C. McInnes, 'A Different Kind of War? September 11 and the United States' Afghan War', Review of International Studies, 29 (2003), pp. 175–6.

27 S. Biddle, Afghanistan and the Future of Warfare: Implications for Army and Defense Policy (Carlisle, PA, 2002), summarized in 'Afghanistan and the Future of Warfare', Foreign Affairs 82/2 (March–April 2003), pp. 31–46.

28 For early comments, A. and H. Toffler, War and Anti-War: Survival at the Dawn of the 21st Century (London, 1993); G. R. Sullivan and J. M. Dubik, Land Warfare in the 21st Century (Carlisle Barracks, PA, 1995); E. H. Tilford, The Revolution in Military Affairs: Prospects and Cautions (Carlisle Barracks, PA, 1995); A. Irvin, 'The Buffalo Thorn: The Nature of the Future Battlefield', Journal of Strategic Studies, 19 (1996), pp. 238–40, 245–6; L. W. Grau and T. L. Thomas, 'A Russian View of Future War: Theory and Direction', Journal of Slavic Military Studies, 9 (1990), pp. 508–12; C. Gray, The American Revolution in Military Affairs: An Interim Assessment (Camberley, 1997). More recent work includes B. R. Schneider and L. E. Grinter, eds, Battlefields of the Future: 21st Century Warfare Issues (Maxwell Air Force Base, AL, 1998); B. S. Lambeth, The Transformation of American Air Power (Ithaca, NY, 2000); C. Gray, Strategy for Chaos: Revolutions in Military Affairs and the Evidence of History (London, 2002); C. Coker, Waging War Without Warriors? The Changing Culture of Military Conflict (Boulder, CO, 2002), pp. 182–95.

29 C. Parry, 'Maritime Manoeuvre and Joint Operations to 2020', in M. Duffy, T. Farrell and G. Sloan, eds, European Defence in 2020 (Exeter, 1998), pp. 45–63.

30 P. J. Dombrowski, E. Cholz and A. L. Ross, 'Selling Military Transformation: The Defense Industry and Innovation', Orbis, 46 (2002), pp. 526–36.

31 M. Fitzgerald, 'The Russian Military's Strategy for "Sixth Generation Warfare"', Orbis (1994), pp. 457–76.

32 S. Rynniny, Changing Military Doctrine: Presidents and Military Power in Fifth Republic France, 1958–2000 (Westport, CT, 2001).

33 B. S. Lambeth, The Transformation of American Air Power (Ithaca, NY, 2000).

34 R. E. Harkavy and S. G. Neuman, Warfare and the Third World (New York, 2001).

35 W. Maley, The Afghanistan Wars (Basingstoke, 2002).

36 G. Goodwin-Gill and J. Cohn, Child Soldiers (Oxford, 1994); A. Clayton, Factions, Foreigners and Fantasies: The Civil War in Liberia (Sandhurst, 1995).

37 W. Reno, Warlord Politics and African States (Boulder, CO, 1999); K. Fukui and J. Markakis, eds, Ethnicity and Conflict in the Horn of Africa (London, 1994).

38 G. Prunier, The Rwanda Crisis (New York, 1995).

39   J. Cilliers and C. Dietrich, eds, *Angola's War Economy: The Role of Oil and Diamonds* (Pretoria, 2000).

40   D. Lan, *Guns and Rain: Guerrillas and Spirit Mediums in Zimbabwe* (Los Angeles, CA, 1983); H. Behrens, *Alice Lakwena and the Holy Spirits* (Oxford, 1999).

41   T. Negash and K. Tronvoll, *Brothers at War: Making Sense of the Eritrean–Ethiopian War* (Oxford, 2000).

42   R. Harkavy and S. Neumann, *Warfare and the Third World* (Basingstoke, 2001).

Chapter 8: Conclusions

1   As pointed out in C. S. Gray, 'The Revolution in Military Affairs', in B. Bond and M. Melvin, eds, *The Nature of Future Conflict: Implications for Force Development* (Camberley, 1998), p. 65.

2   J. Clarke, 'On the Once and Future RMA', *Historically Speaking*, 4/4 (April 2003), p. 12.

3   A. J. Bacevich, *American Empire: The Realities and Consequences of US Diplomacy* (Cambridge, MA, 2002); W. Murray, 'Does Military Culture Matter?', in J. F. Lehman and H. Sicherman, eds, *America the Vulnerable: Our Military Problems and How To Fix Them* (Philadelphia, PA, 2002), pp. 134–51.

4   C. C. Crane, 'Transformation Plans and Barriers', in Crane, ed., *Transforming Defense* (Carlisle, PA, 2001), pp. 93, 97.

5   M. Evangelista, *The Chechen Wars: Will Russia Go the Way of the Soviet Union?* (Washington, DC, 2003).

6   University of London, King's College, Liddell Hart Archive, Fuller papers 4/6/24/2.

7   D. M. Drew, 'US Airpower Theory and the Insurgent Challenge: A Short Journey to Confusion', *Journal of Military History*, 62 (1998), pp. 809–32, esp. pp. 824, 829–30; C. Malkasian, *A History of Modern Wars of Attrition* (Westport, CT, 2002), p. 205; H. P. Willmott, *When Men Lost Faith in Reason: Reflections on War and Society in the Twentieth Century* (Westport, CT, 2002), p. 259.

8   P. Bracken, *Fire in the East: The Rise of Asian Military Power and the Second Nuclear Age* (London, 1999).

9   See, for example, M. Melvin and S. Peach, 'Reaching the End of the Rainbow: Command and the Revolution in Military Affairs', in G. D. Sheffield and G. Till, eds, *The Challenges of High Command. The British Experience* (London, 2003), pp. 177–206.

10   R. H. Scales, *Yellow Smoke: The Future of Land Warfare for America's Military* (Lanham, MD, 2003).

11   J. R. Cooper, *Another View of the Revolution in Military Affairs* (Carlisle, PA, 1994), p. 40.

12   S. Metz and R. Millen, *Future War/Future Battlespace: The Strategic Role of American Landpower* (Carlisle, PA, 2003), p. 32.

13   W. Owens, 'The Once and Future Revolution in Military Affairs', *Joint Forces Quarterly*, 31 (2002), pp. 55–61.

14   K. P. Werrell, *Hitting a Bullet with a Bullet: A History of Ballistic Missile Defense*

(Maxwell Air Force Base, AL, 2000).

15 J. T. Richelson, *America's Space Sentinels: DSP* [Defence Satellite Program] *Satellites and National Security* (Lawrence, KS, 1999).

16 N. E. Sarantakes, 'The Quiet War: Combat Operations along the Korean Demilitarized Zone, 1966–1969', *Journal of Military History*, 64 (2000), pp. 439–58.

17 R. Kagan, *Of Paradise and Power: America and Europe in the New World Order* (New York, 2003); although see C. A. Kupchan, *The End of the American Era: US Foreign Policy and the Geopolitics of the Twenty-First Century* (New York, 2003).

18 D. Priest, *The Mission: America's Military in the Twenty-First Century* (New York, 2003).

19 D. G. Muller, *China as a Maritime Power* (Boulder, CO, 1983); J. W. Lewis and X. Litai, *China Builds the Bomb* (Stanford, CA, 1988) and *China's Strategic Seapower: The Politics of Force Modernization in the Nuclear Age* (Stanford, CA, 1995).

20 D. Shambaugh, *Modernizing China's Military: Progress, Problems, and Prospects* (Berkeley, CA, 2002), p. 327; T. M. Kane, *Chinese Grand Strategy and Maritime Power* (London, 2002).

21 B. D. Cole, *The Great Wall at Sea: China's Navy Enters the Twenty-First Century* (Annapolis, MD, 2001).

22 P. Bobbitt, *The Shield of Achilles. War, Peace and the Course of History* (London, 2002), pp. 759–60.

23 M. van Creveld, *The Art of War: War and Military Thought* (London, 2000), p. 209. See also, Creveld, *Nuclear Proliferation and the Future of Conflict* (New York, 1993) and *The Rise and Decline of the State* (Cambridge, 1999), pp. 337–54, and E. Luard, *The Blunted Sword: The Erosion of Military Power in Modern World Politics* (London, 1988).

24 J. Record, *Making War, Thinking History: Munich, Vietnam and Presidential Uses of Force from Korea to Kosovo* (Annapolis, MD, 2002), p. 162.

25 S. Biddle, *Afghanistan and the Future of Warfare: Implications for Army and Defense Policy* (Carlisle, PA, 2002), esp. pp. 43–4, summarized in 'Afghanistan and the Future of Warfare', *Foreign Affairs* 82, 2 (March–April 2003), pp. 31–46.

26 E. O. Goldman and L. C. Eliason, eds, *Diffusion of Military Knowledge, Technology and Practices: International Consequences of Military Innovations* (Palo Alto, CA, 2003).

27 J. F. Clark, ed., *The African States of the Congo War* (New York, 2002).

Selected Further Reading

M. J. Armitage and T. Mason, *Air Power in the Nuclear Age, 1945–1982* (London, 1985)

I. F. Beckett, *Modern Insurgencies and Counter-Insurgencies* (London, 2001)

H. Behrens, *Alice Lakwena and the Holy Spirits* (Oxford, 1999)

B. Berkowitz, *The New Face of War: How War Will be Fought in the 21st Century* (New York, 2003)

P. Bobbitt, *The Shield of Achilles: War, Peace and the Course of History* (Harmondsworth, 2002)

A. Bregman, *Israel's Wars, 1947–93* (London, 2000)

J. Buckley, *Air Power in the Age of Total War* (London, 1998)

W. K. Clark, *Winning Modern Wars: Iraq, Terrorism, and the American Empire* (New York, 2003)

A. Clayton, *Frontiersmen: Warfare in Africa since 1950* (London, 1998)

M. Clodfelter, *The Limits of Air Power: The American Bombing of North Vietnam* (New York, 1989)

S. P. Cohen, *The Indian Army: Its Contribution to the Development of a Nation* (2nd edn, Berkeley, CA, 1991)

P. Dimes, *Images of the Algerian War: French Fiction and Film, 1954–1992* (London, 1994)

N. Friedman, *Terrorism, Afghanistan, and America's New Way of War* (Annapolis, MD, 2003)

D. Gates, *Sky Wars: A History of Military Aerospace Power* (London, 2003)

M. R. Gordon and B. E. Trainor, *The Generals' War* (New York, 1995)

L. W. Grau and M. A. Gress, eds, *The Russian General Staff, The Soviet–Afghan War: How a Superpower Fought and Lost* (Lawrence, KA, 2002)

R. Hallion, *Storm Over Iraq: Air Power and the Gulf War* (Washington, DC, 1992)

—, ed., *Air Power Confronts an Unstable World* (London, 1997)

R. Harkavy and S. Neumann, *Warfare and the Third World* (Basingstoke, 2001)

D. Lan, *Guns and Rain: Guerrillas and Spirit Mediums in Zimbabwe* (Los Angeles, CA, 1983)

D. A. Macgregor, *Transformations under Fire: Revolutionizing How America Fights* (Westport, CT, 2003)

C. Malkasian, *A History of Modern Wars of Attrition* (Westport, CT, 2002)

W. Murray and R.H. Scales, *The Iraq War: A Military History* (Cambridge, MA, 2003)

T. Negash and K. Tronvoll, *Brothers at War: Making Sense of the Eritrean–Ethiopian War* (Oxford, 2000)

G. Perkovich, *India's Nuclear Bomb: The Impact on Global Proliferation* (Berkeley, CA, 1999)

G. Prunier, *The Rwanda Crisis* (New York, 1995)

W. Reno, *Warlord Politics and African States* (Boulder, CO, 1999)

L. E. Russell and A. Mendez, *Grenada, 1983* (Oxford, 1985)

R. Sisson and L. E. Rose, eds, *War and Secession: Pakistan, India and the Creation of Bangladesh* (New Delhi, 1990)

S. C. Tucker, *Vietnam* (London, 1999)

—, ed., *Encyclopedia of the Vietnam War* (Oxford, 1998)

H. P. Willmott, *When Men Lost Faith in Reason: Reflections on War and Society in the Twentieth Century* (Westport, CT, 2002)

Index